AMERICAN TOY CARS & TRUCKS

AMERICAN TOY

CARS & TRUCKS

1894–1942

Lillian Gottschalk
PHOTOGRAPHS BY BILL HOLLAND

348

Abbeville Press · Publishers · New York

Affectionately dedicated to 'Willem,'
whose help, encouragement,
and confidence were unfailing.

Designer: John B. Cooper
Production Supervisor: Narisa Levy
Editorial Director: Allen Levy

First edition published in Great Britain by
New Cavendish Books, 1986.

ISBN 0–89659–653–2

AUTHOR'S PREFACE

The field of toy automobiles is so vast and varied that deciding how to segregate the various types into separate categories is very different from other fields of toy collecting. Once the toys are separated by material; that is, tin, cast iron, wood, etc., they can be sorted again by function, age, manufacturer, country of origin, size construction and logo (make of car). Then again other factors which could be taken into consideration are the finish . . . painted or lithographed metal, comic toys or construction kit types, etc.

While advanced collectors have acquired the ability to locate the toys they seek in books, for others who do not know how to begin, tracking down the toy can prove frustrating. After considerable thought, it was decided to arrange chapters according to the material used or the major function of the toy, whichever was more notable. In fact, the division follows a pattern which the majority of toy collectors have adopted themselves and followed for many years.

A word of caution about toys which fall into several categories. Where the toy is a candidate for such a cross-over, the most commonly known classification is used. This usually centers on the most important characteristic of the toy. For instance, a pressed steel, friction-drive fire engine is found in the Friction chapter. Toy collectors consider the friction mechanism the most outstanding feature of the toy. A Buddy L Ford coupe is found with Buddy L trucks and other heavy pressed steel toys. Collectors would not think of it first as a pleasure car, which it most certainly is, but rather as being most notable in the toy world for its steel construction.

There will always be cast iron collectors who do not touch tin, collectors who look with disdain on cast iron, American collectors who adore only foreign tin and still others who appreciate the jumbo proportions of two-foot long vehicles and nothing else. Many comprehensive collectors, like myself, love all of the above, but divisions must be made somewhere. It is the propensity of the majority of collectors to specialize in one field and that has determined the order of this book. If you are not a collector, perhaps, the separate chapters will act as a guide to help you get started.

Finally, if in doubt, consult the extensive index.

Contents

ACKNOWLEDGMENTS

The author wishes to express her deep gratitude to the various private and institutional sources that have assisted in the preparation of this book.

Thanks for excellent data or significant help is gratefully given to Lee Barber, David Bausch, Jane Coleman, Ray Crilley, Dave Davison, Paul Dunigan, Rosemary and Richard Goodbar, Diane Greenblatt, Robert R. Grew, Rosella Harper, Russell Harrington, Dale Kelley, Barbara Klausner, Dr. David Knoop, Martin Kohn, W. A. Krause, Selma and Alvin Levin, Alfred Marwick, Mary Ann Sandoro, Raymond Spong, and John West.

Special credit is extended to the following persons, institutions and companies that provided assistance and are warmly thanked: Lee Whitehead, Greyhound Lines; Larry Massini, Chein Corporation; Dr. Robert Strohacker, Stephenson County Historical Society, Freeport, IL; Barbara Leysock, A. C. Williams Company; Mrs. Frank Proster, president, Friends of Geneva Library, Geneva, OH; Ralph Maynard, former vice-president of Champion Hardware Company; Roger Heatherman, Kingsbury Machine Tool Corporation; and Greg Lennes, archives, of International Harvester.

Expressions of gratitude are also extended to the following persons for valuable assistance: Eric Matzke for information on Louis Marx & Company; Robert I. Saylor for research relating to the companies of Kenton Hardware and Jones & Bixler; Maury Romer who solved the Kelmet mystery; Marty Cramer and his mother who delved into Wyandotte's past; Samuel C. McCluney who provided first-hand information on the Metalcraft Corporation; R. A. Gibbs, a direct descendant of the founder of Gibbs Manufacturing Company; and the late Jacob E. Brubaker, designer of Hubley toys, and his son J. Clarence Brubaker for information on Hubley's early years.

Significant information was also provided by the following sources and is greatly appreciated: the National Motor Museum, Beaulieu, Hampshire, England; Playthings Magazine, New York City, NY; Lancaster Public Library, Lancaster, PA; Library of Congress, Washington, DC; Library of The Antique Automobile Club of America, Hershey, PA; Enoch Pratt Library, Baltimore, MD; The Classic Car Club of America; and The Antique Toy Collectors of America.

It would be impossible not to acknowledge my debt to Sandra Whitson, who typed and re-typed the manuscript, and her father Frank Whitson, who willingly acted as courier for the manuscript and photographs.

Last but not least, to my good friend, Bill Holland, who brought his extraordinary talent to the splendid photographs, a special thanks.

To the above whose kindnesses and encouragement sustained my efforts and to any who may have been inadvertently omitted, I am very grateful.

Lillian Gottschalk
Parkton, Maryland

The first automobile license tags issued in Pennsylvania were of leather with metal numerals attached. Number thirteen was destroyed when no one was willing to accept it! The license plate on this Chein bus clearly illustrates one clue for dating toy automobiles. The year is 1930. The additional number could be either the manufacturers code or catalog number.

Introduction

European toy collectors proclaim in their books that the golden age of toys occurred before 1915. In America, the golden age was just getting started. European settlers in this country brought the skills and trades they had learned to America's melting pot of cultures. Toy designs varied as much as the heritage of the people who created them. The earliest settlers, the English of New England, the Dutch of New York, the Germans in Pennsylvania, the Swedish, Scottish and Irish, all contributed special skills and designs that synthesized into a distinct American style . . . one that is indigenous to America. It is actually a mixture of European cultures.

Americans have long been obsessed with the biggest, the most, the best, the first, etc. The obsession began with the necessity to compete at a time when America was making great strides in growth. The machine age would make America the greatest power in the world and the immense automotive industry would become the nucleus of it all.

Toy automobiles follow automotive history and document the struggles of pioneer toymakers who persevered through some turbulent periods in American history, including two World Wars and a Great Depression. These manufacturers were challenged to devise new methods of doing things and continually improved on previous designs to keep pace with changing tastes.

With a constant climate of change, toymakers were in a lucrative business situation. Toy autos were products with a planned obsolescence. These toys were produced in a durable form required by parents to withstand the punishment meted out by children, but were replaced by a newer, more advanced form for the ensuing year or next sibling.

This continuing search for novelty has many advantages for the antique toy automobile collector. A horse is a horse. Its outline has remained the same since it marched off Noah's Ark and longer. But, the automobile has been in a constant state of change from its inception. Whereas the history of toys is comparatively scarce, the history of the automotive industry is well documented. Cars can be traced by manufacturer and styling dated by year. By making comparisons between real cars and toys, it is possible to identify and date the toys. Where toymakers produced popular sellers over a long period of time, often changes in construction or attempts to modernize the wheels or other parts are clues for dating.

This book is mainly a continuing, detailed account of machine-produced toy automobiles made in America or imported from Europe from 1894 through 1942, the most widely accepted cut-off date for antique toy collectors. After the Second World War, plastics and diecast materials were more viable than cast iron and tin. Furthermore, a design revolution radically changed the appearance of real cars and the toys which followed.

Dates used in conjunction with the toys have been determined by early catalogs (some reprints), flyers, advertisements in magazines, and from factory employees and associates of the original companies. In fact, direct interviews with persons who created the history were responsible for much fresh information and new facts contained in this book. All were keen for the history to be recorded.

Often, my search led me to interesting people, like Jacob E. Brubaker, designer for Hubley from 1914 to his retirement in 1951. Jake was a Mennonite minister and wood craftsman. He combined all these careers from age 15 and continued his woodworking and ministering duties after leaving Hubley. At 83, he had a remarkable memory, and was able and spry, and could recite dates, names and incidents at the drop of a hat. Much that he chose to recollect at our weekly meetings had never been published.

When Bill, my husband, and I missed a Friday meeting one week due to other commitments, Jake got some friends to drive him to Baltimore from Lancaster. He appeared at my door one Valentine's Day with a heart-shaped wood vase he made on his wood lathe. I shall always remember Jake with that pink cedar vase in hand, a black string tie and smile. In the six months since we first met, we became fast friends. He not only knew the ins and outs of the Hubley Company during the time he worked there, but knew a lot about people and the world in general that cannot be found in books. His missionary friends brought him rare and exotic woods for his woodwork and tales of faraway places which he would repeat to interested listeners.

Jake was pleased to learn that someone thought enough of his work to record it, and often stated that had he known how important his toys would become some day, he would have made ample provision by saving a few. Jake died the week this book was finished. His death only served to emphasize the importance of not putting things off.

I met many other people associated with toy factories: managers, jobbers, salesmen and their descendants. All had something to contribute. Often, they disputed previously written material and commenced to put the record straight.

Locating some of them was not easy. The work had much in common with Sherlock Holmes and Dr. Watson routines. Often as not, my investigations led to a deadend. For instance, I learned that Mary Wilkins, wife of toymaker, James Wilkins, died in 1935 at age 77. Her death certificate lists a daughter, Mary Hymers of Newton, Massachusetts. At the time of writing, I am still trying to trace the daughter. Perhaps she can shed some light on her father's history.

One day my curiosity was aroused by the similarity of truck parts found in Gilbert Erector kits to Kelmet trucks. Names used on later kits like 'Trumodel' were also used in earlier Kelmet advertising. And, there were other factors which pointed to Gilbert. Until now, Kelmet history could not be traced. When no Gilbert authority could be found among toy auto collectors, I turned to the toy train collectors. A call to Alvin Levin gave me Maury Romer's name. I think you will find that the Kelmet history is a strange and interesting one, and it's time it was told.

Another 'scoop' was uncovered with the help of my sister-in-law, Diane. I assigned to her the job of calling all the names associated with Metalcraft in the St. Louis phone book. One call gave us the lead to Samuel C. McCluney, Jr., son of a former Metalcraft director living in retirement in Pennsylvania.

Letters and phone calls to Louis S. Bixler, son of the former owner of Kenton Hardware, put me in touch finally with Ohio collector Robert Saylor, who had spent many years gathering material on the company as an outgrowth of his interest in Kenton toys. He even searched court records of bankruptcy of Kenton. Many of his findings proved shocking to Bixler. For one thing, Bixler had not known his own father was a former Hubley foundryman. This proves the historian sometimes knows more about the manufacturer than the family. There is much to be learned while searching court records.

It is impossible to cover every toy automobile classification between the covers of one book. The field is too large for that. My final selections were based on a cross-section of material geared for the novice as well as the advanced collector. The toys range from exceedingly rare types shown here for the first time to some later automotive toys well worth collecting, all vividly portrayed thanks to the photo artistry of Bill Holland.

Tootsietoys and other 1/43 scale toys have been well covered in recent books and articles and therefore are omitted. Other omissions are large wheeled vehicles or so called 'pedal cars.' These toys which were produced by about 50 manufacturers over a 47-year span between the 1890s and 1940 are a subject matter that should be pursued separately in the future. Japanese toys, rubber, pot metal, and diecast toys are also left for another time. I have purposely avoided repeating toys shown in other recent books unless there was something more or new to add in the way of information.

Toy automobiles are not antiques in the true sense of the word. The U.S. Customs Office defines an antique as being 100 years old or more. Anything less is subject to duty. While the Antique Automobile Club of America accepts cars 35 years old or more for competition, toys have settled into a pattern of separation at the Second World War. They are called antiques if made before the last war, and collectibles if they were produced after then, providing they have some special quality to warrant saving them.

Measurements for toys in the book often vary from the original manufacturers' catalogs. Some toymakers rounded out the measurements using quarter inches, while many jobbers' catalogs exaggerated lengths by adding to them, often as much as 1½ inches per toy! Measurements are used to help identify a toy in hand especially when more than one size was made. Keeping this in mind, where possible, the toy's actual length is used.

During visits to homes of collectors of real cars, I noticed that amidst the flotsam and jetsam men collect to decorate their surroundings, invariably there are a few toy cars. Sometimes, these were saved from their childhood. I was struck with the realization that grown men who once played with toys and *looked* at real cars, now *play* with real cars and look at toys!

While I was growing up, I was imbued with the philosophy that if you take something good from life, it is your duty to put something back in order to perpetuate excellence for the future generation. While this theory was intended for community service, I have always kept it in mind for my hobby. I would like to think that this book is a particular contribution for the many pleasures antique toys have brought me over the years.

Pleasure Cars CAST IRON

Research shows that motortoys were developed as copies of real automobiles. Therefore, the history of the U.S. automotive industry and its designers is our greatest aid to understanding the parallel development of motortoys and their makers. World events and economic and business climates were but some of the steps in progress which played a major role in the ongoing production of these playthings.

← **1.** 1923–31. USA
ARCADE 7¼″ long
Andy Gump and Old 348 Cast Iron

1923 advertisements proclaimed the introduction of Andy Gump, a toy that immediately became a leader in sales for its manufacturer.

Comic strip cartoonist, Sidney Smith, licensed Arcade's use of his characters, including Andy, a tall chinless, wispy-haired man; his wife Min, and his son Chester.

The ridiculous proportions and huge disc wheels of Andy's clunker car contributed to the comical look of the toy. Many variations were offered, such as nickel-plating in lieu of painted wheels. A front crank and license were options.

Arcade has a history of being an enterprising company that took advantage of every business opportunity, no matter how small. In 1930, due to increased demand for the replacement of lost or broken parts, as well as requests for the optional parts, Arcade began filling small part orders for customers direct from the factory.

Like many toys of its era, Andy Gump fell victim to hard times and was not offered after 1931.

Released as a companion for his father, Chester in his bright basket weave pony cart attained equal popularity for a while. Chester vanished from the cart in 1931. The empty cart, now painted red and pulled by a green pony, rolled off into the sunset the next year.

2. 1922. USA
ARCADE 9″ long
Coupe Cast Iron

This coupe's spare tire carries the number 1922 on the license plate. Although Arcade made no such claim, the toy is in fact a line-for-line copy of the 1922 Dodge Coupe

right up to the license plate which attaches to the center of the spare bracket.

This toy is a wonderfully preserved plaything. Its white 'balloon' tires show the wear typical of automotive toys that were much loved and traveled many miles with their original owners.

3. 1923. USA
ARCADE 7″ long
Chevrolet Touring Car 3¾″ high
Cast Iron

Open cars were extremely popular, simply because they were cheaper than closed models. A four-door touring car was more suited for family use, but had the obvious disadvantage of being uncomfortable in cold or inclement weather. Many motorists simply

stored their cars and used public transportation during the winter season. A street car ride never cost more than a nickel in the early twenties!

Arcade supplied the Chevrolet touring car to match Dad's. You're right if you think it resembles a Ford touring car in some ways, but a screen radiator makes it a genuine Chevy. Arcade Fords have solid patterned cast iron radiators.

9

4.   1922. USA
ARCADE   6½" long
Model T Ford Touring Car   Cast Iron

The last brass radiator on a Ford car was in 1916. Radiators were henceforth painted black, and when Ford offered nickel-plated radiator shells in the early 1920s there were few takers due to the added cost.

The touring car was the Ford Company's

5.   1923. USA
ARCADE   6½" long
Center door Model T Sedan   Cast Iron

When center door Model T Ford sedans appear at antique car shows, they always attract attention. The placement of the doors never fails to elicit comments from even the most casual viewers.

Designed to allow easy entrance to front or

rear seats, the model was unpopular with customers, who complained it was an awkward arrangement. The car was also slow, top heavy and expensive.

The least popular model in the line, the real car was manufactured for the last time in 1922 after a six-year production span.

The distinctive oval rear window allows the collector a quick identification of this toy model.

most popular model. Similarly, the touring Ford toy was Arcade's best selling Ford. At times, Arcade decorated the radiator shells with silver paint. There was no extra charge.

→

8.   1925. USA
ARCADE   6½" long
Model T Ford Touring Bank   Cast Iron

To extend the successful Model T line, Arcade added the T touring bank. While the Yellow Cabs continued to maintain their lines, the Ford Model A made all T's obsolete in early 1928 causing the elimination of these toys from the Arcade line. Consequently, this bank was produced for only a short period.

The slot in the rear window accepts pennies, nickels, dimes and quarters, and the bank can hold more than $5.00. Once deposited, the coins are hidden from view. The nickel-plated driver is removable.

6.   **1924. USA**
ARCADE   6½″ long
Model T Ford Fordor Sedan   Cast Iron

The Ford illustrations in Arcade's catalog for this year show toys with twelve-spoke wheels exactly like the real cars. In fact, the actual number of spokes on the toy wheels were eight. Collectors should be aware that illustrators often exercise artistic license in attempting to project realism.

Model T Fords did not have four-wheel brakes. Henry Ford claimed they 'grabbed' and were unnecessary. He first used four-wheel brakes on his 1928 Model A's

The Fordor (a term originated by Henry Ford) sedan was the most popular model for families. Dubbed the 'tin Lizzie', this model became the favorite of college boys in the late 1920s and 1930s because it provided cheap, dependable transportation.

7.   **1924. USA**
ARCADE   6½″ long
Model T Ford Tudor Sedan   Cast Iron

The first Model T Ford was produced in 1908. By 1924, both the real Ford and the Arcade toy line were quite extensive. This Tudor (an original Ford term) model was updated with a straighter roofline, fewer but larger

windows and a shorter, lower body.

A toy collector could actually specialize in Ford toys. By 1925, Arcade offered eight different models plus a Fordson tractor!

9.   **1925. USA**
ARCADE   6½″ long
Model T Ford Tudor   Cast Iron

Before 1914, Model T Fords came off the assembly line enameled in colors. After 1914, all Fords were painted black at the factory, in line with Henry Ford's drive to build cars for a lower price. As legend has it, Ford issued his famous edict: 'They can have any color they want, so long as it's black!' By 1923, every other car was a Ford, and people were tired of black. It was not unusual for some car owners to have their cars repainted in colors to suit themselves. By 1925, Ford was again producing cars in colors.

Arcade immediately got the message. Its 1925 catalog offered a Ford Tudor Sedan in four bright colors. Apparently they also tired of looking at black Fords!

11

10.
ARCADE
Ford Coupe

1923–4. USA
6½″ long
Cast Iron

Arcade's advertising stressed a realistic toy without 'springs or gears to bring it to the repair shop.' Trying hard to catch up on its growing business, Arcade was late with this Model T, whose real life counterpart was introduced in 1922.

Outdated by 1925, the large, roomy driver's compartment is typical of cars of this period. Practically devoid of trunk space, packages or luggage had to stored inside or on the running board, protected by a luggage rack.

11.
ARCADE
Ford Coupe

1925. USA
6½″ long
Cast Iron

The change from Arcade's first Model T coupe (fig. 10) is evidenced here by a more compact and modernized driver's compartment devised to make additional trunk space. Straighter lines and a sun visor are other body style alterations.

12.
ARCADE
Ford Coupe

1927. USA
6½″ long
Cast Iron

Known as a doctor's coupe from the very first, due to the preference shown for them by physicians when making their house calls, the coupes gained a reputation for quick, reliable transportation.

The 1927 coupe was rendered obsolete when Model A's appeared in 1928. By then, all makes of cars were taking on new body shapes. They were lower, and had added curves which became the vogue. In addition there were substantial mechanical changes.

Car manufacturers were learning, through trial and error, to make the automobile a reliable, permanent form of transportation. They stressed performance, comfort, dependability and value, but used new and exciting body styles to capture the buyer's attention.

Arcade's 1927 Ford was made only for a short period. By 1928, boys were looking for Model A toys, just like Dad.

13.
ARCADE
Chevrolets
Coupe, Roadster, Sedan

1924. USA
7″ long
Cast Iron

Chevrolet was General Motors' entry into the vast automobile market. Price was a big factor. Ford cars were the cheapest on the market! The Chevrolet Motor Company, Detroit, Michigan, provided plans for the toys that were faithful to the car's design so that in keeping with Arcade's motto – 'They look real.'

The famous 'bowtie' logo is now known worldwide and was stamped in white on the radiators and spare tire carriers of the Chevrolet toys. White rubber tires could be ordered for an additional charge. Collectors today prefer the all cast iron wheels, for they eliminate the problem of flat or decayed rubber. Through increased popularity of toy automobiles, businesses which provide replacement rubber tires for antique toys are now in existence.

Chevrolet toys were made to appeal to children and parents alike. The all-black cars with gold trim can be identified by their screen front radiators.

14.
ARCADE
Buick Coupe and Sedan

1927. USA
8½" long
Cast Iron

Arcade plied every market and used Buicks, Fords, Taxis, Chevrolets and Plymouths to make up promotional toys for advertising. Its efforts resulted in its becoming the largest cast iron toy manufacturer in the United States by 1927. Arcade's merchandising ability would ease it through the tough financial years to come.

The five-passenger coupe and sedan are sometimes found with stenciled advertisements on their roofs. Shown here are the optional rubber-tired wheels which mothers preferred for inside play.

During the Depression, Arcade abandoned the Buick, some Fords, taxis and other slow-selling models, in favor of more lucrative toy models.

The weighted tin stenciled sign was actually a paperweight giveaway from Buick dealers.

15.
ARCADE
Chevrolet Coupe

1925–8. USA
8¼" long
Cast Iron

The Chevrolet Motor Company introduced its new model in January 1925. Shortly thereafter, Arcade produced this coupe along with a companion sedan. Featuring cowl parking lights and disc wheels, the pair of toys was promoted through regular outlets by Arcade. The Chevrolet Motor Company offered its dealers the toy cars with promotional advertising on the roof. Orders were sent directly to Arcade (see fig. 380).

One reason for Arcade's success was an outstanding ability to quickly copy and market the newest and most successful automobiles of the times.

When Chevrolet changed the designs of its cars in 1928, buyers lost interest in this toy, although it was still offered in the 1928 Arcade catalog.

16.

ARCADE Model A	1928. USA
	6¾" long
ARCADE Service Station	1938
	12" × 5½"
A. C. WILLIAMS Gas Pump	c. 1928
	4¾" high
	Cast Iron

In the late 1920s, Chevrolet started moving into first place with a new six-cylinder car, thus giving the Ford Company its first real competition. Henry Ford did not give up the Model T easily, but the time had come for a more competitive car. Ford's answer was the now immortal Model A. Four and a half million real Model A's were made and remain in evidence today as one of the most

recognized of all antique vehicles.

The real model A failed to maintain the longevity of the Model T. It ceased production in 1931 and was replaced by the V-8. These changes were rapidly copied by Arcade.

The 50¢ toy is equally loved by Ford collectors; their bright colors breaking the monotony of black Model T's.

17.   1928. USA
ARCADE   6¾″ long
Model A Sedans   Cast Iron

A Tudor model on the left and Fordor are part of a new line of Fords which revolutionized the car industry and world. No sooner was the real car off the production line than Arcade was ready with a complete line of Model A cars and trucks as advertised in its 1928 catalog.

    Arcade's Model A's sold themselves – cars so well known needed little promotion.

    An Arcade cast iron street sign from the 1920s marks the road.

← 18. →   1931–3. USA
ARCADE   9⅜″ long
Reo Coupe   Cast Iron

Toy companies favored accurate copies of real cars and trucks. Permission to copy would first be obtained from the car manufacturer in order to avoid repetition. Arcade embossed the name 'REO' on the rumble seat of its Royale Coupe, leaving no question of its identity. Arcade, unquestionably the largest cast iron toy manufacturer of its day, maintained its own salerooms at the toy centers in New York and with few exceptions marked all its toys.

    The designer of the Reo Royale, Amos E. Northup of Murray Corporation of America, established a new trend in the car industry when he unveiled his latest creation in October, 1930. The fluid contours accentuated the length of the car. The '31 Reo was the first mass-produced car to resemble a custom-built product.

    Reo-Royale. A majestic name. Both the real car and the toy were and still are collectible. The Reo was carried by Arcade for three years, with changes in color only. This yellow Reo, in original condition, denotes a 1932–3 issue.

    Adding to the play value of the Reo is the detachable body and sidemounts which are fastened together by means of screws and nuts. The chassis and wheels remain intact, making reassembly a simple task.

← 19.

19.   1933. USA
ARCADE   7¼" long
Silver Arrow   Cast Iron

Pierce-Arrow did not build cheap cars. The famed Silver Arrow model caused a sensation at the 1933 auto shows. The sleek futuristic styling was far ahead of its time. Embossing the name on the side of the toy car was a publicity gimmick done on special order from Pierce-Arrow, who used the toys as favors at promotional dinners. The pictured toy is blue, but it was also available in assorted colors, including the famous silver.

A post mortem: the toy was a success, but the real car failed. Only five were made and sold for $10,000 each. These were built for the Chicago Century of Progress Exhibition. Only three of the original five are known to exist today.

21.   1937. USA
ARCADE   Sedan 5½" long
Ford Sedan   Trailer 6½" long
& 'Covered Wagon' Trailer   Cast Iron

Cars were fast losing their boxy looks by 1937. Arcade began producing newer restyled cars and dropped outdated toys.

Manufacturers were forced to work fast in order to keep up with a rapidly changing market, influenced by its recovery from the Depression years. All automobiles took on a totally new look. Headlights were incorporated into the fenders. Automatic transmission, new highways and more trouble-free cars, enticed travelers to take to the roads with house trailers.

The original owner of these toys chose two different colors for his travel set. Though sold as separate units in some sales catalogs, they were meant to be paired.

Interiors and drivers were eliminated on this issue, and rubber tires were now standard equipment – parents preferred their silence to the clanging of cast iron wheels.

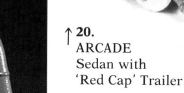

20.   New in 1939. USA
ARCADE   9" long
Sedan with   Sedan 5⅞"
'Red Cap' Trailer   Trailer 2½"
                  Cast Iron

HUBLEY   Front 1939. USA
Auto and Trailer   6¾" long overall
                  Cast Iron

The real Mullins 'Red Cap' trailer was a product of the early thirties, a handy car

22.
HUBLEY
Speedsters & Touring Car

c. 1911–28. USA
Top 7½" long
Left 7" long
Right 7" long
Cast Iron

In the early part of 1900, the automotive industry played a vital role in developing a strong national economy. It brought Americans the thrill of owning a car and the freedom to come and go at will.

The two speedsters and open tourer are typical of the styles of cars seen on the road before 1918. The speedster at the top was repeated in Hubley catalogs through 1928. Only a successful sales record could have kept it there.

Despite the appearance and name, speedsters were not produced primarily for racing. They were stripped-down cars used for quick, cheap transportation.

accessory for travelers in need of luggage space.

This car and trailer, like most cast iron toys made in the late 1930s, performed additional duties during the war years when there was a shortage of playthings.

In medium and small size sedans and trailers, detail is lost. The absence of nickel plating and separate parts were changes prompted by the price factor.

Notice the decreased size of the wheels and fenders of the lightened version. 'Slots' cut into the body, along with larger front and rear windows, smaller axles and rivets and a thinner body wall are measures taken to reduce the weight and material content of cast iron limousine and other toys in 1916.

24 & 23.   1918. USA
HUBLEY   7″ long
Limousine   Cast Iron

Landaulet. Cabriolet. Brougham. Cloverleaf body Chummy roadster. For anyone except the seasoned antique car collector, the terminology used to describe old cars can be very confusing.

A limousine is a closed car. It usually has a glass divider between the driver and passengers. Sometimes, folding seats, called jump seats, were placed in the rear for carrying extra passengers.

Hubley's limo came in various sizes and was a good seller. It remained in the line until the late 1920s, although by then, it was lightened with 'slots' (a term used by Hubley workers) and newer, smaller wheels. To further lighten the toy, front and rear windows were enlarged and the walls of the car cast thinner. Nothing was overlooked to cut corners on shipping costs. Flashing was trimmed off, and smaller axles and rivets completed the transformation.

Toy manufacturers' catalogs seldom pictured these skeletal options but would list them under the heavy toy with a weight difference. Most of these lighter iron toys were intended for regions west of the Mississippi. Traditionally, shipping costs were 10% higher west of the Mississippi.

25.   c. 1920. USA
HUBLEY   10″ long
Touring Car   Cast Iron

A fashionable lady and her little seated dog enjoy a spin in their open touring car with lines reminiscent of a 1912 car.

Older models were preferred by some toy buyers as evidenced by the large number of outdated models still offered in Hubley's catalog that year.

Toy production came to a halt during the First World War, but when the war ended, toy manufacturers geared up for production again. Hubley's 1920 catalog shows mostly pre-war toys whose production was resumed.

New offerings included the cape top roadster along with other cars in newer styles. Such early Hubley cars have the very flat, cast spoke wheel seen here. The blue paint run on the door is a factory original.

27 & 28. 1927. USA
HUBLEY 11" long
Packard Straight 8 Cast Iron

The 1928 catalog pictures this Hubley masterpiece, considered the ultimate cast iron toy. No other toy auto of the late 1920s is more desired by collectors of elite cars.

The toy shares the mystique of the Packard auto, 'The Symbol of Respect'. According to legend, James Ward Packard gave the message, 'Ask the Man Who Owns One', to a prospective customer when printed literature had run out. It became Packard's slogan.

The person who owns an intact specimen of this exact replica of a classic Straight 8 Sedan will tell you that he is indeed fortunate. This was an expensive, luxury toy in its day.

The collector's appetite is further whetted by the piece's rarity. The production period was cut short in 1929 by the Depression, when Hubley had to weed out higher priced and slower moving toys to focus on new models that matched the streamlined newcomers on the streets. Like most multi-piece toys held together by a couple of screws, the toy is often found minus major parts.

Another interesting feature is that among cast iron toys, only on this Packard and the companion 'Red Devil #5 Racer' can one raise the hood to expose a detailed cast motor.

Long, low-slung, with painted disc wheels, the Packard toy features front doors that open to detailed seats, plus lamps, bumpers and license plates, all in realistic detail usually most difficult to capture in cast iron.

29.
HUBLEY
Coupes

1928–34. USA
9½", 8½", 7" long
Cast Iron

Not only a size for every pocketbook, but for the hand that holds it, Hubley's cast iron coupe is a composite of every closed coupe that traveled the roads in its day. Surely this was its intention, so a child could give it his own identity. The lines are those of a mid-1920s car, but owners kept their cars longer in those days, perhaps because the cars held up so well, as have these toys. Hubley carried the largest coupe in their line through 1934, after which streamlined cars took over, in keeping with a changing world.

30.
HUBLEY
Auto and Trailer

1936. USA
14" long overall
Sedan 7¼" long
Trailer 7⅛" long
Cast Iron

The real V-12, ultra-streamlined sedan offered by the Ford Motor Company, had an engine powerful enough to pull a house trailer. 'Streamlining for realism' was the description used for the Lincoln Zephyr and its house trailer.

Separate nickel-plated bumpers and grilles add substance to the toy.

31 & 32.
HUBLEY
Airflow Chrysler

1934. USA
8¼" long
6¼" long
4½" long
3" long
Cast Iron

Though engineered and planned many years before its release in 1934, the car with a grille described by writers as a 'waterfall' was not a success. It is interesting that Hubley managed to patent these Airflow toys late in 1933 (patent #1943160).

The Airflow toys, like the real cars, were before their time and are avidly collected as historic automobiles.

A permanent turnbuckle which can be seen underneath the center of the car operates battery lights. The windshield frame is formed of pressed nickel-plated steel. An ingenious arrangement permits disassembly of parts which are locked together by the spare tire.

The real Chrysler Airflow was a commercial failure, although it continued to be manufactured through 1937.

33.
IVES
Motor Hunting Trap

1895. USA
6½″ long
Cast Iron
Clockwork

IVES
Early Transitional
Automobile

1895. USA
7″ long
Cast Iron

Sometimes called a shooting brake, the original vehicle was used on large estates to hunt game in areas traversable by automobiles. The hunter faced the rear to lessen the danger of accident and interference with the driver and passenger up front. They were also built for park use and summer touring. The De La Vergne Refrigerating Machine Company of New York produced a hunting trap of this style in 1895. A manufacturer of ice-making plants, the company experimented with gas motors as a source of power for its ice business before turning to auto production.

Ives did not mark its automobiles or toys before 1907.

Some ancient overpaint on the body of the toy is overlooked due to its age and extreme rarity.

35.
(*Left*) Probably IVES

(*Right*) KENTON

Horseless Carriages

c. 1898–1905. USA
6″ long
Cast Iron
6″ long
Cast Iron
Clockwork

Ives was known to have made some automobiles but for many years they could not be identified. Little by little they have surfaced and each one has proved radically different. It has taken careful study to positively identify Ives toys since it is presumed no catalogs exist which show the automobiles.

A consensus attributes the automobile on the left to Ives. The clockwork mechanism is identical to one found in a Hubley Roman Gladiator, a turn of the century horse-drawn toy, but Hubley company experts deny the car is one of its issue.

Clockworks for toys were supplied to Hubley and Ives from the Westbury Button Company of Connecticut. It was a common practice throughout the cast iron industry to sell and exchange wheels and parts, especially automotive wheels which differed from buggy and carriage wheels. The earliest automobile wheels carried more spokes than later cars, a

carry-over from the first real automobiles which were made in buggy and wagon shops.

A wire holds the tiller tight for directional steering or it can be set to run in a circle. A cast-in hole, adjacent to the tiller, is found on another Ives toy which was used for comparison (see fig. 34). Although this earlier car is transitional, with a removable front end, the springs in both toys are identical castings.

Our photographer used a Karl Bub key. This is ironic because clockwork cast iron toys were America's attempt to compete with Europe's mechanical tin toys. Buyers were fascinated with the action.

Precious few of these clockwork iron toys remain. When they are found, often the

Probably Ives' first toy automobile. A differential on the rear axle is the telltale addition which marks this carriage design as an automobile.

Ives replaced a front-end hitch for horses with a pivotal wheel unit. This copied wagon shops of the period which went into the business of building automobiles using carriage designs for bodies.

clockworks have been removed and lost, leading one to surmise the repairs were either unsuccessful or abandoned. Proof of a former clockwork toy is the special hole cast into the toy to hold the key and obvious wear around the place where the motor was installed. To properly repair the motor in an Ives toy, the entire toy must be disassembled.

A simplified clockwork was used on the Kenton toy which winds from the left side of the car. The vehicle's direction cannot be controlled once it is set to run. Its uncontrolled course must have provided a thrill for the young owner!

↓ **37.**

37.
JONES & BIXLER
(later Kenton)
Left
'Red Devil' Touring Car

c. 1910. USA
9¼" long
Cast Iron

Delicate cast iron posts supporting the roofs of early toy cars were susceptible to breakage in the hands of children. Like Murphy's law, anything bad that could happen would . . . and did! Consequently, few touring cars with this type of cast iron roof have survived intact. In 1910, the name 'Red Devil'* was associated with fast cars. This one is painted blue and has tiller steering.

JONES & BIXLER
(later Kenton)
Right
'Red Devil' Open Automobile

c. 1912. USA
9" long
Cast Iron

Before 1910, cars had no doors on the driver's compartment. Motors were hot, and so were the driver's feet! Later, when improvements diverted heat from inside the car, doors were added. Wheel steering was introduced in America in 1900, superseding tillers, although some manufacturers were slow to make the change. Toy autos with tillers are found to about 1911.

↑**36.**
JONES & BIXLER
(later Kenton)
Runabout

c. 1906. USA
8" long
Cast Iron

Antique car collectors have always called the rear single seat a mother-in-law seat. Wishful thinking, perhaps, but it was actually a place for the chauffeur when the owner wished to take the wheel.

This early version of a sports car was made before bumpers appeared on cars. The toy and the real car it copies are both rare.

* Jones and Bixler used the brand name 'Red Devil' for their toy automobiles. When Kenton assumed production of the J&B toys, they continued the use of the name for a while.

Was the slanted hood meant to copy a Franklin car or possibly a Renault? No. Toy manufacturers were bright businessmen. Toy automobile designs were not intended to pinpoint a specific make of car unless success depended on it. Ford and Chevrolet were already household words. Of the hundreds of makes of other real cars, many had the same or similar outward appearance, including a slanted hood. Toy cars listed in early manufacturers' catalogs were simply called roadsters, tourist cars (meaning touring cars), or sedans. A parent or child could call it any make and often they did. In this way, toy makers vied for designs which would represent a multitude of cars on the road and have the widest appeal to the biggest number of buyers. Still, it was important that the car looked up-to-date and realistic. Hubley designer, Jake Brubaker, told me his boss once sent him to New York City to view and copy the designs of taxis on the street because such an overview could not have been obtained in the little community of Lancaster, Pennsylvania in the early 1920s.

38.
KENTON
Automobile

c. 1900. USA
7" long
Cast Iron
Clockwork

The turn-of-the-century design of Kenton's clockwork car is just one step from a carriage. The high square form with tiller steering and its prim and proper looking occupants can steer the car in a circle.

Clockwork cast iron toys are rare in all forms. They simply did not sell well for various reasons. They were costly, and

parents as well as children wanted them to work well.

Toy manufacturers bought their clockworks from specialty companies that made them to order.

To repair a broken spring required a blacksmith to first remove the contraption; a patient clock repairman to fix it; then, back to the blacksmith to – well, you see what I mean!

An historically important toy and so American in feeling! One of my favorites

↑ 39. c. 1905–8. USA
KENTON 6″ long
Early Automobiles Cast Iron

Styled as Locomobiles, these cars are the same with one exception. The car on the right has a new, improved tiller with horn attached, a necessity for increasingly crowded roads. In 1900, cars were both right- or left-hand drive depending on the maker's design. Drivers used either side of the roadbed as well! Then, as now, some drivers thought their half was in the middle. Driving laws soon settled the confusion.

→ 42. 1906–11. USA
KENTON 6½″ long
'Red Devil' Automobile Cast Iron

By 1906, most automobiles had engines in the front. Kenton's fenderless runabout was not designed for serious driving. This was still a time of rough, rocky, dirt roads and sometimes no road at all! Fenders, designed to protect passengers from road dust and stones were optional equipment on some makes of cars.

The toy shown has a horn attached to the tiller steering column. Some of Kenton's early figures of drivers were adapted for use in autos from horsedrawn toys. Thus, the loop in this driver's hands was designed to hold horses' reins.

Listed only as 'automobile' in early Kenton literature, in 1911 this toy was named 'Red Devil', a name used mainly by Jones & Bixler with whom Kenton had involved business dealings for many years (see J&B history).

↑ 40.
JONES & BIXLER
Manufactured by Kenton
around 1910
Tourist Car with top down

c. 1908. USA
9¾" long
Cast Iron

Although the Tourist Car is fashioned after a
1904 design touring car, the earliest
verification for the production of this toy
dates from 1908.

Jones and Bixler were skillful casters using
simple and beautiful designs in their early toy
automobiles. The early 1900s mark an era
when time was taken to achieve pride in
workmanship.

Smaller numbers of this toy have surfaced
than its companion with the roof up (fig. 41).
Both cars are visual beauties. They are nicely
proportioned and hold removable drivers and
passengers.

41.
JONES & BIXLER
(later Kenton)
Tourist Car

c. 1908. USA
9¾" long
Cast Iron

Folding tops on the earliest open touring cars
required two people to raise and lower them.
In 1910, the use of a one-man top was
adopted which rendered unnecessary the
braces which formerly attached to the back of
the front seat.

This toy has simulated curved braces cast
with fine detail on its roof. A most beautiful
and graceful cast iron car that is rarely found
intact. In 1912, the toy was updated by the
addition of front doors.

43.   ← c. 1911. USA
KENTON   8″ long
Alphonse and Gaston   Cast Iron
Automobile

These two comic strip characters were best
known for constantly bowing to each other,
making sweeping gestures with their hands
and uttering statements such as, 'After you,
Alphonse.' 'No, after you, Gaston.' This
resulted in widespread public mimicry of the
gestures and remarks for many years.

   An unsuccessful attempt to propel cast iron
toys with clockworks led to Kenton's use of
animated action by connecting the jointed
bodies of Alphonse and Gaston to the
movement of the wheels. Alphonse is the
bearded passenger.

← N. N. HILL BRASS CO.   c. 1908. USA
Happy Hooligan Automobile   6″ long
                                   Cast Iron

Looking on from the rear is Happy Hooligan
in his soapbox automobile. Sold as a bell toy,
the car resembles a home-made sidewalk toy
of the period. A stovepipe, miner's lantern
and box with the word 'Soap' are cast into
the body. The nickle-plated bell under the toy
seems secondary to the importance of this
comical toy. Happy, who wore a silly grin
and a spinach can on his moveable head, was
the inspiration for many toys made of tin,
plaster, china, wood and cloth, as well as cast
iron.

44 & 45.   c. 1917–22. USA →
WILLIAMS   11¾″ long &
Touring Cars   9⅛″ long
                                   Cast Iron

This big tourer is well made and typical of
the average car on the road from 1917–22, the
same period this toy was made. The smaller,
cheaper version has updated disc wheels of
1922.

46.   1923. USA   →
KENTON   9¾″ long
Touring Car   Cast Iron

Kenton was so positive this touring car was a
winner that they offered it in three variations.
Seen here is the stripped down version. The
same car with an additional folded down top
and another with an open full top have the
extra weight that came with optional
additions.

   Suppliers often used open spoke wheels as
a means of conserving on shipping weight
and costs.

47.　　　　　　　　　　1927. USA
KENTON　　　　　　　10¼″ long
Sedan　　　　　　　　　Cast Iron

Antique car collectors will recognize this sedan as a 1927 Nash, Special 6.

By the late 1920s, Kenton, like its competitor, Arcade, had a modernized factory with new automatic casting machinery. Production was speeded up and toys were manufactured with a smooth uniformity not possible using hand-worked methods. Car forms could now take on a more realistic shape when cast in sections, and assembly of pre-painted parts speeded up production.

48.
KENTON
Sedan

1927. USA
8½" long
Cast Iron

New in 1927, the five-wheel sedan with its lady passenger travels a rocky road. The slanted windshield is unique to Kenton toys but copied from real cars of the period. Some Kenton sedans are discovered painted in taxi colors.

Road building was progressing at a fast pace in the 1920s; and sales of automobiles were booming, enabling the urban populace to reside farther from the centers of cities.

Nevertheless, imperfect coordination of road improvements left many rough areas to be traveled by hardy souls and their sturdy cars. Typically, this was a basic sedan, painted a dark color, and invariably with spare wheels!

49.   i927. USA
KENTON   10¼″ long
Wreck Car   Cast Iron

In the late 1920s, small garage owners and independent mechanics could buy good used cars for very little money. After cutting the car bodies down, they added wrecker cranes which were available as separate units and small enough to be installed in the rear spaces of cars. More important, these cranes could be operated by one man. The completed compact wreckers occupied minimal storage space and were ideal for towing small, light

cars. On this toy version, a crank pulls the cable and a ratchet holds the 'wrecked' Ford in position.

KILGORE   1924. USA
Ford Coupe   6″ long
                               Cast Iron

Kilgore's entry into the toy auto market was somewhat slow because of the small size of the company.

It was no small feat to come up with something different for the Ford car, but Kilgore had a better idea! There would be no

advantage in tampering with the body style of a Ford, thus spoiling the resemblance to the real coupe. Instead, Kilgore created a newer, rounded, nickel-plated wheel and occupants that bob on springs, thus creating movement within the car.

By 1923, Ford owners had tired of black exteriors and were custom painting their old cars, so Kilgore gave its 1924 toys corresponding colors. These variations plus craftsmenlike casting made the Kilgore Fords effectual challengers of Arcade's product.

→
50.   1930–1. USA
KILGORE   10½″ long
1929½ Pontiac Roadster   Cast Iron

GIBBS   1925. USA
Filling Station   15″ long × 9″
                               wide × 7″ high
                               Paper & Wood
                               Pressed Steel

Many stories have been written over the years about Kilgore's wonderful multi-piece roadster. Though the stories differ, they have one thing in common. Each identifies the toy as a Stutz. Wrong!

For many years, I searched among full-size cars for the prototype of this toy without success. None even came close. One 1930

model Studebaker President suggested many parts, but it was not quite right. I can't describe the excitement I felt when, quite by accident, I spotted *IT*. I was at an antique auto meet, taking a shortcut through the show field. Coming to an abrupt halt, I let out a whoop, startling everyone within earshot. Wishing to keep my secret, I refused to reveal the reason for the yell, no doubt adding fuel to the rumors of my craziness.

Eureka! Every detail matched exactly – vertical louvers, small cowl lights, a medallion on the radiator shell, the door handles, two-tone finish, and even the tail light and license plate – the same. A search of the reference books confirmed everything once again. Why not a Pontiac? It makes

sense. One of the best-selling General Motors lines of 1930–1, it was familiar to children. How many of them knew about the costly Stutz at the height of the Depression?

Pontiac was named after the powerful Indian leader who allied seven tribes by treaty into one confederacy. The radiator cap is ornamented by an Indian brave with swept-back feathers on his bonnet. The Fisher-body roadster was light, powerful and good value for money. Called a 1929½ because it was released so late in the year, the real auto had wire wheels with large hubcaps. Kilgore's toy Pontiac had disc wheels. Note, however, the large center disc on the toy wheel, Kilgore's compromise between practicality and fidelity.

52 & 53.　　　　　　　　　1934. USA
KILGORE　　　　　　　　　Coupe 6¾″ long
Ford V-8 Coupe and Sedan　Sedan 7″ long
　　　　　　　　　　　　　Cast Iron

This pair of nickel-plated showroom samples
were obtained from Kilgore when it closed its
doors for good. Plated toys were intended to
avoid chipping of paint, rust and wear from
constant handling of samples.

　The separate body and chassis interlock by
means of a special wire designed by Kilgore
for quick assembly. Although these toys are
unmarked, their method of construction and
assembly acts as a means of identification. A
separate unit contains the radiator,
headlights and bumper.

　The real '34 Ford V-8 had several
improvements over the first model. Two
handles were placed on the side of the hood
in place of one. The windows could slide back
a little for ventilation as well as roll up and
down in the usual way and the steering
turned in a smaller radius. 1934 models can
be identified by a modified grille which is
wider, has a straighter front and is heavier-
looking than earlier models.

← 51.　　　　　　　　　1931. USA
MAKER UNKNOWN　　　10½″ long
probably KILGORE　　　Cast Iron
Reo Royale Victoria

The Reo Royale was the first American car to
introduce streamlining. Shown in Europe, it
won various Concours d'Elegance prizes for
its advanced design, usually credited to
European cars at that time. The selling price
was comparable to Rolls Royce and other
such fine cars in Europe as well as America.

　The colors and construction of the toy car
point to Kilgore as the maker. However, no
1931 Kilgore catalogs can be located, so
this fact cannot be confirmed.

55.　　　　　　　　c. 1927. USA
MAKER UNKNOWN　　　11½" long
Roadster with Rumble Seat　Cast Iron

Weighing in at almost four pounds, this big, clumsy-looking car utilizes pressed steel wheels with black rubber tires like those found on Hubley racers and fire engines of the same period.

A steel spring is positioned to rub against the spokes on the inside of a rear wheel to create a clicking sound when the wheel rotates. This noise was intended to simulate the sound of a motor. This same design was first used by Hubley on their motorcycle line It is also found on Vindex racers.

Jacob E. Brubaker, toy designer for Hubley from 1914 to 1951 examined this toy and rejected it as a Hubley. The wheels and tires were designed by Brubaker, but subcontracted for manufacture by another company who probably provided the wheels for this roadster. The rubber tires were molded by an Ohio rubber company for Hubley who, no doubt, provided them for Vindex and others.

This toy is found in several variations. Some cars are fitted with cast iron bumpers, others with wire ones. Some models are minus the children in the back seat and it is also found with the rubber tired spoke wheels.

This roadster is a real whodunit!

↑ **54.**　　　　　　　　c. 1940. USA
MAKER UNKNOWN　　　12" long overall
Dream Car with House　Cast Iron
Trailer

A 'dream car' was a designer's conception of a car of the future. Most designs never got farther than drawings or a scale model. Sleek, futuristic designs were usually too impractical for road use or production and almost all were years ahead of their time.

The few 'dream cars' that reached production were failures. The Pierce Silver Arrow (fig. 19), and Chrysler's Airflows (figs 31 & 32) are prime examples. Buckminster Fuller designed a car on three wheels with the single wheel at the rear in 1933. Called a Dymaxion, it was shaped like the body of an airplane. Only three were built. It was a flop.

A few toy designers got a chance to see their 'dream cars' in production in the late 1930s. Hubley, Wyandotte, and Champion, are a few American companies that added dreams to their line. Alas, the late 1930s were not times for new toy ideas. Fate intervened with the Second World War and deemed these cars failures. Instead of being too early, they were too late!

The fast-back toy car shown with fender wheel covers has design features which would eventually evolve in the late 1940s. The high, narrow windows would be considered out of date by then.

56.   1940–1. USA ↑
MAKER UNKNOWN   6⅝″ long
Packard Sedan   Cast Iron

The toy was cast in two parts with the bumpers as an integral part. This gave an interesting design to the headlights which flow into the body in a surrealistic manner. This scarce Packard toy was made close to the Second World War period when toy production finally came to a complete halt.

The Packards' classic styling and distinctive radiator were excellent selling points. The style and quality of the cars contributed to their appeal. The last Packard was built in 1958, after a long troubled financial decline.

57.   c. 1924. USA
WILLIAMS   8¾″ long
Lincoln Touring Car   Cast Iron

Made in several sizes, the tourer was called a 'Baby Lincoln' in Williams' advertisements. In 1922, The Grigsby Auto Supply Co. of Columbus, Ohio, sold a radiator cap embellished with a shield and embossed with the name 'Baby Lincoln'. It was intended for sale at $1.00 to Ford owners. The toy was $1.00 in 1932; 50¢ for 7¼″ long size.

Sprues shown hanging from the base of the running board are part of the casting process. They were usually ground flush with the part before leaving the factory.

58.
VINDEX
Oldsmobile

1929. USA
8″ long
Cast Iron

The F-29 model coupe was one of a limited number of cast iron transportation toys manufactured by Vindex as a sideline in 1929 and for a short period in 1930 before their toy operation was dissolved.

Vindex manufactured transportation toys with a limited market value like a Packard Victoria and Autocar truck. Their toys were well-made, but double the cost of well-established lines, which were having their own problems during a depression. The Vindex Pontiac roadster did not compare in value and quality to Kilgores's multi-piece (fig. 50) 1929½ Pontiac. The scarcity of Vindex toys today is due to the company's short business span.

The wheels on the 'Olds' are out of scale (undersized), but original. The assorted wheels found on Vindex toys leads to speculation that they were purchased from established specialty manufacturers.

59.
BUDDY 'L'
Dump Truck

c. early 1920s.
USA
24″ long
Pressed Steel

Heavy baked enamel finish on 20 gauge automobile steel made a toy so durable it served several generations.

The first of a stream of toymakers using auto body steel, Buddy L remained a leader in the field and set a precedent for those who followed, such as Keystone, Steelcraft, Sturditoy, and Kelmet.

Repurchases depended largely on new models, additions to a family, and word of mouth. The Buddy L's were the brutes of the toy world. Designed for outdoor play, they were constructed to withstand every conceivable punishment.

Buddy L's, the best-known pressed steel line, will still be here when we are all gone. Posed on a fence post, a dump truck with cord and crank-operated hoist stands ready for work in a cornfield.

Pressed steel of 20 gauge or more is identical to the weight used for real automobiles and trucks. Known as auto body steel, it was used for Buddy L's. The strength and durability gained with the use of auto body steel justified the high cost and was instrumental to the initial success of the toys. For the first time, toy trucks and automobiles could go outdoors and stay there.

Though not advertised as such, toy buyers were aware the Buddy L line was geared for 3 to 10 year-olds. Buddy L included girls in its advertising, but in a very subtle manner. They showed a little girl at play with toys and made reference to the female gender only slightly. Perhaps they had a tomboy in mind. More often, the company referred to the rugged abuse its toys could withstand, the jobs they could perform, and stressed outdoor play.

62. 1924. USA
BUDDY 'L' 12½" long
Flivver Delivery #210 Pressed Steel

The first real roadster pickups were conversions from runabouts with the stock rear deck removed and a pickup body installed with flare board sides and drop end gate.

Buddy L wheels were cast from aluminum and after polishing at the circumference, the centers were painted.

61. 1924. USA
BUDDY 'L' 12" long
Flivver Roadster #210A Pressed Steel

The first vehicle in the real Ford Series, this model was the most frequently used style for after-market conversions. A $25 Pickup Body could be ordered to replace the real roadster deck in 1926. The deck and box were restyled in 1926 to accommodate a canopy roof.

Buddy L Fords are sturdy, well-made toys

that have lived up to the company policy of playthings 'built to endure'. In 1925, the company claimed its toys would outlast several generations. To ensure this, toys were spot welded and riveted like the real cars and trucks they copied.

60. 1925. USA
BUDDY 'L' 12" long
Flivver Coupe #210B Pressed Steel

The only action on the Flivver was the front wheels. These could be turned with the steering wheel.

Buddy L toys were given two coats of enamel and then baked, like real cars, to give them a hard durable surface. Still, they were small enough to come indoors when needed.

The coupe appears to have been a favorite of mail order houses. It appears often and over a long period of time. Priced at $2.65 in 1928.

63.
BUDDY 'L'
Ford Dump Cart #211

1924. USA
12½″ long
Pressed Steel

Advertised as 'a realistic copy of a truck used extensively on construction work for hauling concrete, cinders, and other material', the toy copied a Dempsey Dumpster body, made by the Dempsey Company in the early 1920s for an after-market Model T conversion. The real model was operable by one man, and in the toy the body was also balanced on the frame over the axle so it would automatically tip and discharge the load when the catch was released.

64.
BUDDY 'L'
Dump Truck #211A

1924. USA
11¼″ long
Pressed Steel

The Flivver series trucks were ideal for the smaller child who could imitate older ones at play with a toy scaled for his size. Dump trucks were a favorite body style of buyers and the model which sold in the greatest numbers in all manufacturers' toy truck lines. They also received the most use and as a result are not all that plentiful today.

65.
BUDDY 'L'
One-Ton Ford
Express Truck #212

1925. USA
14¼" long
Pressed Steel

The real truck was introduced to the public April 29, 1925. Like the 212A Delivery Truck, the pickup did not have a long life span due to the radical changes that were to take place in the truck and toy industry in the late 1920s.

At age 59, this truck has developed a cancerous looking condition which should serve as a warning for toys kept in a humid climate. My policy is to keep the original paint 'as is'. This condition drives a perfectionist crazy and is the perfect example of when a repaint is warranted. The eating-away of the metal can only be stopped if the truck is stripped and the metal thoroughly cleaned. Decals are available these days and restorers are willing to take the work.

Both the One-Ton Express and the 212A Delivery are scarce toys.

66.
BUDDY 'L'
One Ton Ford Delivery
Truck #212A

1925. USA
14½" long
Pressed Steel

An express body with canopy top and closed cab made these trucks ideal for produce. With the addition of screen sides, the 'huckster' became a mail truck.

Buddy L added screen sides to this model about 1927, and though the real T's were already out of production, the toys remained favorites for a little while longer. Stores were still promoting Model T toys in 1928.

67.
BUDDY 'L'
Coal Truck #202

1926. USA
25½" long
Pressed Steel

'Built exactly like the big city trucks used in hauling coal to be delivered by chute through basement openings', reads the catalog. A tapering body insured a steady flow down the flanged and angled coal chute with a little help from the coal man to nudge it along.

68.
BUDDY 'L'
Sand and Gravel Truck
#202A

1926. USA
25½" long
Pressed Steel

Four compartments with latched hinged doors allow separation of material. The sloping floor ensures the material will flow freely, very important for busy little construction workers. The body partition is removable.

Buddy L trucks were strong enough to hold a child seated on the roof . . . and often did.

Top
BUDDY 'L'
Dandy Digger #2025

c. 1932. USA
38" extended
Pressed Steel

On the ground or in the sand, the digger turns around and digs by a push and pull of the levers. Boys could excavate a hillside or dig clams at the beach with this toy without sitting on the ground or tipping over.

One of Buddy L's few reasonably priced toys, the digger was featured in F. A. O. Schwarz's 1932 catalog for $1.00!

71. 1923–30. USA
BUDDY 'L' 27″ long
Fire Department Truck Pressed Steel
#205

Combination hook and ladder and wrecking truck was designed for multiple play use. A brass bell and railing add sparkle to a truck with ladders that could be extended to a height of six feet by use of interlocking clips and a windlass. The pull cord is original and was supplied with each new truck.

California Notions and Toy Company, offered the fire truck in its 1928–30 catalog for $9.00 each. This price is astounding for a toy offered during a depression, as well as being proof of a successful toy carried in stock for many years.

Despite the fact that this toy was never played with, it has aged from the passage of time.

← 69. 1926. USA
BUDDY 'L' 25″ long
Lumber Truck #203A Pressed Steel

One of the most attractive toys in the line, the lumber truck has many interesting parts. Two stake sections anchor each side. The bed is fitted with three steel rollers and a crank at the end so loads can be rolled off with ease. The cord tied to the windshield post is original and as delivered in the box. This exceptional toy has *never* been played with and carries its original load of lumber.

← 70. 1925. USA
BUDDY 'L' 26½″ long
Street Sprinkler #206 Pressed Steel

Street sprinklers disappeared with paved roads, but are still the only means for keeping down the dust at new construction sites, race tracks, and other open dry places in the summertime.

A fillable tank with a brass spigot to regulate the flow must have thrilled youngsters. Dirt and water – a combination my son could never resist when he was a little boy!

Buddy L swapped the sprinkler attachment for four special oil cans which were placed in the racks alongside the tanks and called the variation a #206A Oil Truck.

72.
BUDDY 'L'
Ice Truck #207

1926–9. USA
26½" long
Pressed Steel

An important industry before the advent of home and store ice makers and even afterwards. The iceman delivered for special occasions, like parties, weddings, and also supplied fish and meat markets, restaurants and bars.

Standard equipment for the toy was a pair of steel ice tongs and three pieces of glass imitation ice.

←73.
BUDDY 'L'
Wrecking Truck

1932. USA
26½" long
Pressed Steel

A standard Buddy L chassis is fitted with the latest rubber-tired wheels and a special body. The well-designed boom swings in an 18-inch circle by means of a turntable and wheel operated by the owner. Cable drums either lift or pull up to 20 pounds and lock with an automatic ratchet.

A quality toy and hard to find.

75.
BUDDY 'L'
Robotoy

New in 1932
USA
22" long
Pressed Steel

An unusual toy in its day and a total departure for the Buddy L Company. By pressing or releasing a button on the control box, the truck steers forward, backs up, the dump lifts and it can go into neutral – all by remote control. A 21-foot electrical cord limits the traveling distance, but not the fun a child must have experienced with this toy, which was certainly a futuristic design.

Buddy L toys were never cheap, but the $12.50 price tag was considered an extravagant sum in 1932 for the Robotoy truck. Very few of these toys remain today. Directions for operating the toy boast that it will perform on *any* strength current!

A pressed steel gas pump, 9" high, holds a removable '5 gallon' glass tank which actually holds liquid. The pump handle and hose are for make-believe. Besides, no gas was needed for this customer! The mid-1920s gas pump sold for 19¢.

←74.
BUDDY 'L'
Express Line #204A

1930–2. USA
25" long
Pressed Steel

A removable heavy screen side body with double lockable rear doors and a drop tailgate provide multiple use for this attractive and well-built truck. Original accessories include the baggage cart and skid with Buddy L decals. Though made for outdoor use, this model has been well cared for. The dual rear wheels copy real Railway Express trucks of that year.

Prices for this truck ranged from $6.75 to $8.99, depending on dealers and location across the United States.

76.
AMERICAN NATIONAL
Packard Roadster

c. 1928. USA
28½″ long
Pressed Steel

A large outdoor toy, too small to ride in and too heavy to lift, but a very realistic model of a classic of its day. No 'motor', just a pull rope attached to the bumper.

American National was a large manufacturer of sidewalk toys and regular pedal cars. They were aiming for a market size a little bigger than the Buddy L's and a little smaller than their own juvenile pedal cars, into which children could fit and drive.

A roadster with the top down was also available. Either Buick or Stutz logos could be bought with a different color scheme. American National also turned the cars into a Red Fire Chief's Model; the radiator ornament exchanged for a bell.

The roadster was carried in jobbers' catalogs from 1928–30, selling for $6.75 wholesale. The oversize pull toys were not seen again after 1930.

77. →
CORCORAN
DeSoto Airflow Sedan

1934. USA
17″ long
Pressed Steel

Chrysler Motors produced 6,797 DeSoto Airflows in 1934. Like the Chrysler Airflow, this car was considered a disaster. Despite the problems encountered with the real vehicle, the design continued to appeal to toy manufacturers.

A Corcoran advertisement in an April 1934 issue of *Toys and Novelties*, a toy buyer's guide, claims this toy, which is 'scaled to an actual twelfth', was 'built for the builders of the AIRFLOW car – to be used as extra help to fast moving sales. This miniature will please parents and children alike.'

The real DeSoto suffered badly from the Depression and lagging sales. There is no evidence to support Corcoran's claim that the toy was used as a promotional item, although it seems entirely possible that the toy was originally intended for this purpose. The wording of the ad suggests that something may have gone wrong with the plan.

This model is a pull toy with battery-operated headlamps.

78. →
CORCORAN
Chrysler Six Passenger
Airflow Sedan

1934. USA
17¼″ long
Pressed Steel

Remarkable lines for pressed steel, which by its very nature resists fine details. Extremely well-made, the one-twelfth scale Chrysler Airflow sedan operates by a strong steel spring 'motor' which utilizes space in the rear compartment.

Wooden front seat, cast iron steering wheel, and rubber tires are a melange of material which makes this perfect scale model a copy of the real car.

Real seats were 50″ wide. Head and legroom was increased substantially by the strong, streamlined beam and truss body. The basic design was supposedly taken from an airplane. An engineering success, the much-admired Airflow was a financial disaster. This startlingly different car is easily recognized today, but was too far ahead of its time.

79.
EMMETS
Concrete Mixer Truck

1920s. USA
19½" long
Pressed Steel

The husky cab and chassis on the concrete mixer is constructed of 16 gauge steel; heavier than the steel used on Buddy L and Keystone toys (the heavier the steel, the lower the gauge number).

    The drum rotates with the help of string and wooden pulleys and can hold whatever its owner desired. I found stones and bird feathers, well mixed, when I acquired the truck. The drum is set in motion when the truck is pushed forward.

    A well-made and heavily constructed steering wheel occupies the entire center space of the windshield area. Someone forgot to plan ahead.

80.
KELMET
Dump Truck

1925. USA
25" long
Pressed Steel

The White brothers, Windsor, Rollin and Walter, had their initial success with steam vehicles and showed their first gasoline truck at the New York Auto Show in 1910. An outgrowth of their father's sewing machine business, the sons reorganised The White Company to become the White Motor Company in 1915. Pioneers in the truck industry, the Whites were to leave a

well-respected and established name.

    This toy is a true replica of the real White truck with dual rear wheels, steering gear and dumping mechanism. The six solid rubber diamond tread tires were standard equipment. Some toy companies charged extra. However, the price of the toy in December, 1925, when it was featured for Christmas was $7.65, a goodly sum for those days.

A relatively scarce toy today, even the best, like our spotless example shown here, have trouble keeping the aging tires rolling.

    The screen-vented hood on the White radiator and special artillery wheels distinguish the 'Big Boy' line of Kelmet trucks. The lithographed cardboard box in which it was packed was imprinted as a White Service Station, a nice additional feature.

81.
KEYSTONE
Dump Truck #41

1925. USA
26″ long
Pressed Steel

Before the advent of the large pressed steel trucks of the early 1920s, toys were flimsy and not suited for rugged outdoor play. Keystone, Buddy L's closest competitor, stressed the strength of their pressed steel product by picturing a 250-pound man standing on top of the toy. Their earliest trucks used a baked enamel finish and had solid metal wheels with polished tires which resembled Buddy's. Later issues were to have rubber tires.

   Each toy manufacturer of big pressed steel dump trucks searched for a way to make his truck stand out from the others. Keystone used a Packard radiatior that actually carried the Packard logo, even though real Packard trucks had ended production in 1923. The front crank with a worm gear elevates the dump body. A drop end gate contains a chute door and a signal arm is located on the driver's side.

82.
KEYSTONE
Water Pump and Tower
#56

1928. USA
29″ long
41″ high with
tower extended
Pressed Steel

This working toy directs a stream of water 25 to 35 feet from its water tank by a brass pressure pump. The Klaxon horn and brass bell give warnings.

   A never-used plaything that has some flaking typical of Keystones. The original tag hangs from the front with the original pull cord.

← 83. 1925. USA
KEYSTONE
U.S. Mail Truck 26″ long
18 gauge steel

1928
U.S. Mail Plane 26″ long
17 gauge steel 24″ Wingspan
Pressed Steel

A mail plane prepares to land. The mail truck and plane are in official U.S. Government colors of the period.

The airplane sold in small numbers during financially hard times. It cost $3.00 in 1928. The truck retailed for $7.50.

↓ 84. Late 1920s. USA
KEYSTONE 26″ long
U.S. Army Truck #48 Pressed Steel

Americans were not eager buyers of military toys in the post First World War era, but accepted those without artillery such as this transport truck.

Acquired from an estate where it had been the purchase of a grown man for himself in the late 1920s, the truck lay in a store room from its first day. The pull cord is still in the original factory-tied position on the dash.

Keystone toys were spray-painted over bare metal. Evidence that the paint does not hold up without a base coat can be seen in flaking in the hood area. The decal across the radiator departed for the same reason. No maker of large pressed steel toys would ever equal the quality finishes of Buddy L. Still, Keystone had one main attraction. They copied the Packard truck for their designs and were quick to realize the importance of rubber tires and novel designs.

Kingsbury Motor Truck, No. 318. 25 inches long. Handsomely finished in two colors of enamel, with rubber tires, cushioned bumper. Winds up crank-fashion from the front. A toy that will make thousands of American children happy this Christmas.

Load it up and start away!

HAVE a trucking business all your own! Load up to capacity at your "warehouse." Crank your motor—which winds the strong powerful spring. All set! Put the motor into gear with the lever beside the driver's seat. And away you go.

Around the corner a package to be delivered. Pull back the lever at the driver's seat—brakes on—the truck has stopped. Deliver your package and you're off to the next stop. Don't stop yet to crank—your truck will run 200 feet before this is again necessary.

Here is a real toy that will make you he envy of every boy on the street. It is the finest toy we have ever built—and Kingsbury has built fine toys for over 35 years. Price $15. $16 50 west of the Mississippi. Other toys from $1. up.

Better put this on your "Christmas Stocking List" right NOW.

KINGSBURY
MOTOR DRIVEN TOYS

This wonderfully lifelike motor truck is just one of an almost endless series of mechanical and pull toys made in Keene, N. H. by Kingsbury. You ought to have the Catalog that shows and describes them—Fire Engines, Ladder Trucks, Hose Wagons, Busses, Delivery Wagons, Tractors, Trolley Cars— every kind of wheeled toy you can think of, all finished in lifelike natural manner, and priced in a range within everybody's means. If your dealer

is not now showing Kingsbury Toys for Christmas, write for this book and we will tell you how you may secure Kingsbury Toys quickly.

This Non-Skid Eraser, 10c

Send 10c coin for this miniature disc wheel whose balloon tire is really a rubber eraser for school or home use.

KINGSBURY MANUFACTURING COMPANY, 80 Myrtle St., KEENE, NEW HAMPSHIRE

Dealers Note: Our complete line sold and displayed by Reimann-Seabrey Company, 215 Fourth Ave., New York City

85.
KINGSBURY
Chemical-ladder Truck

1925. USA
34″ long
without ladders
Pressed Steel

Kingsbury was engaged in manufacturing fire toys from the early 1900s and established markets for new models which they continually updated and released.

One marketing strategy used by Kingsbury was to set up special toy displays and demonstrations for children during fire prevention week, usually held in October. Special backgrounds and accessories enhanced the appearance of the toys. It also gave parents time to plan Christmas purchases, once their children had been captivated by the trucks.

A companion aerial ladder truck was available in 1926. The spring motor driven fire engines sold for $11.00 to $13.00, depending upon location and outlet. This was a substantial amount for 1925. Prices varied with the times. The higher-priced fire engines were reduced to $10.00 in 1929 to promote sales. A detachable handle for pulling the toy was included.

86 & 87.
STURDY
Police Department Truck
Contractor's Dump Truck

1929–33. USA
26″ long
26″ long
Pressed Steel

Buddy L, Keystone, Kingsbury, and Kelmet, among others, paved the way for buyers' acceptance of large pressed steel trucks. Sturdy tried to infiltrate the market with its line of toy trucks in 1929, at the worst possible time.

Looking for all the world like a copy cat, Sturditoys were electrically welded and riveted on a chassis built to withstand the weight of 175 pounds. Construction and body styles similar to other lines were offered, including comparable prices. Bowing to financial difficulties and established firms, the line was advertised at half-price in time for the Christmas trade in 1930. It didn't help. The company was phased out in 1933.

The police van with screen sides was an uncommon body style and one not found in competitors' lines. It appears to have been Sturditoy's most saleable truck. A high-sided dump and a side-tilting dump were other unique body styles in the line.

Dump trucks were competitive and almost always the least expensive toy in a manufacturer's line. Open cabs were preferred by buyers for access to workable steering wheels.

Many Ohio rubber companies were involved in making rubber tires for automotive toy manufacturers in the 1920s and 1930s. Sturditoy snagged Firestone, the only famous name on its toys.

88.
TURNER
Fire Pumper

Late 1920s. USA
29″ long
Pressed Steel

A well-proportioned and substantially constructed pumper, minus the flywheel motor found on most Turner toys. The added weight of a motor large enough to move this heavy toy would hamper its action.

While fewer disc wheels appeared on real cars and trucks, they were preferred by toymakers as being easier to manufacture and paint. They provided extra strength for outdoor toys and there was less chance of breakage compared with spoke wheels.

89.
WYANDOTTE
Cord Coupe Model 810

1936. USA
13″ long
Pressed Steel

A line-for-line copy of the 'coffin-nosed' Cord coupe designed by Gordon Buehrig in 1935 for the Auburn Automobile Company. The advanced styling included headlamps concealed within the fenders and a wrap-around grille.

Children have always been big fans of outrageous automobile designs. While adults stood and stared at the innovative designs of Airflows and Cords, they failed to buy them. The toy copies, were in contrast, bought in large numbers.

The toy is pressed from extra heavy steel which has been enameled and baked.

Propelled by a reverse-wind-up spring motor concealed by a plate covering the entire base, the mechanism is unusual for Wyandotte. To wind up the spring, the toy is pressed to the floor while pushing backwards. When hands are off, the toy will move forward. No keys clutter the body design of this flamboyant classic. Rubber tires are mounted on large wooden wheels shaped to simulate the large hub caps on the real Cord.

A very heavy toy for its size and a nice model of the true car, it is surprisingly well detailed. The only toy of its type, it sold well into 1937, when E. L. Cord's empire collapsed.

Cars and Trucks LIGHT PRESSED STEEL

90.
ACME
Curved Dash Oldsmobile

1903. USA
11″ long
Pressed Steel

The curved dash Olds bears the distinction of being America's first mass-produced automobile. Completed in 1900, it sold for $650. After the song, 'In My Merry Oldsmobile' was written by Gus Edwards in 1905, the car and song were to become equally famous.

The Oldsmobile was designed as a very simple car so it could be easily serviced and the design was suited to mass production.

Acme duplicated the simple design in a well-made and durable toy using a pivotal front axle brace reminiscent of earlier Hafner cars. The crank handle for the concealed clockwork motor is an original innovation and afforded easy access for the child from the top of the toy. The reinforced spoke wheels were patented.

Acme also produced a truck with a canopy roof. Both toys bear a stenciled 'A' monogram on the side.

→
92.
CONVERSE
Touring Cars
Pierce Great-Arrows (2)
Buick

1908. USA
16½″ long
Pressed Steel
16½″ long
Pressed Steel

The pair of touring cars in the upper part of the picture have long been known as Pierce Great-Arrows to antique car collectors. Although the car was never identified as such with markings, the identity is confirmed by consulting the Pierce Great-Arrows dealers' catalog. Cars by this maker before 1909 were known as Great-Arrows; thereafter the name was changed to Pierce-Arrow. They did not carry their name on the radiator like other cars, as the manufacturer felt such a prestigious automobile was recognizable without its name.

The touring car in front closely resembles an early Buick. Converse made this scale toy available with or without a clockwork motor. Converse produced this series to include a fire engine, pickup truck, speedster, and an open depot wagon. Because they were durable toys, many were pressed into service during the First World War to fill a shortage of metal toys and are often found repainted with the heavy enamels prevalent in those days. No way has been found to successfully remove the overpaint without destroying the original coat.

Doll collectors favor these cars as their roomy interiors are ideal for dolls.

91.
CONVERSE
Auto Hansom

c. 1895. USA
10½″ long
Pressed Steel

Representing a turn-of-the-century electric Hansom taxi used in large cities, this toy is powered by a fine, strong, brass geared clockwork motor. The driver sat up high for better visibility. A quality transitional toy, which copies the very earliest form of taxi service.

The real taxi was steered from the rear axle with a steering wheel. The toy has no place for one. Steering was easier using the smaller rear wheels.

93 & 94. c. 1913. USA
A. C. GILBERT 8″ long
U.S. Mail Truck c. 1914
Dump Truck 10¼″ long
overall
Pressed Steel

Gilbert appears to have copied the slot and tab construction typical of German imports. The windup spring which extends the length of the truck is wound by a crank in front similar to those on real American trucks of the pre-1915 period. The pressed spoke wheels are strictly a copied design, close in appearance to German models.

Changes include an open side window, heavier metal, and a lithographed steel driver holding the steering wheel. The heavier material satisfied an American desire for sturdiness in their toys. The mail truck was advertised for 59¢ in 1913.

To update an earlier truck, Gilbert simply pulled off the straight dash and added its version of the latest design. Hoods were growing in 1910, but not into shapes like this. The spring leads to the motor which is in the rear. Could the flat sides on the hood be Gilbert's version of a Ford? This is one of those toys which is fun, for it always leads to a discussion.

Note: Mail truck has a working rear door.

→
95. 1932. USA
GIRARD 14″ long
Pierce-Arrow Coupe Pressed Steel
12-Cylinder

Pierce-Arrow made fine cars. Beautifully engineered, many sold on their elegant looks alone. Advertisements for their 12-cylinder model was directed at the 'well-bred' Americans who could afford such expensive cars.

Girard gave subtle, but recognizable, styling to its Pierce-Arrow model; a slanted windshield, the large hood louvers, double sidemounts, and single bar bumper were taken directly from the original car in 1932. Battery-operated fender lamps are a clever substitute for Pierce-Arrow's famous trademark – lamps growing out of the fenders. The rose and plum colors were intended to catch a toy buyer's eye. They did, and still do.

The steel used for Hafner automobiles and trucks is very light weight. Once stamped and given a japanned finish,* they closely resemble tin toys. The light metal enabled details to be embossed, and where most American steel toys were constructed by welding or soldering, the Hafners used the tab and slot method of assembly in much of the body. This gives them a European look which is further augmented by their delicate stampings. This is especially noticeable in the auto express. Hafners are stenciled with a small design or lettering.

The baggage truck on the left came with a very old toy shop address card and note. The toy was presented as a gift in 1901. The large cast iron rear wheels confirm the period. This is probably the first or one of the first automotive toys by Hafner.

The Auto-Express truck was a featured special for 67¢ by Montgomery-Ward in 1903.

* A japanned finish on metal toys is achieved with transparent lacquer or varnish which allows the shine of the basic metal to reflect through the paint.

The most popular style car on the road was the single-seat runabout.

This mechanical toy is powered with a clockwork motor which was touted as being 'almost noiseless' in the house. It sold for 68¢ at Montgomery Ward's in 1903 with a japanned finish and gilt trim.

This style automobile is taken directly from a horse-drawn two-seat brake.

The fenderless, tiller steering car with velvet seats copies a transitional vehicle in which the motor was underneath the body instead of under the hood. The tiller turns and sets the front wheels to run in a circle. The wheels are cast of lead and painted. Very few automotive toys were made by American manufacturers during this period.

99.   1904. USA
HAFNER   10″ long
Touring Car   Pressed Steel

A rear entrance tonneau clockwork model with velvet seats and a polished steel hood is characteristic of the real 1903–4 automobiles of the day. Early toy automobile manufacturers copied cars seen on the road. These were still few in number and a novelty. A few early, outlandish models that did appear on the roads, like the 8-wheel car and weird body shapes, were never made into toys.

Hafner's early touring car represents a 1903–4 Rambler. In a 1903 *Automobile Topics* magazine, an article advises the readers that a single-cylinder Rambler has only half as many parts as the 2-cylinder, therefore, is only half the trouble!

Rubber tires are fitted to cast lead wheels on Hafner cars. Made only for a few years in the early 1900s, after which the company abandoned them to specialize in trains, Hafner automotive toys are scarce and treasured by collectors.

100.   1903. USA
HAFNER   9½″ long
Police Patrol   Pressed Steel

The improbable steering wheel works on this clockwork, rear entrance patrol and shows poor advance planning in the design. It would have taken a stepladder . . . a tall one, to get into the driver's seat! The earliest steering wheels were in an upright position.

101.
KINGSBURY
Roadster

1923. USA
11″ long
Pressed Steel

Kingsbury updated its post-First World War line with the addition of bumpers – still an optional purchase on many real cars. Conversely, while headlamps were optional on toys, they were standard equipment for the mass- produced car in the early 1920s.

The outline painting of the door shows that handwork still existed in the company's production lines in the early 1920s. Stamping machines were not yet in use for the addition of body details.

→
103.
KINGSBURY
Dump Truck

1927. USA
14″ long
Pressed Steel

Something about the tipping and dumping action of dump trucks has remained a perennial favorite with buyers.

Kingsbury's trucks from the late 1920s and later had basic, clean lines, and a classical appearance that held up for many years, requiring few changes to remain active sellers.

102.
KINGSBURY
Artillery Truck

1919. USA
12″ long, closed
Pressed Steel
Wood 'Shells'

A khaki tan war vehicle with metal wheels displaying the company's change in name from Wilkins to Kingsbury. Cast iron drivers were absent from many post-First World War toys as Kingsbury lightened toys and eliminated the high-cost material which had risen so dramatically during wartime.

The anti-aircraft gun is removable and rotates. It can actually shoot the wooden ammunition which stores neatly behind the driver's seat.

An unusual toy for Kingsbury which failed to excite the buyers and was short-lived. The hood and chassis style with an integral bumper was used for other truck styles. Vulcanized rubber tires were developed shortly thereafter.

104.
KINGSBURY
Coupe

1923. USA
11″ long
Pressed Steel

This toy was Kingsbury's answer to the popular Arcade coupes which were moving in on the toy market in a big way by 1923. One advantage of pressed steel toys over cast iron ones, was their lighter weight.

Arcade's Fords and Chevys were painted black like the real cars. This was Kingsbury's chance to add color to a non-make. It is interesting that Kingsbury promoted their toys for boys *and girls* in their advertising, though the toys they sold as defined by the standards of the day were totally masculine.

The attractive coupe has a jaunty appearance with its straight, prim passengers' compartment. The rear license plate has an additional spot representing a stop signal.

106.
KINGSBURY
Sedan

1927. USA
14″ long
Pressed Steel

Part of a 'Body by Fisher' label is still in evidence on this toy. The Fisher Body Corporation of Detroit was owned by General Motors who, in the late 1920s, controlled Cadillac, LaSalle, Buick, Oakland, Oldsmobile, Pontiac and Chevrolet. The toy body was designed by Kingsbury and approved by Fisher Body to carry its trademark as a publicity gimmick.

The designs of Kingsbury cars are composites of many GM makes, and not one in particular; they incorporated features from the top of the Fisher lines. By 1930 most Fisher bodies had curved windshield posts.

107.
KINGSBURY
Delivery Truck

1927–8. USA
14½″ long with tailgate closed. Opens to 16″
Pressed Steel

Closed cab trucks with a full-length canopy

105.
KINGSBURY
Roadster

1927. USA
13½″ long
Pressed Steel

A snappy roadster that copies the two-tone colors and striping of the roaring twenties era. Two-passenger roadsters are sometimes called playboys' cars by collectors, as they are totally impractical for family use. The small

top could be fitted with side curtains or screen sides for further enclosure.

This lightweight commercial style truck was made for J. C. Penney and has its paper cigar-band shaped label.

The toy sold for $3.00 in 1927.

driver's compartment enforces close proximity of the passengers and, other than a space for golf clubs behind the seat, there is little room for much else.

Numbers printed or pressed on Kingsbury license plates are the manufacturer's catalog number. Sometimes the rear plate holds a clue to the year of manufacture as well.

Priced at $2.50 in 1927, with 10% more west of the Mississippi.

108.
KINGSBURY
Coupe

c. 1927. USA
14″ long
Pressed Steel

Equipped with battery-operated lights and linkage steering, this car has a lever visible in the driver's compartment which operates the lights. The outstanding feature of this model is its 'radio', actually a concealed music box activated by opening the rumble seat. A variety of popular tunes of the day were used. This one plays, 'I'll Be Loving You Always'. The 'radio' was also offered on 1930s models.

109.
KINGSBURY
Cabriolet

1927. USA
14″ long
Pressed Steel

The cabriolet town car is a composite of body styles, copied mostly from a 1927 Chrysler. The last year in which Chrysler used a Fisher Body was 1928.

In striving for authenticity, Kingsbury pressed its toys from a light-weight steel which allows for sharper detail. The scale and pleasing colors of the toys make them very collectible.

The town car is an elegant addition to any collection.

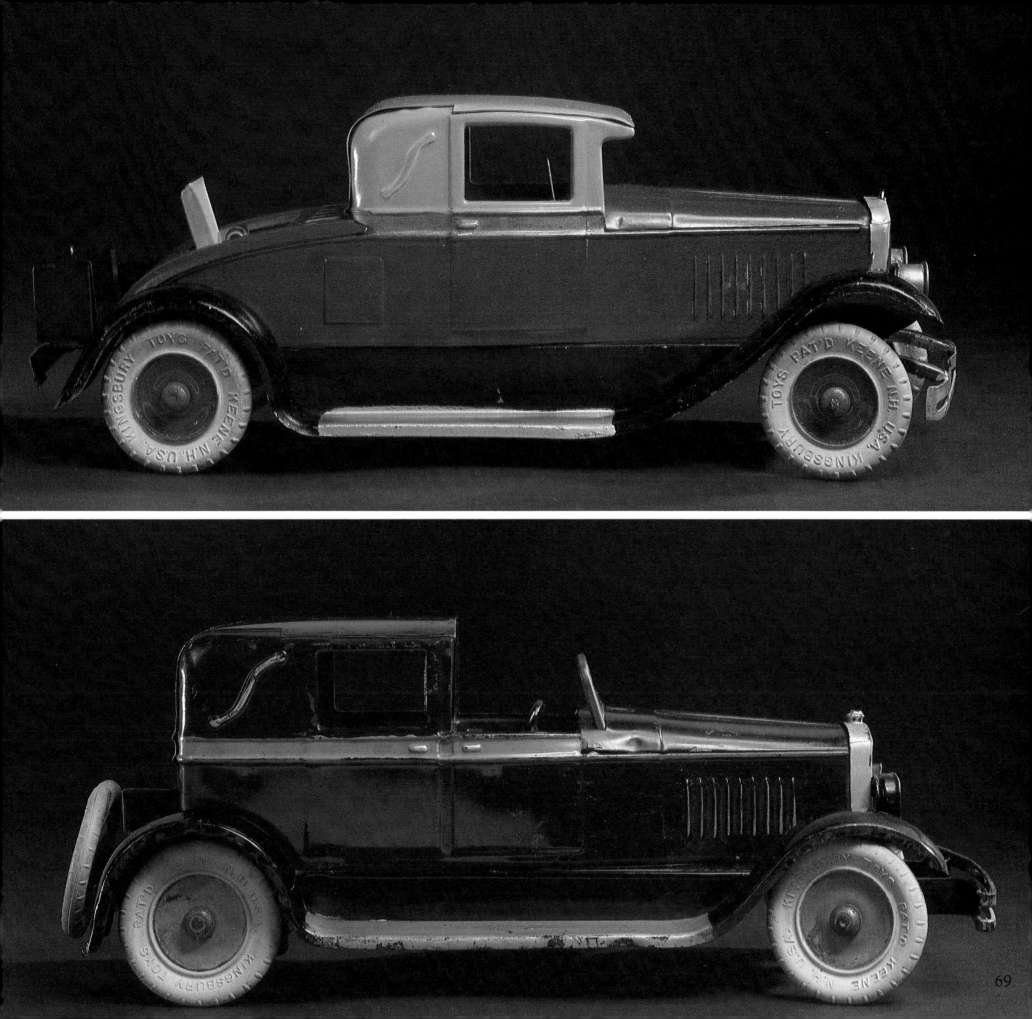

110.
KINGSBURY
Ford Station Wagon

1929. USA
12″ long
Pressed Steel

January 1929 marked the first time a major automobile manufacturer mass-produced a station wagon with a wood body. Classified as a commercial car, the station wagon embodied refinements hitherto found in passenger vehicles. Prior to this time, station wagon bodies were sold for installation on a Model A chassis by independent body builders.

   Made exclusively for J. C. Penney's private label 'Little Jim Playthings', the 'woodie' was made without headlamps.

111.
KINGSBURY
Chrysler Airflow Sedan

1934. USA
14″ long
Pressed Steel

Kingsbury produced the largest line of Airflows of any toy manufacturer and updated these radical cars every year through to the last model in 1937.

   Toy Airflows were offered with horns, battery operated lights, 'radios' (Swiss music boxes with appropriate tunes for children), and an assortment of trailers as accessories. On some models, trailers held the music box and were sold as a car-trailer combination.

   The model shown is in pristine, never-played-with condition. A lever barely visible in the passenger compartment operates the headlamps. Kingsbury clockwork 'motors' were noted for their strength. Most are still found in working order, probably attributable to their concealed springs in sealed units. Tires this year were all rubber with painted centers.

   Airflows were popular best sellers, despite the hard times.

112.   c. 1929. USA
KINGSBURY   14″ long
Sedan   Pressed Steel

The most popular cars in the late 1920s were closed sedans, considered the most suitable for families. 1929 heralded an era of fast automobiles, painted in off-beat colors to match the spirit of the time. This was also a period of elegant cars, or ones which, on the outside at least, were made to look rather special.

A paper label declares the toy as having 'Body by Fisher'.

113.   1935. USA
KINGSBURY   14½″ long
Chrysler Airflow   Pressed Steel

A wash and wax job is responsible for the clean looks of this sleek toy.

The Airflow, conceived in 1927, was kept in the experimental stage until its release in 1934. Aviator Orville Wright recommended that an experimental wind tunnel be set up with scale models for testing the flow of air over the curved surfaces. Six years passed before a satisfactory design was completed and adapted to either two-door or four-door sedans. Though the public was unwilling to accept the design, which followed airplane principles, children loved the car!

Chevron stripes on the radiator grille and redesigned hood identify the 1935 model. The Kingsbury patented clockwork motor was used on all its toys. This model is equipped with a battery operated horn. A 'D' flashlight battery compartment fitted in the floor pan and powered a horn or headlamps, although these were never together on the same toy.

The number of actual Chrysler Airflows sold in 1935 diminished, while the Kingsbury toys sold in increasing numbers. In both the real and toy world only sedan bodies were made.

114. c. 1935. USA
KINGSBURY 11″ long
Dump Truck Pressed Steel
with 'Electric' Lights

If there was ever an uglier toy truck made, I haven't seen it! New axle holes bear proof that the chassis was given lower lines in order to modernize it. Black rubber tires and battery-operated lights were added to updated toys by Kingsbury in the mid-1930s – Kingsbury had all but eliminated cast iron parts on their toys by then. Even cast iron drivers with double pronged pins had completely disappeared. There is no steering wheel or place for one. No hole for a driver, either. This one's a temporary occupant to dress up the seat!

116.
KINGSBURY
1937 Lincoln Zephyr and
Camp Trailer

1937. USA
22½″ long
overall
Sedan 12″ long
Pressed Steel

Not an exact model, the manufacturer took liberties with the design of the headlamps and bumpers to cut costs and speed production. Even so, there is no doubt that the toy was intended to represent a V-12 Lincoln Zephyr to the buyers. The Lincoln Zephyr was the start of a radical styling change for Lincoln and was the first mass-produced car constructed with a unit 'bridge truss' body, thus eliminating the chassis frame. President Calvin Coolidge bought a 1924 Lincoln for his use at the White House and established a precedent for US Presidents to use that marque to the this day.

The 'bustle back' trunk made the luggage compartment accessible through the trunk door this year. Missing are the rear fender wheel covers found on the real cars. The sedan pulls the most uniquely designed trailer in the Kingsbury series, equipped with a removable and folding 'tent' roof. Picnic furniture was included and stored inside the trailer. A stop-start lever on the sealed clockwork motor appears on many late Kingsbury toys.

← 115 & 117.
↓ KINGSBURY
Coupe 'n Trailer

Coupe 'n Boat with Trailer

1936. USA

22½″ long
overall
1937

22½″ long
overall
Pressed Steel

Trade journals reported an enthusiastic reception for Kingsbury's newest additions to its automotive line – the Lincoln Zephyrs.

The toy house trailer could be ordered with a 'radio', Kingsbury's name for a music box. The coupe 'n trailer was the company's main feature toy in the 1936 trade shows.

73

118.
KINGSBURY
Borden's Truck

1937. USA
9″ long
Pressed Steel

The Divco-Wayne Corporation of Detroit, formed in 1927, is still a going business. It introduced a door-to-door delivery truck that could be driven from the folding driver's seat or midway between the front and rear wheels. In 1937 emphasis was on a square-shaped body, enabling the driver to stand and providing greater capacity. The truck also had the ability to idle for long periods of time and thus was ideal for house-to-house deliveries.

The silver colored Borden's truck may have been a special production toy. It also comes in plain white without a name. A stop–start lever can be seen behind the right rear wheel.

Black rubber tires with the Kingsbury name in bas relief help identify those toys as coming from the late 1930s.

119.
KINGSBURY
Sky Roof Sedan

1939. USA
14″ long
Pressed Steel

The Yellow Cab Company used DeSoto sedans, including the sky roof models, to make up a major portion of their fleet in 1939–40. The conservative, reliable sedans were roomy and favored by passengers for sightseeing in major cities across the nation.

The real car had low-set headlamps, but their placement on the toy is ridiculous! The toy 'sky roof' slides open for air and sightseeing.

120 & 121.
KNAPP
Electric Automobile

1899. USA
10″ long
Pressed Steel

A plain-bodied early electric toy with interesting lines except for the precariously high seat which was so designed to hold the wet cell batteries and make them readily accessible. Before the turn of the century, many homes were not equipped with electricity and wet cells were the only source of power for battery-operated toys. Knapp used a substance they called Chromite – actually a bichromate. A 10-ounce bottle was supplied with the toy. The Chromite was activated by adding water, and one single charging provided sufficient current to run the car for up to one hour.

Around 1903, Knapp produced an improved electric car. A back-to-back trap style, it had smaller wheels, lowered seats, and used dry cell batteries. Priced at $5.50, it was higher than the 1899 model which sold for $3.00.

The electric motors on the cars were deliberately left exposed for educational purposes and reveal finely made gears which turn the rear axle.

The manufacturer produced toys specifically to acquaint boys with the wonders of electricity. Most were designed for simple experiments and for 'America Industry in Miniature' as their catalog reads.

122 & 123.
LINDSTROM
Open Bed Express Truck

Mail Truck No. 1

1919. USA

9½" long
overall

8¼" long
overall
Pressed Steel

Lindstrom had its own ideas about how a US Mail truck should look. I suspect that the drivers and wheels were bought in as many American toy manufacturers subcontracted for these parts. The blue painted toys are peacetime vehicles. The USA Army Air Force and Mail Van bear interestng crank wind motors which differ from the Gilbert and German windups. The large gears visible underneath drives the rear axle. When the truck moves, the bell rings.

The heavy, sturdy, American construction is in evidence once again.

Unlike the Gilbert trucks, the Lindstroms are welded except for the seats which use tabs to hold them in place.

→
124.
MARX
Service Station

1930. USA

13½" long
10" deep
5¾" high
Pressed Steel

This is what service stations used to look like. No 'Out of Gas' or 'Pumps Closed' signs. Instead, free air, water, and maps. Sometimes, you could pick up a snack while waiting to get your car serviced.

Our toy has battery-operated lights on the gas pumps and beneath the grease rack which raises with a hand lever. A water can, oil wagon and truck on the grease rack are standard equipment. The entire set was priced at $1.00, including directions.

In 1930, gasoline was 17¢ a gallon!

125 & 127.　　　　　Mid to late
MARX　　　　　　　　1930s. USA
Searchlight Truck　　　9¾″ long
Gravel Mixer　　　　　9¾″ long
　　　　　　　　　　Pressed Steel

Marx adapted its 'dream car' designs to produce this pair of trucks. These exaggerated truck forms did not travel the byways of America except when custom-produced for a specific purpose.

The Buck Rogers and Flash Gordon era gave birth to toy trucks shaped like rockets to the moon. Dream cars and trucks wore fender skirts, even some airplanes sported the wheel covers. The kids were crazy about them.

A battery-operated searchlight mounted on a truck bed is used to spot enemy aircraft or attract people to a special event. The battery fits neatly into an adjoining box.

126.　　　　　　　1907. USA
MASON & PARKER　　7″ long
'Baby Auto'　　　　　Pressed Steel
　　　　　　　　　　Wood hood

The earliest runabouts closely resembled the fenderless buckboard buggies from which they were copied.

In its 1907 catalog, Mason & Parker claim to have been the first to manufacture steel toys. Makers of horse-drawn toys, its first automobiles were made in the early 1900s and were primarily formed of wood with pressed steel used for small parts and wheels.

Most of its toy automobiles and trucks are found using Wilkins' drivers, giving credence to theories that many toy makers bought parts from each other. Some Mason & Parker automotive toys used cast iron wheels which could possibly have been purchased elsewhere.

The tin gravel drum rotates for play value. Colorful, strong, sturdily constructed trucks typify American toys of the period.

GRAVEL MIXER MADE IN U.S.A.

128.
STRUCTO
Roadster #40
Ready built auto

1919. USA
10½" long
Pressed Steel

This toy is a factory-built roadster whose design is a direct copy of Stutz's most famous sports model, the Stutz Bearcat. One major

difference in the toy is the use of round holes for hood vents, while the real car used fine vertical louvers. Stutz and Pierce-Arrow were the last car manufacturers to standardize cars for left-hand drive. The 1919 was a right-hand drive. The toy steers from the center!

Structo gained a reputation for quality construction kits produced from about 1915 through the mid-1920s.

← **129 & 130.**
↙
STRUCTO
DeLuxe Auto #12

1921. USA
16″ long
Pressed Steel

This was the best and most expensive Structo automobile construction kit, priced at $10.00 in 1921.

A separate heavy-duty crank winds the powerful triple-spring motor used on all larger Structo cars and trucks. Solid disc wheels and rounded fenders were improvements on the 1921 Stutz. The slanted windshield, rear spare tire, and lowered body copy the real car.

Structo took many liberties with its Stutz toy design. When the real car finally changed from right- to left-hand drive, the spare wheel was mounted in a unique way. Countersunk into the rear deck at an angle that was almost horizontal, it was secured with a huge wing-bolt-type handle, very different from the conventionally mounted spare on the toy.

Several trucks, a tractor and tank were offered in kit form, along with the autos. The series was intended as educational toys, complete with small wrench and screwdriver.

A car kit was offered with a single spring motor in 1919 for $5.98 through Sears, Roebuck & Co and bore the legend, 'Boys, build your own mechanical auto!'

A view of the works.

Racer Barney Oldfield loaned his name to the tire which was first made by the Firestone Tire and Rubber Co. in 1916. In the mid-1920s when his racing days were almost over, Barney test drove his Oldfield tires on Marmon cars which he endorsed simultaneously with the tires. In this model, one wheel has managed to retain an Oldfield rubber tire.

Toy Oldfield Tires were sold with Structo Stutz kits and assembled cars. When Oldfield Tires closed, the toys reverted to the use of Firestone Tires.

131.
WILKINS
(*Left*) Automobile Phaeton
(*Right*) Automobile Phaeton

1902. USA
8½″ long
1905
9″ long
Pressed Steel
Cast Iron

The name *phaeton* was taken from an open four-wheel carriage usually drawn by two horses. Shortly after the first Wilkins automobile was introduced, the name was transferred from the horse-drawn carriage it copied.

Harry Thayer Kingsbury, owner of the Wilkins Toy Company, was fascinated with real cars and built one which ran on naphtha in 1900.

Wilkins' first toy automobile sports a steering wheel, a comparatively new innovation in American cars at the turn of the century, but one which was quickly adopted for use on toy cars in the U.S. and Europe.

The appearance of hoods and lamps on real cars prompted the restyling of the later Wilkins car which also includes fenders. High rear wheels lasted only a short while. Manufacturers found it more practical to use uniformly sized wheels which used the same spare tire when pneumatic tires came into use replacing hard rubber tires. A touch of whimsy is the cast iron rug with fringe at the feet of the lady driver.

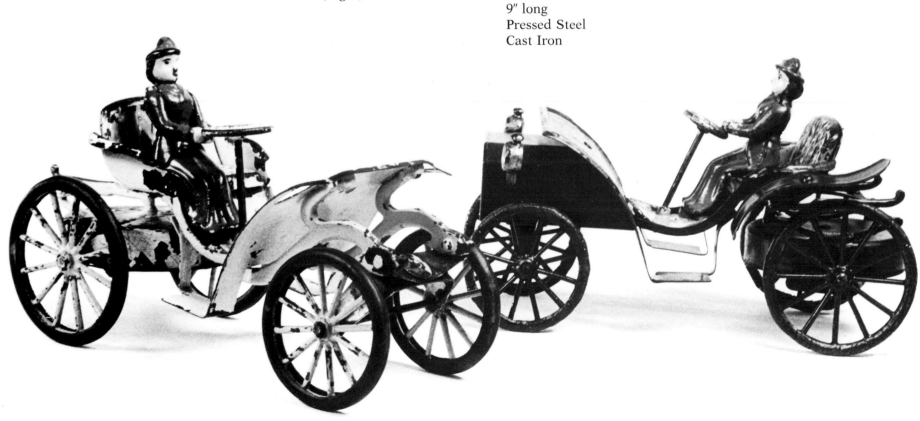

132.
WILKINS
Automobile Surrey

1911. USA
7½″ long
Pressed Steel
with Cast Iron
Wheels

Large rear wheels, the development of the
hood and the general open appearance of this

toy indicate a transitional design developing
from the turn-of-the-century carriage. The toy
is listed in a 1911 catalog, although in real
life the design was obsolete by 1905.

An early pleasure automobile with two
seats and a straight floor was named a
'Surrey' for its resemblance to the horse-
drawn carriage named after the county in

England where it was first built. The Surrey
was introduced in the United States in 1872.

Wilkins and Kingsbury steering wheels
were designed to snap on to the steering rod.
They have a way of falling off with long use.

133.
✓WILKINS
Auto Reversing Motor
Express

1911. USA
11¼″ long
Pressed Steel

An amusing action toy, designed to reverse
itself when the bumpers strike an obstacle
either from the front or the rear.

The cast iron wheels were sheathed in
rubber tires when new. Age and plenty of use
have worn them off on this toy. Wilkins was
one of the first American toy manufacturers
to recognize the value of rubber tires for
automotive indoor toys.

134.
✓WILKINS
Motor Truck Wagon

1911. USA
15″ long
Pressed Steel

1911 was a significant year for the automotive
industry. Henry Ford won the lawsuit
brought against him and other car
manufacturers. A patent lawyer, George B.
Selden, was attracted to a demonstration of a
2-cycle stationary engine exhibited at the
Philadelphia Centennial Exposition in 1876.
Using fuel oil under compression without
exploding, the engine was not too efficient or
practical, but Selden was wise enough to
envision the value it might have to propel
road vehicles. Keeping abreast of the engine's
progress in Europe, he filed for a basic
American patent on the automobile on May 8,
1879. It was granted in 1895, and Selden was
to make history when he sued Ford for
infringement. The case was in litigation from
October, 1903, to January, 1911.

A few auto manufacturers paid Selden
royalties on demand, but not Ford and some
others. They refused to pay or acknowledge
the patent from the start. Henry Ford is thus
credited with the start of free enterprise
within the automobile industry.

Harry Kingsbury received patents for
windup motors on October 14, 1902 and
August 14, 1905. The last included an
improved starting and stopping device used
on this truck. Six barrels were included with
the purchase price. Though this truck is seen
in Wilkins' 1911 catalog, the design is from
an earlier period.

135.
WILKINS
Motor Transfer

1908. USA
9½" long
Pressed Steel

The diamond-shaped windows and curved roof seem impractical when viewed through an adult's eyes; still, this toy is one of Wilkins' most charming toys.

A transitional truck altered from a horse-drawn version to operate with its patented motor, the design reflects an earlier era before motors were in front and under a hood.

In real life this type of truck was utilized to move furniture and household appliances. A chain across the rear and ropes to tie articles to the posts were all that were needed.

136.
WYANDOTTE
Circus Truck and Trailer

1936. USA
19" long
Litho Steel

Introduced in the fall of 1936, this attractive circus truck priced at 50¢ uses embossed wooden wheels.

The truck and trailer with new aerodynamic cab design has removable rear door panels giving access to an assortment of animals.

This was the first notable automotive circus toy seen since the mid-1920s* and its design was totally new.

Nothing in the Wyandotte line has ever equaled their spectacular circus truck.

* 1925–6 Strauss 'Big Circus Show' Truck. See American Tin Section.

Construction, Farm, Utility Trucks

Trucking started in America with small delivery vans. Powered by gas, electric and steam, they came in every imaginable shape and size, proving to the world that motorized transportation could perform to advantage over horse-drawn wagons.

The truck preceded the automobile, with the first use of a truck for hauling being recorded in America around 1890. It was about 1903 when trucks successfully proved their worth and began rapidly to replace the horse in America. By then, the automobile had advanced and passed the truck in popularity; but before long, the race would become an even one as America awakened to the labor- and time-saving potential of horseless wagons in an increasingly industrial and commercial world. Trucks were off and running!

137.   c. 1920. USA
ARCADE   7″ long
Auto Dump Wagon   Cast Iron

The salvaged end flap from the original box shows an early name associated with horse-drawn toys. Painted red and gold, the toy truck was intended for play with sand. The shovel shown was included. Manufactured and selling well into the 1930s, later versions are painted red and green.

This truck has never seen service.

138.   1924. USA
ARCADE   8¼″ long
Yellow Panel Delivery Truck   Cast Iron

This early model was painted in yellow cab colors and sported a driver plated with a copper wash. In 1925, the small, oval rear window was altered to a larger opening to compete with a similar truck by Dent Hardware. The bigger rear opening was used as a selling feature for boys to 'store small items for pretend deliveries.' This model is scarce and was made in one size only.

139 & 140.   1925–38. USA
ARCADE   12″ long
Mack Dump Truck   Cast Iron

A hoisting rod used pulleys and ropes, activated by a heavy spring, to raise the dump body. Available in blue, grey and green, the truck could be ordered with nickeled wheels, painted wheels, or with disc wheels with rubber tires at an extra charge (see close up).

One of the longest-running toys in the Arcade line and by far the best-selling one of the Macks, it endured until the late 1930s. A durable toy that is the closest copy of the real 1920s Mack.

In 1903, John Mack designed the first vehicle which he and two of his brothers built as a sightseeing bus for tours through Prospect Park in Brooklyn. In 1905 the five brothers settled in Allentown, Pennsylvania, where they found a suitable site for building trucks.

The first AC 'Bulldog' Mack was introduced in 1914. Its outstanding performance record in the First World War provided the necessary business stimulus the company needed to get through the Depression.

The big, rugged toy will always be a favorite for big and little boys; no wonder that the popularity of Mack 'Bulldog' toy trucks continued year after year. Indeed, their success was parallel with the real truck. Arcade copied model after model. Like the Mack Company, Arcade made it through the financially tough years. Both companies had the same secret – they'd latched on to a winner.

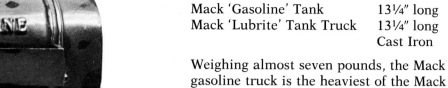

← 141 & 142. 1925. USA
ARCADE
Mack 'Gasoline' Tank   13¼" long
Mack 'Lubrite' Tank Truck   13¼" long
                              Cast Iron

Weighing almost seven pounds, the Mack gasoline truck is the heaviest of the Mack series. The 'Lubrite' truck is identical, except for the extra word.

Like many Depression-era toys which were passed from child to child, this 'Lubrite' truck was found partially covered with repaint. The result of paint remover going too deep in places are the 'measles' which appear on the tank.

This was a professional restoration job when the practice of toy restoration was in its infancy. Paint removal from cast iron toys is tedious work. Areas no more than a square inch are worked on at one time. Each layer is removed and then neutralized with oil. Blending and working on layers is done with cotton swabs. The remover can be dangerous if splashed in the eyes or on the skin, so this work is best left to a professional.

With each 'Gasoline' truck, the 1925 Arcade catalog promised an *experienced* nickeled driver!

This 'Lubrite' truck is possibly a custom order. It does not appear in any available Arcade catalogs.

↓ 143.   1923. USA
ARCADE   9¼" long
Chevrolet Utility Express Cast Iron
Truck

This model appears in Arcade's 1923–4 ads, but by the time it was seen in the 1925 catalog, the real truck had changed its styling. In 1925, Chevrolet introduced a new one-ton truck chassis for general purpose use. The driver's compartment was partially closed for comfort. in a move to bring more

passenger car features to trucks: such as, windshield wipers, inside lights, and protection from the elements. The 1925 Chevrolet body changes were so radical, that the toy copy was hopelessly outdated. Arcade abandoned the toy after 1927. This truck could also be ordered by Chevrolet dealers with a paper label affixed to the panel parallel with the side window.

→ 144.   1925. USA
ARCADE   8½" long
Ford Ton Truck   Cast Iron

A small, light Model T Ford Truck capable of carrying 2,000 pounds was called a one-ton truck and was first built in 1917.

Arcade's model is loaded down with toy cast iron street signs made by Kilgore in the 1920s. Included are a fire plug and manhole flag. The same road construction signs in boxed sets appear in the 1940 Arcade catalog. The line was probably acquired when the American Toy Company closed. (See Andes in Manufacturers' Directory).

← 145.

Top to bottom: Three trucks considered relatively scarce.

ARCADE
Ford Anthony Dump Truck

c. 1926. USA
8½″ long
Cast Iron

To meet the special needs of contractors, road builders and haulers, the Anthony Company of Streator, Illinois made a large variety of dump bodies and equipment for trucks.

The gray body dump truck with an open cab copies the real model. The Anthony name is embossed on the tailgate. A hand lever behind the seat actually works.

ARCADE
Ford TT One-Ton
Stake Truck

1925. USA
8¾″ long
Cast Iron

A place to store small packages, rocks and other treasures made toy trucks with beds the preferred choice of many buyers. The majority of Arcade truck drivers wore nickel plate. Offered for just two seasons, this toy is scarce. An advertisers' label on the body is too faded to read.

MAKER UNKNOWN
Anchor Truck Co.

Mid-1920s
styling. USA
9½″ long
Cast Iron

A search of Arcade catalogs and advertising does not show the Anchor truck. A basic-type, stake body truck, such as this one, would have appeared in Arcade catalogs for several years, providing it was one of its regular toys. I have concluded that the truck is probably a promotional toy or one made to order, not necessarily by Arcade.

The anchor symbol was a trademark of North & Judd. However, no positive connection can be made with this company and the toy.

Very few Anchor trucks have surfaced, making the toy a rare one.

↓ 146.

ARCADE
Ford Weaver Wrecker

1926. USA
11″ long
Cast Iron

The Weaver wrecker is held by a single bolt. It gave children good play value as they could learn to use a mechanism that worked like the real one, using a ratchet, chain and hook to tow a toy car.

Called a 'Ton' truck after its capacity, this open express body was outdated by the Model A toy truck in 1928 and was thus short-lived by toy manufacturing standards.

147.
ARCADE
(*Top*) Carry-Car Truck
Trailer

1928. USA
24½″ long
Cast Iron

The basic toy consists of two pieces, a cast iron cab pulling a welded steel trailer with nickeled wheels. It was offered in 1928–31 with four 25¢ Model A coupes and sedans as shown or with three 50¢ Model A cars.

Revisions in Arcade's 1931 line consisted almost entirely of new colors on old product lines. (New offerings were limited to a line of caterpillar tractors.) Arcade offered many more options by 1932 in an effort to promote business during a depressed financial period. For example, the car carrier became available for purchase without cars. However, the merchandise persisted in copying Model A's and Mack trucks, as those old standbys still ruled the road.

KENTON
(*Bottom*) Car Carrier

c. 1927. USA
10″ long
Cast Iron

This toy was cleverly designed to ensure that no cars got lost. The three Buick coupes were cast in a unit with the trailer. These are *very* low mileage used cars!

148.
ARCADE
McCormick-Deering
Thresher

1929. USA
16½″ long
overall
Cast Iron

Farm toys found acceptance in those regions of America where the full-scale machinery was most visible, such as Pennsylvania and the Midwest. They were often distributed in unorthodox fashion through farm implement dealers, hardware stores and advertisements in agricultural magazines. The toys were also ideal as contest prizes and as premiums for door-to-door sales of such products as patent medicine and magazine subscriptions.

Arcade's faithful models were the first products of a sub-industry which copies contemporary farm machinery to this day. Farm toys are now highly collectible.

149.   c. 1925. USA
ARCADE   7¼″ long
McCormick-Deering Tractor   Cast Iron

Boys who played with cars and trucks in the 1920s had toy tractors too. They could be used in the fields to play farmer, to harvest crops, to load trucks, to tow things. Plows, rakes and trailers could be attached. When seen at antique meets today, they evoke remembrances and stories.

McCormick-Deering tractors are made by International Harvester of Chicago. The toy is a realistic copy. The front wheels and axle are mounted on a swivel which permits the tractor to remain level while passing over uneven ground or rocks. Our driver poses near a real International Harvester tractor.

150.   1929. USA
ARCADE   7½″ long
'Ten' Caterpillar Tractor   Cast Iron

A pull toy with nickeled driver, and tracks which rotate with the wheels. Wide track crawlers were once used in potato and onion farming to prevent the soil from compacting. The Caterpillar lays its own road on which the wheels travel.

Construction workers used crawlers to move over steep inclines or ground where a wheeled tractor could slip or turn over. The Caterpillar Company is still a going concern, making construction equipment in Illinois. The 'Ten' stands for ten horsepower. The driver holds two brake levers. By pulling on one the real machine would make a turn to that side.

White introduced the real truck late in 1928. →
Arcade marketed the toy in 1929 during the worst
of business times. Judging from the number of
these trucks that have surfaced, it can be assumed
few were sold or survived. Shown in the 1930
catalog, it is missing from the 1931 line.

↓ **152.**   1929. USA
ARCADE   12½″ long
Wrecker and Service Car   Cast Iron

A rare accessory, the two-wheeled jack was
packaged with the wrecker in 1932. An
important piece of equipment for automobile
garage owners, the jack fastened onto the
wrecker's axle and was used to tow a truck or
car short distances around the repair shop
lot. The jack is an exact replica of a 'Walker
Auto Ambulance'.

The gentleman who once owned this toy
wrecker replaced his lost Weaver hoist chain
with string and a Hubley hook. He made me
promise to keep it intact so he'd always know
his toy if he saw it again. He passed away
many years ago, but I have kept my promise.

The wrecker made its first appearance in
1929 as an addition to the popular large
Arcade Mack truck series.

TOY WHITE DUMP TRUCK

No. 249X. Length 11½ inches, width 4½ inches,
  height 5¼ inches bed down, 6¾ inches bed up.

Color: Assorted, red, green and blue.

Wheels: Nickel plated tires. Real rubber tires at
  small additional cost. Dual rear wheels.

Packed: 1 in a carton, 1 dozen in a case.

Case net weight 60 pounds, gross weight 65 pounds.

Case measurements 24x15½x13 inches.

No. 249

← 153.　　　　　　　　　　　1930. USA
ARCADE　　　　　　　　　　　10¾″ long
'International' Dump Truck　Cast Iron

In 1930 International Harvester dropped the name Harvester and called its new models 'International' trucks.

   The toy is copied from a model with 6 cylinders; a 3-ton truck capable of 65 miles per hour with a 5-speed transmission. The new A-5 was equipped with dual rear wheels and was available in a stake body in both toy and real form.

← 151.　　　　　　　　　　c. 1928. USA
ARCADE　　　　　　　　　　　12″ long
'Milk' Truck　　　　　　　　Cast Iron
also known as Stake Body
Truck

Sometimes seen with the word 'Milk' lightly stenciled on the body panel, the letters have worn off on most trucks.

   A favorite with farm boys and city boys alike, and a nice truck to find with the stakes intact.

TOY TRUCK-TRAILER

No. 233

No. 233, The truck with two separate bodies—a stake body and gas tank. The gas tank actually holds water.

The truck chassis may be backed up to each of these bodies. It slides under and fastens securely to the trailer.
Packed: 1 in a carton, ½ dozen in a case.

The tanker-trailer pulled by a Model A cab appeared in Arcade's 1930 jobbers catalog. The tanker was replaced by an all cast iron side-dump trailer in 1931.

↓ 154.　　　　　　　　　　1929–30. USA
ARCADE　　　　　　　　　　11⁵⁄₁₆″ long with
Stake Truck Trailer　　　　one trailer;
and Ford Cab　　　　　　　added trailer
　　　　　　　　　　　　　　6½″ long
　　　　　　　　　　　　　　Cast Iron

Farm produce intended for markets was loaded into open bed trailers. When full, they were attached to the cab for hauling. The truck chassis was backed under the trailer and made a solid connection when the coupling was in place. Extra trailers could be added if desired for use with trucks or farm tractors.

   In 1930, a gasoline tank which held water was included as a second trailer to stimulate lagging sales.

   When I was a young girl, I recall trucks just like this hauling sugar beets to the refinery in Southern California. Heaped sky high in the trailers, I was always afraid they'd come rolling off if we passed them. It never happened, I'm glad to report.

155.
ARCADE
Mack High Dump

c. 1930. USA
8½″ long
Cast Iron

Balanced, nickel-plated levers mechanically raise the dump bed. An end gate opens by means of a thumb lever on the dump body. Toys that worked and simulated real trucks gave boys a reason to play out of doors and were popular selections by parents.

To promote the toys in 1932, one-half pound of imitation coal was supplied with the 8½″ toy, and one pound with a 10″ long truck.

156.
ARCADE
Mack High Dump

1931. USA
12⅜″ long
Cast Iron

Arcade expanded the large Mack truck series regularly despite the Depression. Some models were updated, but primarily additional sizes of older models were used to increase the line.

The 'coal' truck is sometimes found without the stenciled name. It appears in the 1931 catalog for the first time and was carried through 1933.

157 & 158.
ARCADE
Mack Ice Truck

1931. USA
Large 10¾″ long
Small 8½″ long
Cast Iron

Home and store delivery of ice was still big business in the early 1930s. Restaurants, dairies, fish markets and butchers still required the service.

The Mack series trucks were top sellers in the Arcade line. By simply changing the red wrecker body to blue and adding an end gate to retain the glass 'ice', Arcade had a new model for their '31 season.

Most of the ice trucks I have seen are quite worn. This means that they have been well liked and used. The ice tongs and ice are harder to find than the truck!

160.
ÅRCADE
Ambulance

1932. USA
8″ long
6″ long
Cast Iron

Ambulances are rare in automotive toy lines. They were produced as an adjunct to fire engines and war toys.

Sold individually for a few years, the smaller truck was relegated to a boxed fire toy set by 1935. Four 25¢ toys that included two fire engines, a fire chief's car and the smaller ambulance sold for $1.00.

← **159.**
ARCADE
Ford Truck with Weaver
Wrecker
ARCADE
Garage with Cast Iron Gas
Pumps

1928. USA
8¼″ long
Cast Iron
1936. USA
12″ deep × 10″
wide
Pumps 4¼″
high
Cast Iron &
Wood

A 1928 Model A truck with a Weaver wrecker is ready for a service call at Arcade's service station.

The Weaver Auto Crane by Weaver Manufacturing Co. of Springfield, Illinois, could be operated by one man with one hand. It was a compact, self-contained unit designed to be mounted in the bed of a service truck, leaving space for other equipment. The size was ideal for the Model A, and an important piece of equipment for small automobile service garages.

Arcade's first toy garage was constructed of paper. In 1926, a wooden garage was used at the toy fair for display purposes, later launching a line of wood garages with metal doors and cast iron gas pumps to be sold singly or as a set. Initially offered to dealers as a display unit, the company made double garages available at the 1929 toy fairs. This cream-colored wood garage with green roof has a tin overhead door that works, allowing toys to be stored inside, stenciled windows, and a pair of cast iron pumps with round iron globes which were ideal for boys playing 'fill-er-up'. Pumps are anchored on square wood bases for safety.

The gas pump was offered alone for 10¢. For the well-heeled there was a 5⅞″ model for 25¢ which was scaled for large toy trucks.

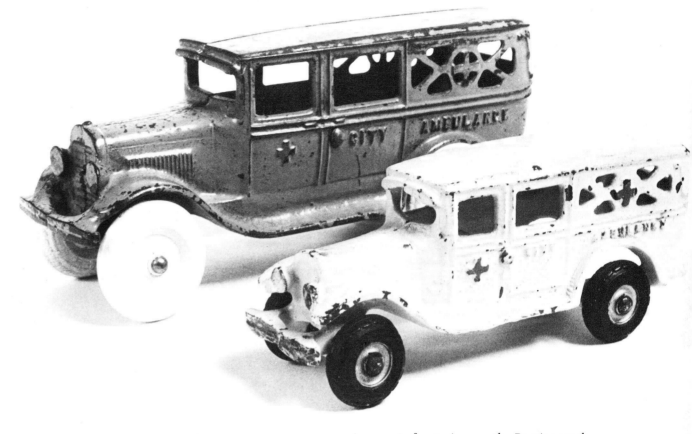

A separate front piece on the Pontiac truck corresponds to the famous 'Silver Streak' bands of chrome used by Pontiac along the center of the hood. This was an exclusive feature of Pontiac hoods for almost 20 years.

25¢ toys from a 1936 Arcade jobbers catalog. Copy of a small wrecker which was sufficient to tow all passenger cars of its day.

No. 2020X Ford Wrecker

Length 7 inches, width 2¾ inches, height 3 inches.
Color: Assorted, 6 red, 3 green, and 3 blue, with sloping nickeled radiator and bumper. Nickeled crank and reel and wire hook on end of cord. Ratchet crank winds cord. White rubber wheels centered red on blue and green toys, wheels centered blue on red toys.
Packed 6 in carton, 3 dozen in case.
Case net weight 56 lbs., case gross weight 62 lbs.
Case measurements: 12x12x22 inches.

No. 2390X Pontiac Stake Truck

Length 6¼ inches, width 2½ inches, height 2¼ inches.
Color: Assorted red, blue and green. Nickeled radiator, hood center, lights and bumper. White rubber wheels with red centers on blue and green toys, blue centers on red toy.
Packed 6 in box, 3 dozen in case.
Case net weight 38 lbs., case gross weight 42 lbs.
Case measurements: 11x12x20 inches.

"THEY LOOK REAL"

161.
ARCADE
International Delivery Truck

1936. USA
9½″ long
Cast Iron

The 1930s ushered in the widespread use of all-steel roofs which could be formed in an upsweep for added head room in cars and trucks.

Arcade's closed delivery van has a separate nickel-plated radiator with headlamps and bumper cast in one piece. For some reason, these vans along with most immediate pre-Second World War cast iron toys, are rarely seen. Collectors reason that, too new for sentimental attachments, most were tossed into scrap heaps during the wartime drives for metal. Earlier toys seem to have survived in greater numbers. Alternatively, it could be that they just did not sell well.

Trucks pictured in a 1936 Arcade jobbers catalog are actually 1935 models. Arcade devoted a major portion of their 1936 line to toy vehicles with fender skirts and the curved, sleek lines spawned during the 30s era. These trucks were priced at $1.00 each retail.

No. 3090 International Stake Truck

Length 12 inches, width 3⅜ inches, height 3¼ inches.
Color: Bright green with nickeled radiator, lights and bumper. White rubber wheels with red centers. I. H. Co. decalc. on side of door.
Packed 1 in carton, 1 dozen in case.
Case net weight 45 lbs., case gross weight 51 lbs.
Case measurements: 12x14x26 inches.

No. 3030 International Dump Truck

Length 10½ inches, width 3½ inches, height 3¼ inches.
Color: Bright green with rear chassis in red, green dump box, nickeled dump lever and rod. Nickeled radiator, lights and bumper. White rubber wheels with red centers. I. H. Co. decalc. on side of body. Dump body raised by pulling lever. End gate opens.
Packed 1 in carton, 1 dozen in case.
Case net weight 39 lbs., case gross weight 45 lbs.
Case measurements: 12x14x17 inches.

162.
ARCADE
'Yellow Baby' Dump Truck

c. 1935. USA
10¾" long
Cast Iron

The International Harvester 'Red Baby' was renamed 'Yellow Baby' and painted a color which corresponds to the name. Contrary to Arcade's quest for toys that 'look real', correspondence from International Harvester confirms that a real 'Yellow Baby' truck was never produced by that company, nor is it listed in Arcade's catalogs. It may have been issued as a special promotional order.

American toy manufacturers worked hard to pull out of the business slump of the early 1930s. The ones that made it had sales representatives on the road as well as at toy fairs. At times, they would offer certain toys which were painted in special colors or decorated to the customer's specifications as a sales promotion. The offers usually accompanied a price break. The toys were always older patterns and factory overstock.

On a few occasions, the toys were assembled from assorted overstock parts, giving way to variations from catalogued items (see fig. 229). Top salesmen could work out special deals this way with their favourite customers.

163.
ARCADE
Transport

1938. USA
18½" long
Sedans 4¾"
long
Cast Iron &
Pressed Steel

In 1929, The Motor Car Carrier Company made news when it exhibited a double-deck semitrailer used for delivering real automobiles from the factories in Detroit to car dealers in Michigan.

Four toy sedans in assorted colors ride on a welded steel double-deck trailer considered a modern design in 1938.

Arcade's predilection for specific cars is absent here, but it seems the sedans are based on 1938 Chevrolets, the only car with a slash line on the body during that period.

164.
ARCADE
Army Tank with Gun

1940. USA
8″ long
Cast Iron

Although the war was accelerating in Europe, American toy manufacturers still managed to avoid making military vehicles in appreciable numbers. By 1940, Arcade's only venture into war toys was a limited number of boxed sets, consisting of cast iron soldiers and this army tank in camouflage green and brown colors.

The top of the toy forms a hopper to hold steel balls which can be shot 15 to 25 feet in the air by a spring-controlled crank attached to the side.

The army tank is a scarce toy. A contributing factor could have been the missile range damage caused by the flying balls. The most likely reason was the state of national affairs. President Roosevelt declared a national emergency on May 27, 1940. The toy fair held in February, just three months earlier, hardly had a chance to promote toys for the 1940 season when raw materials were given a priority status for war preparation.

Arcade had a long, successful association with Mack Trucks. It is an interesting observation that in 1940, Mack started building military vehicles under government contracts. One of its first products was a monster Army Tank. Understandably, Arcade's toy is *not* an exact copy!

One of the earliest truck designs, called cab-over-engine was revived in 1934 in order to alleviate the problem of trucks that were too long. It placed the engine under the driver's seat and enabled him to get a better view of the road.

This pair of model D–400 trucks were offered by Arcade in their 1940 jobbers catalog, the same year they were introduced by International.

No. 2600 International Stake Truck

Cab-Over-Engine Type. An exact miniature in detail.

Length: 9½ inches, width 3½ inches, height 3⅞ inches. Cast iron.

Finished: in bright yellow with nickeled radiator, lights and bumper, rubber wheels with colored centers.

Packed: 1 in a carton, 1 dozen in a case. Case net weight 36 pounds, total case weight 38 pounds. Case measures 18x15½x11 inches.

No. 3710 International Dump Truck

Cab-Over-Engine Type

A faithful copy in miniature of the latest design of truck models. Loads of "play" value.

Length: 9½ inches, width 3¾ inches, height 3½ inches. Cast iron chassis and dump body. A new type of snap-spring mechanism effects the dumping action. This mechanism is actuated by a lever on the side of the toy.

Finished: in red and green, chassis red, dump box green, nickeled radiator, lights and bumper. Rubber wheels with red centers. Dual rear wheels.

Packed: 1 in a box, 1 dozen in a case. Case net weight 32 pounds, total case weight 36 pounds. Case measures 18x12½x10 inches.

No. 2600

No. 3710

→
166.
ARCADE
Ice Truck

1941. USA
6¾″ long
Cast Iron

The last such model made by Arcade, the cab over engine (called C.O.E. in the trucking world) carries on its door the emblem of the White Company of Cleveland, Ohio. White, a maker of trucks since the turn of the century, currently operates as Volvo-White.

With the advent of automatic icemakers, the demand for ice trucks was eventually eliminated.

165.

One listing caught my eye in a sale notice for the contents of a long-closed orphanage. It read, 'Old iron toy trucks in good, clean, usable condition. Only 106 previous owners!'

Without a second thought, I knew I'd be the next owner no matter what the toys looked like. Here, you see them! Toys that survived the Second World War and constant playing by orphanage boys. If, for no other reason, they should be saved and kept together as a relic of 106 childhoods – with time, perhaps 107!

ARCADE	1941. USA
(*Rear*) International	9½″ long
Harvester Pickup	Cast Iron

Late cast iron toys are more scarce today than some 1930s toys. Produced for only one year due to wartime restrictions on manufacturers, many of these toys were lost in the metal scrap drives of the 1940s.

ARCADE	1941. USA
(*Front*) Dump Truck	6½″ long
	Cast Iron

A stylized Ford truck in a medium-priced toy designed for outdoor play.

Arcade's Last Hurrah!

167.

ARCADE	1941. USA ↘
International Harvester	11″ long
Dump Truck	Cast Iron

A heavy coil spring aids the dump bed to empty its load. One of the very last toys made by Arcade before the company converted to wartime production, the realistic 'K' line model is Arcade's farewell to cast iron automotive toys. Dual rear wheels add to realism.

By 1940, Arcade's line no longer featured traditionally popular makes of trucks and cars. Carry-overs from previous years filled its catalog and deluxe size automobiles, trucks and accessories were conspicuously absent. In their place was a large line of boxed sets of toys. Included were several kitchen and laundry sets for girls, road and construction sets made up from toys in previous catalogs, and newly designed scenic boxes which served as background for the multi-piece sets.

DENT   c. 1923. USA
↑**168.** NY–Phila. Express   16″ long
←**169.** American Oil Truck   15½″ long
↙**170.** Stake Truck   15½″ long
↓**171.** Dump Body Truck   15¼″ long
172. →   Cast Iron

Dent Hardware was well-established in business when Mack started its factory to build trucks in nearby Allentown, Pennsylvania. Like many truck manufacturers, the Mack brothers started with a wagon shop, building bodies for horseless carriages, sightseeing buses and many different style trucks. However it was their AC Mack 'Bulldog' model which led them to fame.

Big and tough, these powerful trucks needed no reason to change their appearance and remained the same style, overlapping one year after another. The Mack was given its nickname 'Bulldog' by the American doughboys because of its ferocious look.

The four toy Macks by Dent show off the manufacturer's ability for fine castings in extra large sizes, especially in the New York to Philadelphia express, where the open grill work required special skills.

The stake truck was suitable for lumber, barrel and boxes – real or toy. A dump truck should work, and Dent's will tip with a hand lever.

'Built like a Mack truck' is an expression still heard today. The 'Bulldog' is gone, but not forgotten.

←173.
DENT
(*Top*) Breyer's Ice Cream
Truck

c. 1930. USA
8½″ long
Cast Brass

Shows refrigerator doors on right side.

←DENT
(*Middle*) Parcel Express
Truck

c. 1925. USA
8″ long
Cast Iron

A large rear opening provides space for small packages. An attractive well-made toy by any standards, but it was no match for a similar model made by Arcade.

←ARCADE
(*Bottom*) White Delivery
Truck

1931. USA
8½″ long
Cast Iron

For details, see Advertising chapter.

↓174.
DENT
Dump Body Truck
Wrecker Truck

1930–2 USA

11″ long
10½″ long
Cast Iron

Dent automobiles and trucks display a uniform sense of delicacy, yet are totally functional. The castings have a unique quality that makes them readily identifiable. This is especially true of their cars and trucks from 1920 through the early 1930s. Dent did not mark its toys.

The 'bare bones' wrecker copies old, used, or wrecked trucks purchased by garages and repairmen of the Depression era. After stripping off the bed, a specially ordered one-man wrecking crane would be installed. Custom-built wreckers were not only expensive but rarely available on small trucks.

Dent designed its own wrecking crane but did not bother to give it a name.

175.
HUBLEY
Open Bed Auto Express

1910. USA
9½″ long
Cast Iron

A tin roof supported by posts was optional, as was a load consisting of barrels and boxes to fit the truck bed. Shipping weight, cost and personal preference made the difference. The wheels of early Hubley automotive toys were always cast iron and beautifully clean castings. For lovers of Americana, this truck has a special appeal.

176.
HUBLEY
Auto Express with Roof

1910–28. USA
9½" long
Cast Iron

Pennsylvania, home of Hubley toys, was named the Keystone state from its central position among the original 13 states. The Keystone emblem embossed on the side of the truck is a key to the identity of the maker of some of the finest early cast iron toys in America. Hubley was one of the first toy manufacturers to produce an extensive line of automobiles and trucks.

The auto express has tremendous charm. Though more susceptible to breaks, the roofed version was carried into 1928 and, therefore, probably survives in equal numbers as the roofless version, which was made for a short period. An identical Negro driver was made by Kenton.

177.
HUBLEY
Five-Ton Truck

1911. USA
17½" long
Cast Iron

Carbide lamps help date this old-timer. Though one is shown in a 1920 Hubley catalog, it was altered to include newer 'electric' head lamps and the single front 'cyclops' lamp was removed (fig. 181).

Successful companies began to purchase fleets of the real 5-ton trucks for their use, but problems arose when inexperienced drivers without mechanical skills ruined the trucks with recklessness and inadequate knowledge of the motors. With time, drivers were trained and these problems solved. By 1910, Anheuser-Busch operated more than fifty trucks to deliver its beer. Twenty of these were the 5-ton size. A special effort was made to educate drivers and maintain the fleet properly.

Hubley sold its 5-ton toy truck into the late 1920s. When the cost of iron and shipping began to escalate along with the Depression, it forced a cutback both in size and price of toys. The demand for large expensive toys had diminished. The big market was now for N.D.Q. toys.*

* Nickel, dime and quarter.

178.
HUBLEY
Auto Dump Coal Wagon

c. 1920. USA
16¼″ long
Cast Iron

The recent history of this particular piece illustrates the necessity for the collector to learn to distinguish old cast iron from reproductions and alterations. This truck was

completely repainted when I received it, but appeared to be sound, so I took a chance on it. A professional restorer removed *six coats* of paint, each a different color! The original red paint was present as I had hoped. Those six coats of new paint had, in fact, preserved and protected the original coat. The slight bleaching of the original paint is due to the action of the paint remover. Periodic oiling restores the luster.

Most antique toys are found with their original paint. When a cast iron toy is found completely repainted, or with no paint whatsoever and rusted, it pays to take a close look. Extremely durable (the coal wagon weighs over 10 pounds without the coal), some were repainted to pass down to another child or were rescued and 'restored' by charitable organizations as a Christmas project for poor children. However, a repaint sometimes conceals a repaired break. Carry a magnet to check for unauthentic lead, epoxy, brass and copper. Toys are sometimes rusted to make them appear aged, or an effort is made to obliterate the fresh paint on a new reproduction. Memorize the outlines of reproduced toys so you will learn the difference.

If you are unsure of a toy, the best policy is to ask the dealer to give you return privileges in writing, specifying a reasonable time limit, so that you may have an expert inspect the toy for you. If the dealer does not agree, you have grounds for suspicion. I have always sought out and patronized dealers who have agreed to such requests, and after establishing myself as a customer, have accepted their handshake or word as readily as the paper.

179.
HUBLEY
Auto Truck

1918. USA
10″ long
Cast Iron

A no-nonsense, practical-looking truck with built-in driver and heavy-duty 'artillery'

spoke wheels. This is a composite design from real trucks, which by now were serving most of the needs of business, construction and farming but also providing employment for millions of Americans.

→
180.
HUBLEY
Auto Truck

c. 1920. USA
17½″ long
Cast Iron

This 5-ton truck of massive proportions was a good seller and remained in the Hubley toy line for over ten years – a long period for automotive toys which changed styles rapidly.

Hubley's keystone emblem is found here and on many of its larger-size trucks.

The green color is rare. Yellow is the standard color for 5-ton trucks, which are favorites of collectors.

181.
HUBLEY
Five-Ton Truck

c. 1920. USA
17″ long
Cast Iron

This stake truck of large proportions was made during a period when casting was a fine art.

Cast iron artillery wheels on real trucks used solid rubber tires due to severe vibrations and strains. Lighter truck engines and pneumatic tires were not far off.

In the old days, when heavy meant quality, the 5-ton truck had plenty of it! A steel seat and truck bed helps lighten a hefty toy.

182.
HUBLEY
Merchants Delivery

1925. USA
6¼″ long
Cast Iron

The range of the motor truck soon made door-to-door delivery a new trend and merchandising asset.

Toys with cast-in names are desirable and charming additions to a collection reflecting the extra work involved in their design and execution. The lettering on many toys was replaced by lower-cost decals in the 1930s, or left blank as a cost-saving measure.

183.
HUBLEY
Road Roller

c. 1927. USA
8″ long
Cast Iron

The first road roller was pulled by eight horses and revolutionized road building. By 1923, over 26,000 miles of new roads were constructed under a Federal aid program to help solve urgent transportation problems. Road construction equipment was visible in almost any metropolis, along with trucks used to haul the equipment to work sites.

The Huber Manufacturing Company of Marion, Ohio, made threshers, engines and tractors, as well as road rollers.

The steam traction road roller was copied by Hubley as closely as possible in cast iron. The toy was a workhorse designed to roll stones and dirt for make-believe roads.

184.
HUBLEY
Huber Road Roller

1927–8. USA
15″ long
Cast Iron

Road building was a serious never-ending business in the 1920s and continued as such through the Depression.

Hubley was continually expanding its line of construction, road and farm toys, and, with exclusive rights from Huber, produced several copies of Huber's machines.

Weighing over ten pounds with its standing driver, the pull-toy roller must have provided real exercise for a small child, not to mention its potential dangers. Nevertheless, the big chunk of cast iron is design in motion to some collectors, and is not easily lost or overlooked.

The nickel-plated scarifier works as does the steering wheel. The rest of the work is yours! Two dollars was the 1930 wholesale price.

185.
HUBLEY
Borden's Milk Truck

1930. USA
7½″ long
Cast Iron

In 1856, an American, Gail Borden, received a patent for the first successful milk condensing process, leading to the formation of a company to sell his product. The rapid growth of cities gave rise to an industry which provided home delivery for milk and dairy products. By 1930, Borden was a household word. Today, the company is a leading producer of chemicals and powdered dry milk, most of which is sold overseas.

Hubley's toy is an exclusive copy of the Divco trucks in Borden's fleet. The Divco

remained unchanged in style from 1929 through 1933. One divergence from the design of the real truck is a single, rear, swinging door, hinged from the top. Hubley utilized this door on its motorcycle delivery sidecars. No doubt, quick assembly and the need for fewer parts inspired this design.

Little by little, Hubley was forced to drop

the larger, more expensive cast iron toys from its line during the early 1930s, but the Borden truck remained a popular item. A cost-cutting measure in 1935 was a decal label in place of raised iron letters and the introduction of rubber tires on iron wheels. This variation was carried through part of 1936 before the milk truck was finally discontinued.

← **186.****186.** 1930. USA
HUBLEY 8½″ long
Elgin Street Sweeper Cast Iron

Possibly the most complicated and beautiful casting of an automotive toy made by Hubley. Well detailed with attachments and external extra parts that screw on, the toy was also a lesson in how street sweepers function, for this one actually works. A brush sweeps dirt into a bin in the body, where it can be released by a dumping lever. A pretend 'vacuum' is at the end of the hose.

The uniformed sanitary engineer was designed especially for this toy and fits no other.

↑**187.** c. 1928. USA
HUBLEY 11″ long
Mack Dump Truck Cast Iron
c. 1930. USA
KENTON 15″ long
Fairfield Ditcher Cast Iron

Building continued despite the Depression through the 1930s. Special construction equipment was an aid to getting the job done in a more efficient manner. Engineering developments followed, producing such machines as the Fairfield Ditcher. Meanwhile the heavy, powerful Bulldog Mack trucks were the epitome of success in the trucking industry.

The toy truck and ditcher are a perfect combination for digging, loading and hauling.

188.
HUBLEY
Bell Telephone Trucks

1930. USA
7", 5½", 3¾"
long
Cast Iron

Sold in five sizes, the telephone truck was an immediate hit. To accommodate the tremendous interest in the toy, Hubley made it available with or without accessories, and with a variety of wheels. For Ohio buyers, the truck was finished in red, while the eastern states bought the familiar olive green toy. The auger, derrick and windlass can actually be

made to dig holes and install the toy telephone pole.

In the largest model, it appears the pattern maker failed to plan ahead. The crowding of the letters on the truck are evidence of his misjudgment. The smallest truck carries a ladder cast into the sides and is driverless.

The telephone trucks were a favorite toy, then as now.

189.
HUBLEY
Bell Telephone Truck

1930. USA
10″ long
Cast Iron

Starting with the 1920s, the telephone industry was one of the fastest growing businesses in America. The United States was populated by hundreds of small independent telephone exchanges organized to serve rural communities. These companies provided the service, but the Bell Telephone systems provided equipment, installation and repairs for a majority of these small companies.

This exposure made Bell Telephone an easily recognized symbol across the entire country.

190 & 191.
HUBLEY
Trukmixer

1932. USA
8″ long
Cast Iron

A new offering to the toy trade in January, 1932, the mixer cylinder actually rotates when the toy moves forward. This action is served by cast iron gears, as shown in close-up. Hubley favored construction toys and was a leader in this field of cast iron. It had many outstanding road and farm toys that were never copied and today are highly collectible items. The cement truck is one of them.

192.
HUBLEY
Nucar Transport

1932. USA
16″ long
Cast Iron

Designs of automobile carriers changed radically in the 1930s. With sales of cars climbing, along with transport charges, it was necessary to find a means to move cars more economically. One way was to use carriers that could be loaded and unloaded by one man.

The Nucar Transport is copied from a real carrier used until the start of the Second World War. The Nucar toy was supplied with four vehicles from the Hubley Midget line.

Only the racer parked over the driver is from the original set. The remaining three pieces are by A. C. Williams of about the same period.

Rubber tires, though preferred by parents when the toys were new, deteriorate with time. Collectors found this a problem until a few years ago, when some enterprising collectors began molding replacements to meet the demand. The Nucar Transport wears two new tires.

193.
HUBLEY
Ingersoll-Rand Compressor
Truck

1933. USA
8¼″ long
Cast Iron

Only Yankee ingenuity would put a compressor on a truck bed to then be hauled to the construction site by a Mack cab. The plaything copied the real truck, but there was a big difference. The real one worked. All the boy could do was look at the toy and the buyers did not do that for very long.

Manufactured under an exclusive right with Ingersoll-Rand, the compressor truck is precious due to its short run.

194.
HUBLEY
(*Left*) Tractor Shovel
DENT
(*Right*) Street Sweeper

1933. USA
8½″ long
Cast Iron
1932. USA
8″ long
Cast Iron

Whether by design or not, rival toymakers did not seem to produce many identical toys. However, it often seemed that a new product from one toymaker would be copied and modified by its competitors.

Arcade introduced a sand loader in 1932. Shortly after, Hubley adapted a tractor with a shovel for use as a sand loader.

Hubley's Elgin street sweeper was probably the inspiration for Dent's street sweeper of an entirely different design. A geared left wheel provides the action to rotate the brush.

Neither of the above-mentioned toys attained success. Both were discontinued within two years.

→
196.
HUBLEY
Panama Shovel Truck

c. 1934. USA
13″ long
Cast Iron

'Panama' trucks got their name when they were used to dig the Panama Canal. The unmistakable Mack Trucks were known by every man and boy. They were without question one of the most powerful heavy duty trucks around. This copy of a live steam boiler operated by two men with a movable scoop and shovel gave boys a chance to play with their favorite material – DIRT!

195.
HUBLEY
General Shovel Truck

1931–8. USA
10″ long
Cast Iron

Dual rear wheels supported the extra weight of heavy construction equipment or large loads to be hauled by trucks.

The shovel operator is posed in the typical stance of a do-nothing worker lending interest only. It takes a real boy to operate the digger.

A post-Depression revision of Hubley toys included cast-in and joined figures when possible to save casting several parts. By 1936, rubber wheels were standard on most Hubley toys, a move to lighten shipping costs which were rising, and cut down on higher production cost of cast iron wheels.

← **197.**   c. 1910. USA
KENTON   9″ long
Auto Dray   Cast Iron

Auto drays were versatile trucks. The wooden slat-sided bed was suitable for short-distance hauling and deliveries of most anything.

With no roof for hindrance, objects of odd shape and size could be stacked and tied sky high and often were covered by a canvas in poor weather. Drivers protected themselves with raincoats during the wet season.

Kenton toy trucks were varied and extensive, but taken from real life. In 1919, the lettering on the truck changed to 'ARMY', the color changed from a sunny yellow to army drab, and the driver became a soldier.

→
199.   1910. USA
KENTON   10″ & 6″ long
Auto Ambulance   Cast Iron

Until 1910, nickel-plate was used ony to highlight parts of a toy such as a wheel or figure. Plating was very expensive, giving the all-nickel-plated toys the nickname 'Princely toys', which would usually apply to toys made of ivory or precious metals like silver or gold.

Plating eliminated rust which could spoil the toy and stain clothing and furniture, as well as go from children's hands to their mouths. Nickel-plated toys were also utilized as showroom samples, where toys received considerable handling.

The ambulance was made during the golden years of Kenton and is an example of an outstanding toy made when perfection was the prime consideration of this manufacturer.

198.   1910. USA
KENTON   9″ long
Auto Express #548   Cast Iron

The bright orange enamel truck trimmed in black still has its original paint. Remarkable, considering the fact that the paint used on early Kenton toys was of a type that dried and flaked with time.

After 1910, doors were added to trucks. Sometimes sold with a white driver wearing driving goggles, and often found in white, blue and red enamel finishes, this truck is a favorite of mine.

Kenton's catalog number is #548. On some Kenton cars and trucks, the number is found on the underside of the toy. This is one clue to the identity of the maker.

← **200 & 201.**   c. 1915. USA
JONES & BIXLER
J & B Express   16½″ long

↓ KENTON   c. 1919.
Army Motor Truck   15″ long
                           Cast Iron

The express truck is a composite of the many trucks visible during the early 1900s but borrows most of its lines from Diamond T trucks.

Jones & Bixler was one of the few iron founders who was capable of producing a toy of this size in 1910.

202.   c. 1925. USA
KENTON
Auto Contractor's Wagon   8½″ long
Auto Coal Wagon   8¾″ long
                           Cast Iron

Truck manufacturers were showing considerable interest in balloon tires by 1925. Heavy loads and inflation pressures required attention and took up time if used on heavy trucks, but in return the ride was much smoother, and balloon tires came into increased use.

Kenton equipped its trucks with new wheels and the new tires – but cast in iron. The contractor's wagon dumps all three buckets with one pull of the lever.

When Kenton acquired the J & B pattern, the express truck was shelved until after the First World War. It then reappeared as the 'Army Motor' truck in a khaki color, remaining in the line until closed cab trucks made it obsolete in the early 1920s.

203.
KENTON
'Overland Circus'
Animal Cages and Calliope

1925. USA
10″ long
Cast Iron

Boys could pretend to be in show business with the only cast iron automotive circus trucks ever to be made. Painted white, yellow and red with gold trim, the toys are also found in blue and orange colors.

These quality trucks are scarce and the calliope rare. Fewer calliopes are found today in proportion to the number of cage trucks. Like the real circus equipment, more cages were needed. A set is most impressive. They are found in Kenton catalogs through 1929. The 'walking' elephant, patented in 1873, was designed to walk down a board.

←

204.   Late 1920s.
KENTON   USA
Mack Contractor's Dump   11″ long
                         Cast Iron

In the late 1920s streamlining in the automotive world was becoming a major factor, forcing toy makers to make parallel changes.

The chain-drive Mack dump truck was a reliable standby in the Kenton line. Pressed steel buckets helped lighten a heavy toy and the newer smaller wheels attempted to lower the body a trifle. Although the wheels appear too small to the adult eye, a child would not have worried.

It must always be remembered that shipping costs and economical shortcuts were a prime consideration in the toy business in 1930.

205.   c. 1930. USA
KENTON   11¾″ long
Buckeye Ditcher   Cast Iron

Ohio, home of Kenton toys, is known as the Buckeye state – a clue when identifying their toys.

For the mechanically minded boy, the series of buckets, chains, levers and hopper offer endless possibilities in conjunction with dump trucks. An amusing and instructive toy.

→

206.   Early 1930s. USA
Front to Rear:
KENTON
Cab with Ice Trailer   16¼″ long
Cab with Speed and Gas
Tank Trailers   10½″ long
                         Cast Iron

ARCADE   1931. USA
Model A Cab with Side   12⅞″ long overall
Dump Trailer   Cast Iron

Economizing on costs was a major factor in the early 1930s. Trucks were designed to move larger loads. For this, stronger cabs pulled bigger trailers. Engines were not yet strong enough for tandem trailers. Still, boys dreamed of the time when trucks would pull a string of trailers as easily as a train. Though the toys were meant to be interchangeable, they often ended up in a series of hookups.

The toys shown above were finished in baked enamels. All have survived the punishment of outdoor play, their hardened finishes still intact.

207 & 208.
KENTON
Auto Contractor's Truck
Auto Lumber Truck

1931. USA

10″ long
11½″ long
Cast Iron

The truck driver was completely enclosed by a cab exactly like real drivers in the 1930s. The separate figure was assembled as part of the toy body to make it permanent. Loss of a figure was a problem for the buyer and seller.

However, Kenton failed to plan ahead for truck drivers scaled to match the newer model trucks. Our cast iron man barely peeps over the cowl of his flat bed lumber truck.

Toy bodies changed as rapidly as progress around them, providing newer and better models. This was a paradox in a business where hand-me-downs have always been a factor. The durability of cast iron toys was constantly stressed as a sales point, though this might not work in favor of the manufacturer or younger children who wanted current models instead of a sibling's cast-off.

The Auto lumber truck was cancelled in 1933.

209.
KENTON
Jaeger Mixer Truck

1932. USA
9¼″ long
Cast Iron

Priced at $1.00 in 1932, the Jaeger Mixer uses the basic chassis design of 1930 Kenton trucks combined with a lower, more modern cab, in scale with the driver. The nickel-plated cement barrel is rigged to roll when the toy is pulled and operates by chains and gears connected at the front and rear. A separate closure on the barrel allows it to be filled. Luckily, this one never was! However, I once saw a toy cement mixer with cement hardened in the barrel! Seldom is a toy found which was used in serious play that does not have string, gum, or candy still attached.

I acquired a monstrous, heavy early cast iron toy automobile many years ago. Dried blood was caked all over the front end. I feared the worst when I first viewed the toy, suspecting that something terrible had befallen its owner. I voiced my fears to the seller of the toy, a cantankerous old curmudgeon, who assured me I feared for the wrong person. The toy had been his, he told me, and he'd used it on the neighborhood bully more than once. Both were tough kids growing up in a rough neighborhood. I needed no further assurance of his success. The evidence was still on the toy!

210.
KENTON
Truck with Trailers

c. 1933. USA
19″ long overall
Cast Iron

Sold as a boxed set, the trailers could be hooked in tandem as shown or used singly. Automotive boxed sets gained popularity in the early 1930s.

211.   1923. USA
KINGSBURY   14″ long
Panama Dump Truck   Pressed Steel

The story of the building of the Panama Canal was a fascinating saga and made the name Panama a household word. Toys designed like those used to build the canal had a wonderful realism that boys loved, and the progress of the canal could be followed in their own yards.

Kingsbury's earth carrier was designed to carry large loads that could be dumped with the flip of a lever.

213.   Mid-1930s. USA
MAKER UNKNOWN   7¼″ long
Stake Body Truck   Cast Iron

By 1935, a return to prosperity was evident for the first time since 1929. Truck production was on the rise and toy manufacturers were updating their toys to keep pace. Curved, deep-skirted fenders were becoming popular for use on trucks, more for design than function.

The body style of high stake sides was designed for the delivery of livestock and farm produce to market. The toy has an all-in-one separate, nickel-plated radiator with lights and bumper.

Constructional methods can sometimes identify a toy. This toy has a three-part construction, incorporating a body, chassis and single-piece grille with headlights and bumper. The assembly is a radical change from established methods.

130

←212. 1930–4. USA
WILLIAMS 12½″ long
Austin Transport Set Cast Iron

The American Austin Car Company produced the Bantam car in 1930 and continued with few changes until the last model in 1941. The Bantam delivered 40 miles per hour in a little economy car, based on European economy cars, but designed specifically for the American market, which was severely depressed. Despite the savings offered by its size, buyers felt it was too small for safety and not large enough for families.

Toy collectors associate Mickey Mouse and comic strip characters with Bantam roadsters. They were often used in comic films as well. Some toy transport sets are found with a Bantam rooster embossed on the doors, in place of 'Austin'. Shown aboard the Model A carrier is the Austin 2 Place Cabin Coupe. The carrier set is the best known of Williams' toys.

↓ **214.** 1932–3. USA
WILLIAMS 7¼″ long
Interchangeable Delivery Cast Iron
Truck

Headlights growing out of the front fenders have always been a Pierce-Arrow trademark. This car manufacturer produced custom cars to order and is known to have made a truck, although probably nothing that looks like this one.

The body of the truck is assembled to the chassis with a single spring clip, developed and patented by Williams in 1932. This spring system could be used to clip on a sedan body instead of the truck.

Often viewed as a station wagon by collectors, the toy is actually a huckster-type truck with side curtains.

Fire Engines and Police Vehicles

Dating fire engines is a difficult task. The real trucks from which toys were copied changed slowly, if at all; and, once purchased, they remained in continuous use for many years in most fire departments. One reason was the high cost of the equipment, as well as the fact that most were custom-made to meet the requirements of a particular community.

By the late 1920s, American cast iron fire toys stressed a massive, heavy look in direct contrast to the lighter, finer castings of the transitional fire toys made in the early 1900s. They would grow even heavier in the early 1930s until finally the 1940s streamline age brought a reversal to a more trim appearance with smaller wheels, lowered body and compact equipment.

215.   1925. USA
ARCADE   21" long
Mack Fire Truck   Cast Iron

A hose reel, removable extension ladders, and a bell that rings, add play value to a toy that was a favorite of buyers for over ten years. Rubber tires were an optional extra.

218.   c. 1920. USA →
DENT   14½" long
Hook and Ladder Truck   Cast Iron

An improbable-looking hook and ladder, so high, light and airy as to appear comical. Oversize, cast iron wheels jutting ahead of the fenders add to the ridiculous proportions. Evident, however, is the open filigree casting so typical of Dent.

Truly a 'childish-looking' toy.

216.
ARCADE
Fire Trailer Truck

1933. USA
16¼" long
Cast Iron

The newly designed two-piece fire engine utilized a four-wheel truck and hook and ladder trailer, a toy

which eventually displaced the Mack fire engines in the Arcade line. Retail price $1.00.

Articulated fire engines were designed to turn corners of crowded, narrow streets. The detachable trailer holds a hose reel with a 47" hose and ladders which extend 23" when

interlocked and are attached to a support on the floor of the trailer.

The cast-in driver and firemen solved a long-standing problem of losing crew before reaching the fire!

217.
ARCADE
Fire Pumper

1938. USA ↘
13¼" long
Cast Iron

Arcade's integral casting incorporates six firemen complete with tools and suction hoses. Even the nickel-plated hose reel is

permanently locked in place to avoid a loss of parts. Colorful decorating makes the details stand out and adds the character needed for

the special appeal of this toy. A clear celluloid window snaps into the windshield frame for a completed look.

Long after running boards became obsolete on automobiles and trucks, they remained an important accessory on fire engines, providing a place for firemen to stand and to hold extra equipment.

Arcade illustrates a toy fire unit built on a 1938 Ford truck chassis. Similar units were offered by Dodge, Chevrolet, International and Studebaker.

The six-man fire engine was short-lived, a victim of hard times and Arcade's conversion to smaller, lighter weight castings and concentration on World's Fair toys for 1939.

133

219 & 220.   1912–20. USA
HUBLEY
Auto Fire Engine   15" long
Hook and Ladder Truck   23" long
                           Cast Iron

The versatile Christie front drive tractor was
pressed into service by large metropolitan fire
departments as a means of converting horse-
drawn fire apparatus to motor power. The
real Christie front was manufactured by the
Front Drive Motor Company of Hoboken, New
Jersey. New York City placed one of the first
units into service in 1912. Hundreds of the
two-wheel bolt-on front units were built from
1912–16. Recognizing their significance,
Hubley produced a magnificent series of
articulated fire toys with Christie fronts.

   The Christie Tractor attached to a
LaFrance steam pumper is the prototype for
the Hubley toy. These toys were marketed
only a short time. Like the real Christie, they
utilized horse-drawn parts in stock until they
were used up.

   The pumper was made only in the 15"
length, but a lightened version holds a
painted boiler, has spoked wheels, and is
minus frills such as the eagle.

←221. 1912–20. USA
HUBLEY 15″ long
Seven Man Fire Patrol Cast Iron

Rear wheels activate a gong bell for the largest fire patrol made to match the articulated trucks. A standing fireman is posted on the rear steps. Some pieces for this series used disc wheels as shown; others were sold with artillery spoke wheels.

Our regular driver is off today. A Wilkins driver takes his place.

222 & 223. 1919. USA
HUBLEY 11″ long
Police Patrol Cast Iron

Hubley offered three policemen with its blue-painted patrol, but space is provided for more figures. A wire attached to the

underside of the rear activates a gong. The same truck can be converted to hold a hose reel as shown in fig. 223.

The openness of the design provided by the cutouts indicates a lightened version necessitated by the high cost of shipping and raw materials.

224.
HUBLEY
Fire Engine

Early 1920s.
USA
10¾" long
Cast Iron

Blue and green colors, not commonly used on fire engines, could have contributed to the short life of this toy.

An interesting combination of styling and parts covered the period from 1910 through the 1920s. Large rear wheels are a transitional carry-over, while smaller front wheels ease the work of steering.

225.
HUBLEY
Ahrens-Fox Fire Engine

1932. USA
11½" long
Cast Iron

The real fire engine produced by the Ahrens-Fox Fire Engine Company of Cincinnati, Ohio was made some years before the toy. The design was so successful, it stayed basically the same in its outward appearance.

Ahrens-Fox fire engines are immediately recognizable by the pumping equipment mounted ahead of the motor and exposed with pride. A uniquely designed truck that was never copied.

The piston pumper with its big, nickel-plated spherical air chamber, two suction intakes and complex plumbing presented complicated castings for Hubley. The toy designers were up to the task, as witnessed by this truck and other toys for which Hubley soon gained a reputation. Hubley was known for its supreme engineering of complicated designs.

This historically interesting toy is a treasure for its attention to detail and wonderful lines.

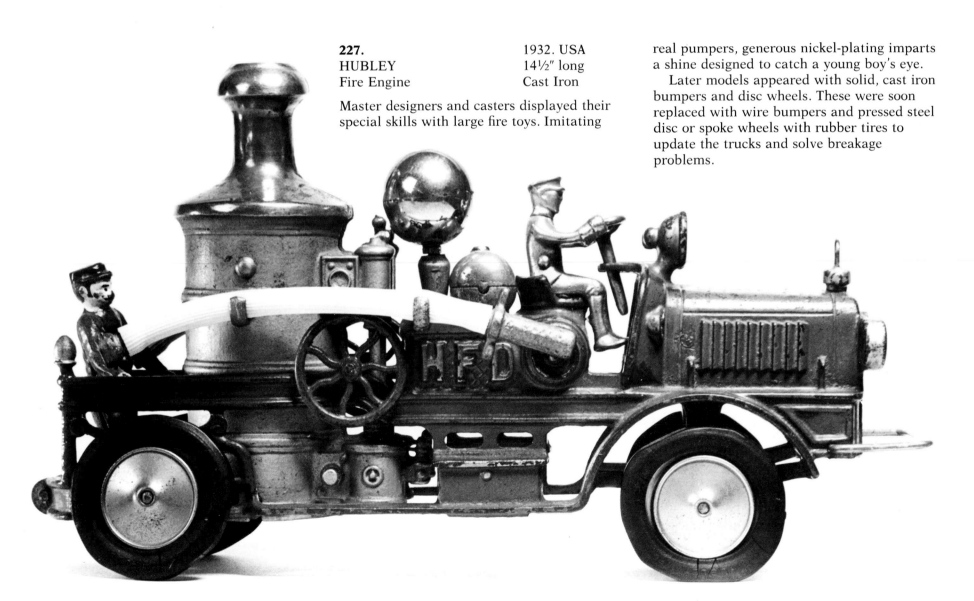

226.
HUBLEY
Hook and Ladder Truck

1926. USA
16½″ long
Cast Iron

Fires were big news and frequent before safety laws were fully enacted.

Made over a long period of time due to the popularity of toy fire engines in the 1920s and early 1930s. This fire truck is special for its sturdy design and pleasing form. The cast-in spotlight, nickel-plated ladders and racks, and spoke wheels are an added attraction. But it is the large cast iron motometer that lures collectors to this toy. A separate casting, it is easily broken or lost.

227.
HUBLEY
Fire Engine

1932. USA
14½″ long
Cast Iron

Master designers and casters displayed their special skills with large fire toys. Imitating real pumpers, generous nickel-plating imparts a shine designed to catch a young boy's eye.

Later models appeared with solid, cast iron bumpers and disc wheels. These were soon replaced with wire bumpers and pressed steel disc or spoke wheels with rubber tires to update the trucks and solve breakage problems.

228.
KENTON
Police Patrol

1910. USA
9½″ long
Cast Iron

Open patrols were a common sight in the earlier part of the 1900s. Here, three policemen ride with their prisoner, showing how America's history is reflected in its toys.

With a change of color and firemen to replace police, the toy was also sold as a fire patrol, thus extending the product line.

KENTON
Auto Hose Wagon

c. 1908. USA
9″ long
Cast Iron

The rear fireman holds the hose in place. This old toy with over seventy-two years of service still retains its original paint. The front crank is lost – but nobody's perfect!

Thin, delicately-cast disc wheels were the earliest offering for this toy.

Caution: Early Kenton toys did not have a primer undercoat. The paint is prone to flake and runs if it gets wet.

229.
HUBLEY
Special Ladder Truck

1938. USA
13″ long overall
Cast Iron

Hubley fire engines were generally a composite of fire trucks seen on the streets, but this ladder truck borrowed many lines from Seagraves, an Ohio firm.

A factory production toy which was never offered through the Hubley catalog, this item was assembled by Hubley from leftover parts. A special nickel-plated assembly mounted in the bed of the truck was designed to hold a ladder with a hand crank used for elevating to a vertical position. Possibly produced to utilize excess factory parts and to be sold as a special promotional order (see fig. 162).

140

230.
KENTON
Auto Fire Engine

1910. USA
12″ long
Cast Iron

High boxy styling typifies early motorized pumpers with rear hose hooks high on the boiler. On later models, the rear hooks are lowered on the framework.

231.
KENTON
Water Tower Truck

1927. USA
19″ long
Cast Iron

The crank and cable hold and lower the tower, which is held in place by a ratchet.

Few automotive water towers were made in proportion to other motorized fire toys, making them scarce items.

→
232.
KENTON
Three-Man Police Patrol

1933. USA
9⅝″ long
Cast Iron

Law enforcement was a vital part of community life, especially during the years between the First World War and the New Deal under President Franklin D. Roosevelt. The roaring twenties signaled a break with the old ways. Open police patrols were used to raid speakeasys and crack down on bootleggers. When caught, high-speeders in automobiles might be escorted to the jailhouse in an open patrol. Open patrols also toured the city looking for trouble spots. In the late 1930s, closed police vans were considered more comfortable and safe, as well as more escape-proof.

White rubber tires were almost universally accepted by the buying public and standard on most cast iron toys. By the early 1930s, the white rubber represented 'balloon' tires, even though real ones were black. Scuff marks on linoleum and wood floors made parents dislike the use of black tires. Later, improvements in black rubber made them more acceptable.

→
233.
KENTON
Fire Pumper

1930. USA
14¼″ long
Cast Iron

This modernized fire pumper shows off wheels with pneumatic tires, lowered body and added hose reel. Another improvement was a lower rear hose hook, which gave firemen access to a hose from the ground.

Other changes for this period were fenders incorporating running boards to give extra firemen a place to stand while hanging on.

Kenton was forced to keep updating its fire toys to stay competitive in the market-place. A still later version was updated with a front bumper and rubber wheels.

143

235. Late 1920s.
KINGSBURY USA
Fire Engine #726 9″ long
Pressed Steel

'Little Jim Playthings' are identifiable by the markings on the wheels. Produced by the Kingsbury Company for J. C. Penney stores and its mail order business, it helped carry the toy manufacturer through a difficult financial period. A cigar-type paper label is also found on some of these toys. Quantity buying gave Penney a cost advantage passed on to its customers at special sales in order to stimulate business.

Kingsbury issued special paint colors for the exclusive use of 'Little Jim' toys. Occasionally a toy is found with Kingsbury's standard colors and the Kingsbury name on the tires but bearing a Penney label. We can only speculate that it was a rush order for the store.

236. Mid-1920s. USA
KINGSBURY 9″ long
Ladder Truck Pressed Steel

Immediately following the Second World War, Harry Kingsbury replaced the pressed spoke wheels on his toys with pressed steel disc wheels, the company name being pressed into the tires. A few years later rubber tires were vulcanized directly on the wheels. The process was developed by the ingenious Kingsbury when he discovered buyers' tastes leaned toward quieter wheels on toys. The secret process was never revealed or duplicated, and the rubber-tired wheels became a trademark of the company.

The austere ladder truck with only the standard windup spring motor was probably intended for the smaller child unable to cope with a springing ladder which might cause injury. (See fig. 241.) A small pair of wooden ladders with wire stock rungs are removable.

144

234. KENTON
Hook and Ladder Truck

1933–41. USA
22¼" long
Cast Iron

There were enough parts on this hook and ladder fire engine to keep two boys busy! The green cast iron and tin hose basket is removable, as are many other parts. Loose parts make it difficult to find multi-piece fire engines complete today. Knowledgeable toy collectors perform a mutual service by searching for parts to trade, thus enabling the completion of toys that would otherwise be incomplete or unsuitable for a collection. More knowledge can also be gained in the process.

237. KINGSBURY
Fire Chief Car

1933. USA
14" long
Pressed Steel

Fire chiefs nearly always had a private car for their personal use. Kingsbury removed the windshield on this 1933 model and gave it a new V-shaped radiator for the purpose of streamlining the car.

Small motorized toy fire chief cars of any material are scarce. Fewer of these pieces were marketed in proportion to other models.

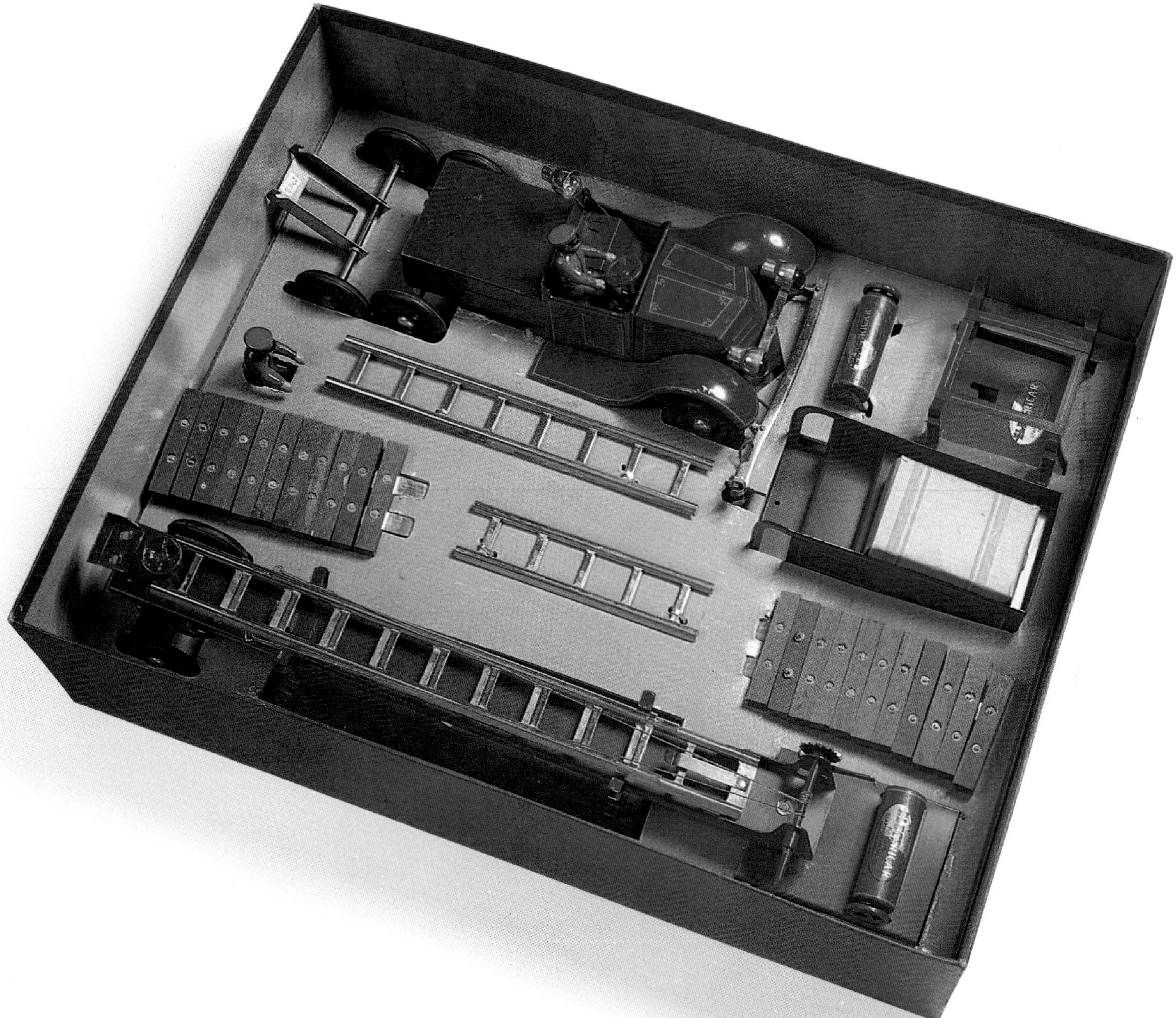

238.
KINGSTON
Kokomo Fire Engine Set

1928–30. USA
Box 23″ × 18″
Pressed Steel

Still packed in its original box, a deluxe set includes a universal chassis with interchangeable bodies to make a complete fire department. Attachments include a patrol wagon body, with chemical tank, hook and ladder, and an aerial truck 29″ long on rubber tires. The 'motor' is powered by contact with an electrically charged fence which operates with a toy transformer similar to that used by toy electric trains.

Its price of $25 for the set was astronomical for 1930. The auto fire set was top of the Kingston line, which included racers and trucks in smaller electric sets, priced from $7.50 to $14.00.

Kingsbury firemen with double-pronged seat pins are used for the toy, evidence of the figure swapping prevalent among toymakers.

239.
STRUCTO
Fire Engine

1927. USA
18″ long
Ladders – 18″
long
Pressed Steel

Structo found a comfortable market in customers who preferred larger pressed steel pull toys for indoor play. A constant stream of new models and custom conversion fire engines on the road gave toy manufacturers a lot of variety and combinations to consider for copies.

This combination hook and ladder truck with hose reel is well made without sharp edges. A touch of luxury is the brass bell, hub caps, and side lamps which copy the brass parts preferred by some real engine manufacturers of the period. This engine sold for $1.75 in 1927.

A 1930s Marx fireman automatically climbs his ladder with the aid of wind-up motor. The clever action of this toy aided its continuance into the 1950s with a molded red plastic hat in place of the tin one. The fireman was one of the Marx Company's best sellers.

240.
WILKINS
(later Kingsbury)
Fire House #8

1911–30. USA
13″ long
Pressed Steel

A staple item in the Wilkins-Kingsbury line, the toy fire house was a consistently good seller, appearing over the years in various jobber and company catalogs from 1911 through 1930. The design was timeless. A 19″ long fire house made to accommodate horse-drawn fire toys, long aerial ladder trucks and a fire chief's car (fig. 237) was also available.

An alarm box, mounted on the right side of the building, conceals a trigger, which when pulled, activates a bell and doors which automatically fly open. The fire engine, its 'motor' wound and ready, speeds out. The alarm then rings a second time and stops.

WILKINS
Auto Fire Engine

1911. USA
11″ long
Pressed Steel

Wilkins automotive toys are not marked. After 1918, when the line was revised and updated by Harry Kingsbury, the company carried his name and the toys were marked.

Early cast iron spoke wheels of Wilkins toys are sometimes covered with a separate rubber tire as shown. The large spoked-wheel fire engine was a transitional toy, adapted from the Wilkins horse-drawn pumper. Kingsbury's patented windup spring motor was added to help it enter the motor age. The fire engine's design was altered several times over the years by simply changing the wheels.

The fire engine and house are an attractive and colorful combination. They were originally purchased as a set in 1911.

241.
WILKINS
Aerial Ladder Truck

c. 1915. USA
9½″ long
Pressed Steel

Painted pressed steel wheels which are unmarked are typical of those used by Wilkins from 1914 through 1918. The wooden ladders are a special play feature. Supported by a strong spring, they quickly rise when the toy strikes an object from the front.

Buses

The earliest motor 'buses' were vehicles not specifically designed for mass transit and were consequently unsuitable and uncomfortable. Often they were touring automobiles in dubious states of preservation. Others began as truck or touring car chassis, which were then fitted with transverse bench seats and folding tops.

While motor buses were used for sightseeing in New York around 1902, the seeds of the commuter and inter-city bus industries in the United States were sown in the newer territories such as Minnesota, Texas, California, the Pacific Northwest and Florida's Atlantic coast. Here 'jitneys' were used to transport workers to mines or oil fields. One such service, beginning with a seven-passenger Hupmobile, eventually led to the famous Greyhound Lines. Operators constructed their own equipment. Thus, as early as 1903, Mack produced a 20-seat open-body bus with a revolutionary feature – a steering wheel instead of a tiller. Another successful production model was the Stanley Steamer 'Mountain Wagon' of about 1915, which transported passengers between rail depots and hotels or resorts.

Several primitive features were universal in bus design through the 1920s. Luggage was carried on roof racks or in a small rear 'boot', as in a stagecoach. When buses became enclosed for all-weather travel, there was still no center aisle, and each row of seats corresponded to an exterior door. GMC's 1924 Model X bus had five doors along one side.

The 'Good Roads' program of the 1920s was a huge factor in making modern bus carriage possible. That program, plus technical advances that contributed to passenger comfort, fostered the growth of the sightseeing bus tour industry. The same decade also saw many significant improvements in vehicle design.

The travel business was helped greatly in its recovery from the Depression by the Chicago World's Fair of 1933–4, which attracted visitors who used bus transportation. Furthermore, the display of innovative, streamlined buses sparked public interest in modern transportation.

242. 1926. USA
ARCADE 13½″ long
Yellow Coach Bus Cast Iron

The first regular bus service began in New York City in 1905. Double-decker buses with their great capacity were popular for use in large, crowded cities. Visitors liked the unobstructed views when good weather prevailed. These buses ran regularly along Fifth Avenue in the 1920s, becoming so well known that American collectors often refer to double-decker buses as Fifth Avenue buses.

This toy underwent the removal of several coats of overpaint which revealed the original coat intact. While at the restorer's workshop, a tornado struck the area uprooting trees and complete houses. The shed where my bus awaited me was blown over. A search of the debris in the area uncovered the bus, which was in one piece, minus two seats and a small dent in one tire. My bus has been through a lot!

The real Yellow Coach was built from 1921 to 1927 in Chicago, Illinois. The toy is an exact copy of the Model Z built in 1926.

150

243. 1925. USA
← ARCADE 11½" long
ACF Coach Cast Iron

A realistic model of the American Car and Foundry streetcar bus. The most distinguishing feature is a front door that opens and closes.

It is possible that the idea for the toy was conceived from the appearance of the real AFC coach in Chicago, just a few miles from the Arcade factory.

By 1925, Arcade successfully produced four large buses, each of a different make.

244. c. 1925. USA
ARCADE 13" long
Yellow Parlor Coach Cast Iron

A sturdily built bus which carries the logo of the Pennsylvania Rapid Transit. Double sidemount wheels add realism. Rubber was costly in the early 1920s and rubber tires were an additional expense. While Arcade was able to cast the iron wheels, it was necessary to buy rubber tires elsewhere.

Note that the yellow coach bus discharges passengers from the rear.

245. 1925. USA
ARCADE 12" long
Feagol Safety Coach Cast Iron

In 1921, twin brothers Frank and W. B. Fageol built the first successful bus for intercity service in America, calling it the 'Safety Coach'.

Built low with full-height doors, the design was eventually to be copied by the entire bus industry. Previous buses had been built on high truck chassis. Fageol was sold to American Car and Foundry (ACF) in 1926. Frank Fageol, who remained with the company, designed and produced two new bus models under the new name, 'Twin Coach'. Stressing comfort and safety, Frank Fageol became known as 'the father of the modern bus industry.' The real 1923 Fageol bus featured forty-eight windows and reclining seats for 28 passengers.

Arcade was a little slow picking the bus for its line, but when they did, it was produced in large numbers in two sizes to meet a great demand. Although considered a common toy, it is a longtime favorite of collectors.

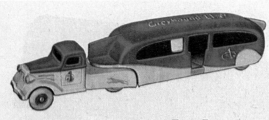

No. 4370 Great Lakes Expo Bus

An exact model in miniature of the Cleveland Exposition Transportation Bus.
Length 11¼ inches, width 2¼ inches, height 2⅝ inches.
Color: Bright blue, white and silver, as illustrated. White rubber wheels with blue centers. Stencilled in white on blue top "Greyhound Lines." Trailer turns on pivot and is detachable.
Packed 1 in carton, 1 dozen in case.
Case net weight 21 lbs., case gross weight 26 lbs.
Case measurements: 10x10x12 inches.

Arcade's catalog for 1936 shows a souvenir bus featured at the Great Lakes Exposition during the summer months and offered to toy dealers elsewhere as well.

No. 3170 Double Deck Bus

Length 8¼ inches, width 2¼ inches, height 3¼ inches.
Color: Green with aluminum bronzed bumper and headlights. "Chicago Motor Coach" stamped in gold letters on both sides. Two red spots on rear to represent "stop" lights. White rubber wheels with red centers.
Packed 1 in box, 1 dozen in case.
Case net weight 22 lbs., case gross weight 27 lbs.
Case measurements: 9x12x16 inches.

Receding fenders and a streamlined body mark this cast iron bus shown in Arcade's 1936 catalog. It was probably produced as a regional souvenir, selling for 50¢.

246. 1938. USA
ARCADE 8" long
Double-Deck Bus Cast Iron

In the United States, buses would eventually carry more passengers than any other form of transportation.

The cab over engine (C.O.E.) bus was a totally new, streamlined style for the late 1930s. The shortened wheel-base made the bus easier to handle and greatly improved maneuverability.

Arcade's faithful copy reflects the popularity of the styles which had taken over by 1938. Almost every leading truck manufacturer including Ford, Chevrolet, Mack and White offered C.O.E. models.

Arcade supplied three nickeled, removable passengers for the upper deck seats.

247.
CONVERSE
Sightseeing Bus

1906. USA
11″ long
Pressed Steel

The Rapid Motor Vehicle Company of Pontiac, Michigan*, started manufacturing commercial vehicles for sightseeing tours in 1904. The seats faced forward and could be entered easily from the side, leaving plenty of space for rubber-necking. Well-suited to journey from railway and bus stations to hotels, 1906 buses appeared with a surrey-type roof and side curtains which were kept rolled up in nice weather.

Winding the toy from the roof was intended to make the task easy for children, although there is a loss of authenticity from the original design. No steering wheel is needed (nor was one ever provided) since the front wheels can be set to run in a circle.

* Formed in 1899. Later part of General Motors.

152

248.   c. 1923. USA
DENT   15″ long
Coast to Coast Bus   Cast Iron

By 1928, all forty-eight states had imposed gasoline taxes ranging from two to five cents a gallon, to cover costs for road building and maintenance. Coast to coast bus travel increased as accommodations became more refined. Bus stops sprouted up between cities, providing relays for the bus drivers and places where travelers could take care of personal comforts before moving on.

This big nickel-plated multi-door toy has a high center of gravity, typical of an early 1920s style bus. Large windows are fine for sightseers. Dent omitted seats and a driver, leaving just a shell to be filled by the child's imagination.

249.   Early 1920s.
DENT   USA
Bus Line Bus   8½″ long
     Cast Iron

Almost all school buses are a bright orange color, borrowing from early Yellow Cabs that needed to be seen from long distances.

Dent's school bus has a roof light to mark it from other traffic on the road and alert school children of its approach.

250. 1926. USA
DENT 14″ long
Public Service Bus Cast Iron

This design is taken from a 1926 Mack 29-passenger City Bus with roof vents – an identifying feature. The Dent factory in Fullerton, Pennsylvania, was only a short distance from the Mack Factory.

A tag attached to this never-played-with bus proclaims the toy a showroom sample, #2292. When outdated, samples were sold. Passed from collector to collector for many years, the wonderful bus came to a full stop at my house almost fifteen years ago. The previous owners – all automotive-oriented today – were not interested in toy cars in those days.

→
252. c. 1906. USA
KENTON 10½″ long
Sightseeing Auto Bus Cast Iron
Seeing New York Bus

The first sightseeing buses were custom-built by early truck manufacturers for transporting spectators at the World's Columbian Exposition. Held in Chicago in May, 1893, the fair commemorated the 400th anniversary of the discovery of America. The innovation proved successful and similar buses immediately appeared on the streets of major cities like New York, Detroit and St. Louis, enabling conventioneers and other riders to tour the local attractions.

Copies of 1904 photographs show as many as 35 passengers piled onto a small bus with five bench seats. Later, larger buses held even more people, while enterprising photographers peddled souvenir pictures and post cards to the passengers.

Probably, the white-painted bus was made first and the New York bus (selling as a souvenir for $1.50) later.

The collector acquired the set of comic figures occupying the bus separately. Their slightly worn appearance suggests the wearying nature of primitive motorized transport! The figures are: The Sailor at the wheel; Happy Hooligan with his spinach can hat; Happy's brother, Gloomy Gus; the Professor; and Mama Katzenjammer with her familiar red hair in a top knot.

251. c. 1928. USA
DENT 9″ long
Interurban Bus Cast Iron

Interurban buses carry passengers between cities or towns. In the early days, drivers

would pick up passengers at any point along the route. The practice was discontinued when passengers increased in number and scheduled stopping places became necessary.

There are no seats or place for a driver in this toy bus.

SIGHT SEEING AUTO 899

SEEING NEW YORK 899

254.
KENTON
City Buses

A pair of cast iron Kenton buses show the evolution of bus designs from 1923 to 1933.

(*Left*) 1933. USA. 6½″ long. Cast Iron

A lower, longer body utilizes space overhead to add seats and safety rails at the top of the stairs. A change in wheels with 'balloon' tires and a lighter green color emphasize the passage of time from 1923. The up and down windows are a charming detail.

(*Right*) 1923. USA. 5¾″ long. Cast Iron

The bus discharges passengers on the left. Large wheels, fewer seats and a high center of gravity help date this double-decker bus.

255.
KENTON
World's Fair Bus

1933. USA
10⅞″ long
Cast Iron

Toy companies were struggling to survive the business depression in 1933. Kenton produced this new and different bus in an attempt to capitalize on the World's Fair. It failed. Arcade, a local firm, dominated toy sales at the Fair, producing not only an extensive line of replica cast iron buses (see fig. 384) and autos, but other souvenirs as well. This detachable, two-piece bus, with its cast-in figures and light blue color, is rarely seen today.

← **253.**
KENTON
City Bus

1927. USA
12″ long
Cast Iron

For its largest, up-to-date, double-decker bus, Kenton supplied the passengers. A clown, fireman, porter and gentleman are identified by the hats they wear.

The bus was produced by Kenton in various models and sizes from 1923.

COAST-TO-COAST BUS

Equipped with extension handle bar for steering. Length 31¼ inches, height 12¾ inches, width 8¹³⁄₁₆ inches.
No. K84 Weight each, 22 lbs.................each $6.75

'Ride-Em' toys appeared in the early 1930s using the same Packard prototype radiator produced by Keystone since 1925.

This illustration, from a jobber's catalog, shows the handle bar which this manufacturer also used on some of its other toys to add steering, and as a selling point.

256.	1927. USA
KINGSBURY	16″ long
Interurban Passenger Bus	Pressed Steel

Public transportation quickly became a vital part of a city's growth. Intercity buses operated on schedules and routes from the first to meet a great need, providing a practical means of transportation for workers and shoppers.

Boys who yearned to drive a bus – a big yellow one – could buy Kingsbury's for $2.00 in 1927. Surprisingly, the price rose to $2.50 in 1929 with a change in color to blue. It was priced 50¢ higher west of the Mississippi, and there called a 'Cross-Country' bus. Still in the line ten years later, the price was back to $2.00 with an extra 10% charge for the Western states.

257.
KINGSBURY
Greyhound Bus

c. 1937. USA
18″ long
Pressed Steel

When boys called 'all aboard,' they referred to their streamlined Greyhound bus with a New York destination.

A well-loved bus with evidence of thousands of miles of service. Surely this toy provided all the satisfaction its manufacturer promised.

Today, the Greyhound Corporation is a world-wide conglomerate. 'Go Greyhound . . . and leave the driving to us' is a famous slogan, telling us the old dog is still alive and thriving.

258.　　　　　　　　　1925. USA
STRAUSS　　　　　　　　12″ long
Continental Flyer　　　　　Litho tin

By 1925, seventy-five bus companies were serving the nation, 60,000 buses were reported in operation, not counting school buses, and over 3 billion passengers had been transported.

Increasing bus travel made it imperative to devise a means for enlarging the carriers. Many bus manufacturers began using the dual rear axle design to lengthen their buses and distribute the load. Some three-axle buses had brakes on all four rear wheels.

Strauss printed catalog numbers on many of his toys and trademarked the names.

259.　　　　　　　　　1926. USA
STRAUSS　　　　　　　　10½″ long
Interstate Bus　　　　　　Litho tin

It is doubtful whether a double-deck bus was ever used to transport passengers between states, but Strauss used this name for his newest bus.

Carrying the familiar green color of a Fifth Avenue bus, the Strauss toy is propelled by a wind-up spring motor and has a double row of seats on the top.

$1.25 in 1926, the Strauss bus is a favorite of collectors. The front wheels can be pre-set to run straight or in a circle.

The Interstate designation disguises the true name of this design. It is a Model Z Yellow Coach bus of the same year. Arcade produced it in cast iron. (See fig. 242.)

260.
STRAUSS
Bus De Luxe

1926. USA
13¾" long
Litho tin

A cross-country touring bus with curtains at the windows creates an 'at home' atmosphere for travelers and is typical of the many highway buses serving the tourist boom of 1926. Adding to their comfort were pneumatic tires. Old hard rubber tires were unkind to kidneys and bones.

Strauss catalog #105 sold for $1.25 retail and made its way across the states by a wind-up motor.

261.
UPTON
Express Bus

1927. USA
8½" long
Litho tin

Shoreline Express buses ran in the Great Lakes area.

This cheaply made toy bus is mostly constructed from folded light-weight tin, using tab and slot construction to sidestep soldering and speed up assembly. Short on details and with no 'motor' to give it the cannon ball speed it implies, it has justified its place in history due to the original 10¢ cost.

Taxis

The first electric-motor-driven automobile for hire in the United States appeared in 1898. The first gasoline model and the first meters came in 1907. Not surprisingly, the advent of motorized taxi cabs in the early 1900s was quickly followed by the development of toy counterparts.

Although it did not operate as a passenger carrier until 1921, the Yellow Cab Manufacturing Company of Chicago, Illinois had been producing taxi vehicles prior to that time.

Yellow Cabs of the 1920s were distinguishable by their headlamps mounted on the cowl (instead of the front of the car) and the horizontal louvers located behind the rear windows. Of course, the bright orange color made them easily recognizable. The driver's compartment was open on both sides to allow the driver to hear calls and handle collections without leaving the cab.

Yellow Cab's closest rival in taxi cab production was the Checker Cab Company of Kalamazoo, Michigan. Checker cabs were similar to Yellow Cabs; however, it was Checker who built a reputation for quality-built cabs.

Arcade produced the first cast iron Yellow Cab in 1921, and was the leader in toy taxi production throughout its existence. Because they were more readily recognized by city kids, toy taxis were most popular in cities. (Similarly, farm and construction toys were most popular where those kinds of activities took place.) In 1925 rubber tires, a must for indoor use, were available by special order. A few years later, rubber tires became standard on some toys, no doubt the result of increased demand from mothers.

By enclosing the passenger compartment and floor of a standard cab, Arcade produced a Yellow Cab bank. The money slot is in the roof or hood. Because they promoted thrift, banks were favored by parents, who, after all, did the buying. Taxi banks are classified as semi-mechanical banks.

Toy taxis were produced in American and foreign models and in such great quantities that it is not surprising to find collectors who specialize in this field alone.

262.

Top left — 1924. USA
ARCADE — 8″ long
Yellow Cab Bank — Cast Iron

Telephone number is from 'motor city', Detroit, Michigan.

Top right — 1925. USA
ARCADE — 8″ long
Green Checker Cab — Cast Iron

In the 1920s, Yellow Cab's closest rival. Except for color difference and Checker emblems, it was hard to tell them apart.

Middle left — 1924. USA
ARCADE — 8″ long
Red Top Cab — Cast Iron

Toy stores could special order taxis in colors to match local fleets. This accounts for the Red Top Cab, and others such as Arcade's Blue and White cab and Brown Top Cab. These taxis are not classified as advertising toys except when imprinted with a message or phone number.

Middle right — 1930. USA
ARCADE — 8½″ long
Limousine Yellow Cab — Cast Iron

The license number 3300 gives a clue to the year of manufacture. It has a money slot in the top of the hood and conceals its loot in the engine compartment.

Bottom left — 1926. USA
ARCADE — 8″ long
Yellow Cab Bank — Cast Iron

Updated with a beltline to copy models on the street.

Disc wheels were quicker and easier to wash. They also eliminated warping, split wood and clinging mud. For these reasons, they were preferred on real Taxis.

Bottom right — 1923. USA
DENT — 9½″ long
Yellow Cab — Cast Iron

This toy came in its original box marked 'Yellow Taxi with blue wheels'. Its true yellow color is a change. The driver bolts to door to ensure togetherness.

265.
ARCADE
Yellow Cab

1925. USA
9″ & 5¼″ long
Cast Iron

Introduced in 1925, the 5¼″ cab was retired from the 1928 catalog.

Made for only a short period, the little Yellow Cab is scarce. The smaller size was also sold in a special finish, although this was not listed in regular catalogs. Special finishes were color painted to customers' requests upon orders of sufficient number. Arcade conducted a business division devoted to advertising and special order items from 1922 to their closing in 1946.

266.
ARCADE
Checker Cab

1932. USA
9¼″ long
Cast Iron

Dwindling toy cab sales prompted a new design in the form of a Checker Cab. This year's model had a yellow body, integral bumpers, and was trimmed in black with a black roof and wheels. Rubber 'Goodrich' tires added a small additional cost, usually 10¢–15¢. A single-piece nickel-plated radiator with attached Woodlites make this toy, made only over a short period, into a deluxe collector's item.

Hoping for increased sales and lower shipping costs, the 1933 model was revised to include a cast-in sign over the windshield with the embossed word 'Checker'. It was offered in two reduced prices and sizes – 8¾″ long and 6⅞″ long. Both were commercial failures.

267.
ARCADE
Ford Yellow Cab
Special Edition for the
Chicago World's Fair

1933–4. USA
6⅞" long
Cast Iron

Arcade introduced the newest Ford four-door sedan as a conventional pleasure car in the 1933 dealers' catalog. Copied line-for-line from the real car, the larger, lower body had a sloping V-shaped grille.

Top speed of 85 miles per hour made the V-8 motor ideal and adaptable for police use. At the same time, a light, fast car was just what notorious gangster John Dillinger needed for quick getaways. He stole a 1934 Ford V-8 for use on his bank-robbing sprees and took time out to write Henry Ford a letter extolling the merits of the car. Shortly thereafter, Dillinger was caught and shot to death.

The Ford Yellow Cab, with 'A Century of Progress' stenciled on the roof in yellow and black taxi colors, was made to be sold as a special souvenir of the Fair. It would never gain the recognition or fame of Arcade's first Yellow Cab.

This toy, like Dillinger's stolen Ford, has traveled on a lot of rough and rocky roads!

← **268.**
268.   1936. USA
ARCADE   8¼″ long
Yellow Cab   Cast Iron

The real Model Y Yellow Cab was built by the Checker Cab Manufacturing Company of Kalamazoo, Michigan and remained unchanged through 1939.

In 1936, the mass market was dealing in lower-priced toys while recovering from the depressed financial climate of earlier years. Arcade promoted its 10 line, 25 line and 50 line, intending to get a share of business in smaller toys. The numbers in the line referred to the retail price of the toys.

← **269.**   1940. USA
HUBLEY   8″ long
Yellow Cab   Cast Iron

Every antique toy automobile has one unique feature which makes it stand out from all others. In this case, it is the folding nickel-plated luggage rack.

To lower costs, new offerings were scaled down in size, including the Model Y cab priced at 50¢ retail, which did not have a driver or place for one. Except for a separate nickel-plated grille assembly and new, streamlined design, this was a simple toy compared to Arcade's previous leading toys. A separate rear license plate, number 6391, fastens with a screw and spells the year of manufacture when read backwards. The new taxi was painted a pure lemon yellow like its real counterpart.

Collectors often refer to this toy as a 'Parmalee', the name of a well-known company that operated taxi fleets in the 1930s.

After General Motors took over the manufacture of Yellow Cabs, Chrysler products became more popular for use in their nationwide fleet, especially DeSoto limousines which proved to be rugged and dependable.

The Hubley cab design is loosely based on the DeSoto.

↑**270.**   c. 1930. USA
DENT   6″ long
Amos 'n Andy Taxi   Cast Iron

'A buck short and an hour late!' is the way a former toy representative explained the failure of this toy. It seems a Marx toy of the same name hit the market first and buyers preferred the erratic-action tin windup toy.

Dent never got into full production on this taxi. A few years ago, an enterprising collector bought up the remaining stock of toys, samples and parts when the Dent factory closed for good. He assembled and painted what he could from the stock and made them available to collectors. He used as his guide an original factory ledger which listed paints, trim and other necessary procedures. Some of the original paints found in the factory were still good in their cans.

It is not known whether any of the toys reached the market in 1930, but the patterns were made and a few taxis cast for samples.

271.
KENTON
Auto Hansom

c. 1908. USA
8½″ long
6″ long
Cast Iron

A pair of early taxis line up for comparison. The largest one transports a lady passenger in a duster. Her bonnet is tied down with a scarf for protection against dirt, which will surely invade a vehicle minus fenders, an indication

that the style of taxi may be earlier, though not necessarily made before 1908. The taxi in four sizes, cast without headlamps but retaining sidelamps, was carried in the line through 1927; a long run for an automobile toy.

272.
TURNER
Yellow Cab

1927. USA
9¾″ long
Pressed Steel
Friction

Using heavy auto sheet steel, Turner constructed toys geared for outdoor play. A

fly-wheel mechanism in a sealed unit between the rear wheels provided the power for movement.

The Yellow Cab is seen with its original 1927 catalog sheet. The occupants are an integral cut-out part of the body. That year,

Turner advertised in national magazines, making the toys available by direct order from the factory in Dayton, Ohio. The taxi was priced at $1.00 retail.

See 'Foreign' chapter for more Taxis.

Motorcycles

The motorcycle is as old as the motor car. In the beginning despised socially and banned from 'nice' neighborhoods, it has survived to enjoy wide acceptance. The first motorcycles are now taking their place alongside antique automobiles at shows and motor museums and are recognized as the unique works of early designers and inventors who dared to be different.

At first various practical problems had not been sorted out and impeded total acceptance of the new machines. Gasoline tanks were naturally much smaller than on automobiles and, with the relative scarcity of filling stations, larger trips were not possible. Lights for night driving were virtually non-existent, except for the acetylene lamps used on bicycles. These needed both water and carbide replacements to operate. Often, the rough road extinguished the lamps and the driver's desire to continue. Accidents and breakdowns created new problems, not to mention exposure to the elements. While the mass-produced motor car continued to make rapid improvements in safety, speed, comfort and price in the 1920s, motorcycles lagged behind and found their main market as vehicles of law enforcement in the police force.

Motorcycle racing events were often a sideshow at county fairs and carnivals, with drivers competing for a purse. Daring drivers drove cycles around the sides of motordromes (enclosed tracks) with almost vertical sides at great speeds without tipping over.

← 273.   1930. USA
HUBLEY   9″ long
Harley-Davidson Sidecar   Cast Iron
Motorcycle

A large line of finely made motorcycles highlights Hubley's 1928–34 toy line. Exclusive arrangements with the manufacturers of the real machines guaranteed an exact likeness. An original 1930 advertising folder furnishes proof that the toys were designed from scale drawings provided by Harley-Davidson, which had the right to final approval of the product.

The casting process limited the amount of detail that could be produced, hence, some forms are merely suggested. The cycle is as near to a perfect replica as a cast iron toy could be. Hubley's toy motorcycles carry the name of the real model either embossed into the iron or on a decal. The nattily attired sports driver in cap, breeches and long socks and his lady companion are classical 1930 figures.

A 'clicker' set between the rear wheels simulates the sound of an exhaust on this pull toy, which was also sold with policemen figures.

274.   1928. USA
HUBLEY   10″ long
Harley-Davidson Parcel Post   Cast Iron

Play value is enhanced with a side compartment which opens to hold small packages and letters. Hubley offered buyers a choice of Indian or H-D toys. These were the two best known makes of motorcycles in America in the late 1920s and early 1930s.

H-D continued to make improvements to the Model 74 from its inception in the 1920s, but the outward design was never radically altered. This fact favored Hubley motorcycles, for they did not appear outmoded from year to year as was the case with many toy automobiles.

Indian Motorcycles

George Hendee, a Springfield bicycle manufacturer, joined with Oscar Hedstrom, who had invented the 'Motocycle', a bicycle equipped with a motor. They formed the Hendee Manufacturing Company in 1901. Later, renamed the Indian Motorcycle Company, it became the first company in the United States to mass-produce motorcycles. By 1905, the twin-cylinder engine was in use, and the front assembly was redesigned for front suspension.

Indian acquired its famous red color with gold script logo in 1910. Previous motorcycles were painted a dark blue. Hedstrom, who had retired from Indian, returned in 1916 to replace Hendee and ensure continuity of management. The company made motorcycles for use in the First World War and continued to prosper in the years to follow, making further improvements and advancements.

Financial problems brought on by the Great Depression made it necessary for Indian to reorganize in 1933. The military Jeep manufactured by Willys and other automobile manufacturers edged motorcycles, including Indian, out of the lucrative defense market during the Second World War. The dwindling company struggled along until it was forced to close in 1953.

275.   1928. USA
HUBLEY   8½″ long
Indian Armored Car   Cast Iron

Motorcycle police were able to join in a cops and robbers fast speed chase when the armored plate was added for their protection. The plate deflected bullets from bootleggers, bank robbers and gangsters in fast getaway cars with a penchant for clearing their exit! Alas, there was nothing to protect the tires from purposeful or stray bullets.

The armored car served all through the Second World War where it was used a great deal and fitted on other makes of motorcycles as well, to escort army convoys.

Real antique Indian motorcycles command a loyal following today, with collectors claiming that once the vehicle has been correctly restored, it is henceforth absolutely troublefree, if ridden with care on smooth roads.

This is a unique toy. The armor plate is removable and designed to fit only this Indian 3-wheeler.

← **276.**   1929. USA
HUBLEY   9¼″ long
Indian Air Mail   Cast Iron

Hubley quickly extended the motorcycle series when the first 1928 models were received enthusiastically by buyers. The new issues would be variations of the real models with sidecars or 3-wheelers as they were known in the industry. By the early 1930s, the United States Postal Service used real 3-wheelers in almost all major cities with pickups for air mail.

Demountable motorcycle drivers are interchangeable on all large size Hubley cycles. A rear door opens on this model for holding mail. A label decorates the sidecar with familiar red, white and blue stripes.

277.   1929. USA
HUBLEY   9″ long
Indian 4-cyl. Motocycle*   Cast Iron

The Indian motorcycle is nicknamed 'Iron Redskin' after its color by collectors and restorers of the real machines. This toy is a model of the most famous early Indian motorcycle, the Indian 101 Scout. So named because it could go 101 miles per hour, it was designed by a former racer and engineer, Charles Franklin, for the Springfield, Massachusetts company. Completed in late 1928, the real cycle made its appearance as a 1929 model and was an immediate sensation for its design, speed and special handling abilities.

Hubley quickly acquired the exclusive right to manufacture Indian motorcycle toys. Like the real machine, the toy prospered.

* The spelling 'Motocycle' was used by the Indian Motorcycle Company and Hubley.

278.   1930. USA
HUBLEY   12″ long
Traffic Car   Cast Iron

Motorcycles became a viable product when their value as economy travel was recognized along with their speed and maneuverability.

Handlebars for Hubley motorcycles were cast from aluminum. Though they could withstand a little pressure without breakage, in time the nature of the metal caused them to become brittle; oftentimes the cycles are found with broken handlebars or with a piece snapped off, like the lamp on this toy. Replacements are readily available today, but are cast in a metal alloy which resembles aluminum. The parts vary in design from one make of motorcycle to another, and the correct piece should be established before seeking a replacement.

Traffic cars were used to transport street signs and emergency equipment to congested road areas and trouble spots in communities without traffic signals in the 1920s and 1930s.

280.
HUBLEY
Motorcycle

1932. USA
7½" long
Cast Iron

Like many motorcycle manufacturers, Harley-Davidson was the outgrowth of a bicycle concern which began in 1901. It was known as the Harley-Davidson Motor Company in 1918. A Milwaukee-based motorcycle company, it is still in business today, despite increasing competition from Japanese imports. It is presently owned by AMF, Inc. At the time of writing, AMF is engaged in negotiations to sell the veteran motorcycle firm to Harley-Davidson's current management.

The 1930 Harley-Davidson Model 74's were noted for their comfort. The simple, rugged design resulted in a mechanically quieter and more smoother-running machine, suitable for touring.

The toy figure is an integral part of the casting, with the exception of a separate head for the driver, which can be turned side to side. Small wheels replace a kickstand to provide balance, a sacrifice to practicality.

Rubber tires became standard on this toy in 1933.

↑

279.
HUBLEY
Hill Climber

c. 1935. USA
6¾" long
Cast Iron

The driver is an integral casting with more detail than is found on most Hubley drivers. His crouched position denotes speed, while a number embossed on his back indicates a racer. Pressed steel wheels were used only for a short period on this light blue Harley-Davidson model. In 1936, Hubley changed to cast iron, nickel-plated spoke wheels and offered the toy in a smaller size as well.

281.
HUBLEY
Motorized Sidecar
Motorcycle

1932–4. USA →
8½" long
Cast Iron
Clockwork
motor

Cast iron automotive toys equipped with clockwork motors were commercial failures. The first ones produced at the turn of the century required very strong mechanisms and, once wound and set, could not be controlled. The impact of cast iron against furniture led to disaster and an increase in nervous mothers, not to mention breakage of the toy itself; there is nothing more brittle than cast iron when it falls with force.

Many years passed before Hubley gave motorized cast iron another chance. Spurred on by tin windups gaining a big share of the market, Hubley came up with a practical solution. It simply added clockwork mechanisms to some of their latest automotive designs, and offered them as an optional extra, choosing toys that could successfully conceal the works, like the road roller or a dump truck.

Pictured is a clockwork motorcycle with the motor concealed in the sidecar. A separate key winds the strong spring.

Named GO-TOYS in 1932, they were gone after 1934.

282.   1938. USA
HUBLEY   9″ long
Popeye Patrol   Cast Iron

Popeye, the famous one-eyed sailor, rides astride a motorcycle designed just for him. A bowl-shaped seat and cast iron handlebars are special design features that separate this motorcycle from all others.

Introduced at the January–February toy fairs in 1938, Popeye was Hubley's lead feature toy for the year; but strangely enough, for all its appeal to collectors today, the toy was not considered an outstanding success by Hubley.

Popeye merchandise sales were an outgrowth from the highly successful King Syndicates comic strip from whom Hubley received copyright permission to use the figure. Popeye wears evidence of the copyright embossed on his back.

Cartoonist Elzie C. Segar created Popeye for King Features in 1929. He drew the character from a real person named Rocky, who was the town tough of Chester, Illinois. Rocky swept out the local saloon. He had a

176

reputation as the biggest, meanest fighter around. Once when three brutes lured him into the woods, he returned unscathed while the three challengers spent weeks recovering. They never went near him again. Popeye's girlfriend, Olive Oyl, with her bean-pole body dropped her steady beau, Ham Gravy, after she met Popeye.

By 1932–3, the readers had fallen in love with the comic strip characters; and a Popeye craze swept America. William Randolph Hearst, owner of the strip, instructed the writers to stop Popeye's swearing and told them to have him fight for a good cause. Popeye was to emerge as a do-gooder. When Swee'pea joined the strip, a new word was added to the American language. It was 'glop'.

Today, Popeye is still a well-known character to young and old alike. Thanks to Bud Sagendorf, who presently continues the strip, Popeye and his friends have not aged a day since 1929. A recent movie, 'Popeye' is further proof of his continued popularity.

283.   1938. USA
HUBLEY   6″ long
Popeye Spinach Delivery   Cast Iron

Popeye credited his legendary strength to the consumption of vast quantities of spinach which he swallowed straight from a can! None for J. Wellington Wimpy, who looks on, thank you. He prefers hamburgers!

The demountable Popeye with stationary arms on his red motorcycle named 'Spinach' is shaped to fit this toy only.

284.   1928–9. USA
VINDEX   9″ long
Excelsior-Henderson   Cast Iron
Motorcycle and Package Car

Brothers William and Thomas Henderson produced their first motorcycle in 1912 and continued production in Detroit until 1917, when they sold the business to Excelsior (originally a bicycle manufacturing company founded by Ignaz Schwinn). The

manufacturing operations were moved to the Excelsior factory in Chicago where the brothers continued their work, with William employed as chief engineer. Excelsior immediately developed an improved four-cylinder engine which they marketed until 1929.

The brothers had left Excelsior in 1919, joining with a group of investors to form the Ace Motor Company, which failed in 1924. The company's assets were purchased by the Indian Motorcycle Company in 1927.

Meanwhile, Excelsior, with the designs of Arthur Constantine, introduced a KJ model, which was an improved and completely redesigned and streamlined motorcycle. The Excelsior factory closed in 1931.

Please note the Vindex wheels as compared to Hubley motorcycle wheels. Except for the name on Hubley tires, they appear identical and perhaps were supplied by the same company.

PDQ, meaning 'pretty damn quick', was a risqué name for a child's toy.

American Tin

← 285.
MARX
Comic Cars

1927–38. USA
7"–8" long
Litho Tin
Windup

A meeting of Marx erratic-action cars from 1928 to 1938. The Komical Kop, Charlie McCarthy, College Boys, and Whoopee Cowboy are much sought after for their brilliant colors and comic movement.

'Ride 'm Rough Tire Co.', printed on the wheels of one car, is a spoof on tire ads of the period.

**286, 287,
288, 289,
290, 291.**

Toy faces of the late 1920s and 1930s. Edgar Bergen's sidekick, Charlie McCarthy, star of stage, screen and television will be remembered as the most beloved face of all.

294.
MARX
College Boy Car

Mid-1930s. USA
8″ long
Litho Tin
Windup

A college boy wears the 'beanie' cap and a silly look probably due to his wringing neck which can turn in a complete circle. He steers in an erratic manner.

Made in vast numbers and with a wide range of different body styles and drivers, these toys which drive a devious course are ideal for the new collector because of their availability.

293.
MARX
Funny Flivver

New in 1926.
USA
7″ long
Litho Tin
Windup

The 'Funny Flivver' caused such a sensation when it was introduced that Marx immediately followed with variations on the same toy to hold the market and ward off competition. The 'crazy' cars were successfully marketed for almost ten years.

Pivoting front wheels and an erratic-action windup motor allow the car to travel in every direction. Right and left, darting backwards and then suddenly forward again, the driver turns his head, a look of bewilderment on his face. Sears, Roebuck & Co. charged 45¢ for this toy from its mail order house.

295.
MARX
Whoopee Cowboy

1930s. USA
7½" long
Litho Tin
Windup

A bucking car replaces the bucking bull.
Designed to bring laughter to little
buckaroos! A rear safety-stop prevents
backward somersaults.

296.
MARX
Charlie McCarthy

1938. USA
7" long
Litho Tin
Windup

Ventriloquist Edgar Bergen and his lovable
dummy Charlie McCarthy are one of the few
combinations that successfully made the
crossover from radio, theater, TV, and
movies, extending into the 1970s, and ending
only with Bergen's death.

 Charlie's erratic-action car is adapted from
an already successful Marx line, but a famous
personality makes it a special collectible.

298.
MARX
Funny Flivver

New in 1926.
USA
7" long
Litho Tin
Windup

The mechanism for early 'crazy cars' was
housed under the body of the driver and,
though the front wheels would lift off the
floor steering the car on an irregular course,
the early car did not have the bucking and
high tilting action of the later models.
Balance and counterweight were achieved
with a shorter wheel base and trunk enclosing
the wind-up motors like figures 298 and 299,
to achieve greater action.

 Sold for 45¢

299.
MARX
Whoopee Car

1930s. USA
7½" long
Litho Tin
Windup

Somehow, Marx seemed able to come up with
continual variations on the college boy theme

297.
MARX
Komical Kop

Late 1930s.
USA
7½" long
Litho Tin
Windup

The Keystone cops of the early 1920s spawned a stream of cops in comic postures for the automotive world. They were ridiculed in movies and comic strips, and were a popular subject for humorous toys.

Where you find automobiles, you'll find cops; but seldom are thy shown behind the wheel of a car in full dress uniform.

To justify this scene, the cop drives a traffic car! Enough to make his head turn in circles, which it does.

for its popular best sellers.

Different expressions, slogans or passengers were used to vary these erratic-action cars. The college boy, wearing a raccoon coat, gives a pair of coeds a lift. The girls are loosely fastened to the trunk, so they flap back and forth with the movement of the car. This was the toy designer's keen sense of humor, designating them roaring twenties flappers, young women who manifested a freedom of conduct and dress from the end of the First World War to the Great Depression. This toy was aptly named 'Whoopee Car' by Marx.

300.
MARX
Dippity Dumper

1930s. USA
9″ long
Litho Tin
Celluloid figure

The erratic-action toy is varied with the introduction of a dump bed and a character in celluloid that looks suspiciously like Bluto, the strongman character from Popeye. He is never identified as such, however, since the ownership of the name belongs to King Syndicates.

301.
MARX
Amos 'n' Andy*
Fresh Air Taxi

1930. USA
8″ long
Litho Tin
Windup

One of the most highly sought after tin automotive toys, valued for its comic appeal. The windup alternately moves and stalls shaking both Amos, the driver, and President Andrew Brown, smoking his usual cigar in the rear seat.

Inherent weaknesses are found in the horseshoe radiator ornament, taxi meter, bumper, crank and figures and these parts are often missing.

Amos 'N' Andy's Fresh Air Taxi Company was a full member of the National Association of Taxi Cab Owners during the early 1930s.

* Given this spelling by Marx. Taken from door on toy taxi.

184

302.
MARX
Jalopy

1928. USA
7¼″ long
Litho Tin
Windup

Jalopies were created by recycling previously owned vehicles, to put it nicely. Used cars – really used – is what they were.

High school and college boys started the rage of painting clever slogans all over the cars to conceal dents, rust and hopeless body conditions. The cars were meant to be comical and attract girls.

Used for parades, football games and fraternity transportation, the old rattletraps were nothing more than 4 wheels and a motor. The decaying cars were simply to get the young through the school years.

By the late 1920s, jalopies were a familiar sight on the streets of America. Marx produced an entire series of them with slogans copied from the real cars and some funny sayings for good measure, like 'Caution: Heart Brakes' on the rear end. The erratic-action windup adds extra comedy.

303.
MARX
(Left) Jalopy Ford

1922. USA
7″ long
Litho Tin
Windup

The earliest jalopy is identified by large, spoke wheels and conservative slogans. This toy is a perfect example of one bearing its birth date on the license plate.

MARX
(Center) Jalopy Ford

1928. USA
7″ long
Litho Tin
Windup

The longtime best seller was updated with smart-aleck remarks of the period and the latest wheels. Brighter colors, a symbol of the times, decorate this model.

STRAUSS
(Right) Dizzie Lizzie

1926. USA
8″ long
Litho Tin
Windup

One version of the car with a breakaway hood and bucking action, which was Strauss's attempt to capture part of the lucrative market for these toy cars. 75¢ retail was the price for a car that shivers and rattles from side to side.

Covered with funny sayings, the graffiti reflect the slang expressions seen painted on real sedans, such as '99 99/100% pure tin' and 'I do not choose to run'.

Early Ford cars were called 'Tin Lizzies'. In a recent newspaper interview, Henry Ford II explained the origin of the name as being derived from the word tin, considered a cheap, thin metal, and lizards with their quick, rapid movements. 'Tin Lizzy' was a slang expression. Actually, Ford cars do not use any tin but auto body steel throughout.

Driving well into the 1930s, real Lizzies were too worthless to sell when their owners went off to war and were simply stored in garages. Many cars lived to see their tired old bodies restored years later and still ride the streets today.

304.
MARX
Tidy Tim

Mid-1930s. USA
7½″ high
Litho Tin
Windup

Street-sweeping machinery and increased traffic are responsible for the disappearance of workers like Tidy Tim of the District Sanitation Commission. For the few that remain in our country today, their job titles have been changed to 'Sanitation Engineer'.

A windup spring motor gets Tim's legs moving. The 'spic and span' cleanup man carries his original push broom.

→

306. Late 1920s.
CHEIN USA
Stake Truck with Earth 9″ long
Roller Litho Tin

Water-filled earth rollers are used to level and pack earth before paving driveways, sidewalks, parking lots, and streets, and to prepare building sites. Later machinery incorporating heavy rollers made truck-transported rollers obsolete.

A winch to lower the roller adds play value to one of Chein's most intriguing toys.

305. Early 1920s.
CHEIN USA
(*Left*) Troop carrier 8¼″ long
Pull toy

CHEIN Early 1920s.
(*Right*) Cannon truck USA
9¼″ long
Pull toy

MARX Mid-1920s. USA
(*Center*) Troop carrier with 10¾″ long
canopy Tin Windup

Cheap, lightweight tin toys in wartime army colors are some of the few post-First World War military vehicles produced in this country. Very few army and navy vehicles appear in old toy catalogs and advertisements. When they do appear, it is often for only a brief period, suggesting that military trucks were not popular in America and did not sell well.

Chein and Marx probably filled whatever demand existed for small inexpensive toys, using the Bulldog Mack of First World War fame to help sell the toys.

Marx used its basic Mack truck design and added various military-type body styles in sizes ranging from 5″ to 13″ long, using a friction-type motor in the smaller toys.

Marx claimed in the 1920s to have perfected a spring that could not be wound too tight and boasted of its toys' durability; a claim that can be justified by the condition of most of its toys found today.

→

307. Late 1920s.
CHEIN USA
Dan-Dee Oil and Skid Truck Both 9¼″ long
Litho Tin

Before mechanical lifts were invented, pull-out metal ramps, called skids, were used to slide boxes and barrels off trucks to the ground.

A lightweight tin toy, selling for 19¢, this truck is remarkable for its condition and age.

Chein produced an extensive line of inexpensive lithographed tin toys, trucks, automobiles, and novelty toys, through the 1920s and 1930s; some selling for as little as 10¢.

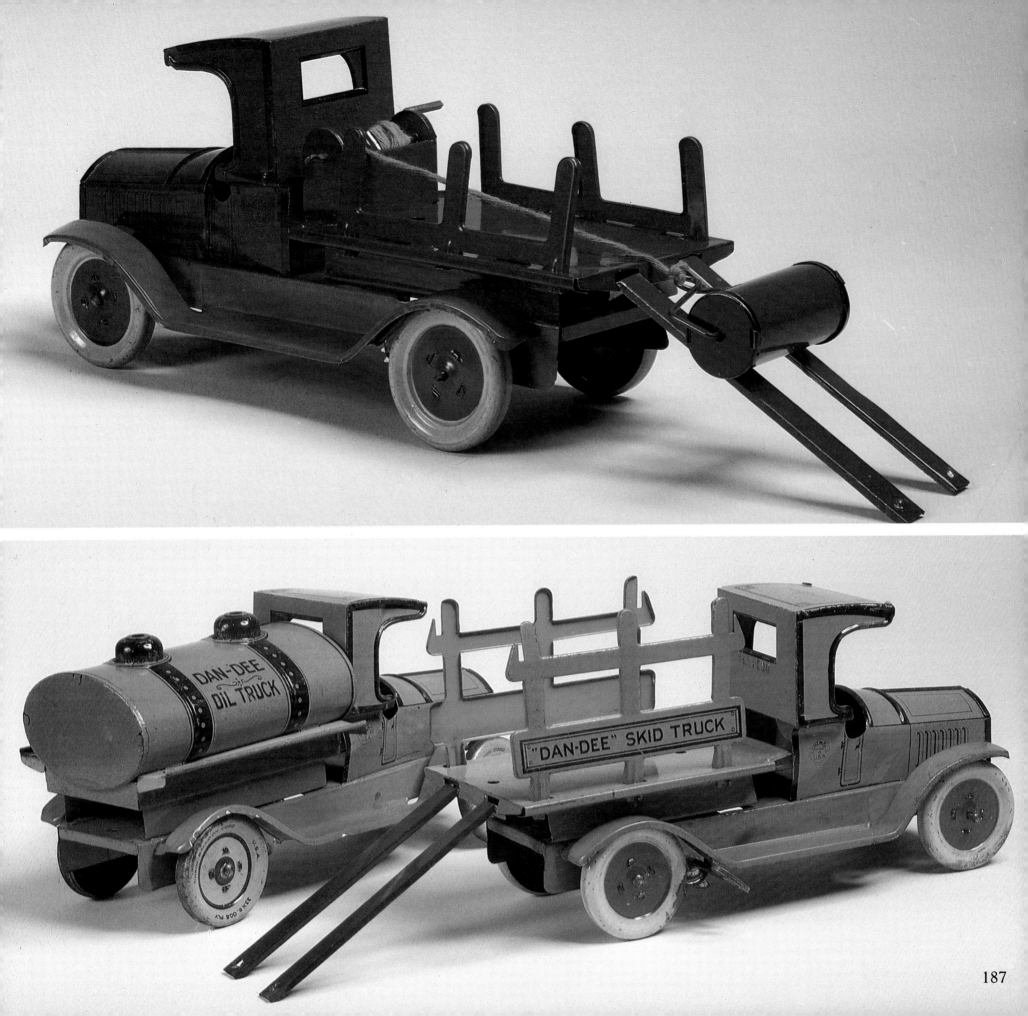

187

309.
FALLOWS
Runabout Auto

c. 1895. USA
7″ long
Painted Tin
Pull Toy

The body of this automobile was already in use by Fallows as a horse-drawn carriage. By removing the horses and adding a string-operated spool 'motor' to the rear axle, the carriage made its transition to an automobile.

Embossed around the hole in the seat, which anchors our drivers are the markings, 'IXL – PAT, AUG, '87'. A printed paper label on the bottom of the toy also carries this information. This date pertains to the patent obtained by Fallows for the process whereby designs were pressed into tin. Fallows used decorative tin for toy kitchens, trains, and horsedrawn toys.

This runabout is the first mass-produced American tin horseless carriage to surface to date. The Philadelphia firm of Francis, Field and Francis is credited with the first mass-produced American tin toys in 1848, some forty-seven years ahead of the first toy automobile!

308.
FALLOWS
Runabout Auto

1890s. USA
6¼″ long
Painted Tin

One of the earliest examples of an American embossed tin runabout with wheels adapted from a horse-drawn cart. Two possibilities exist for setting the toy in motion: the first is a hole for string in the front of the car, and the other is a wire crank handle, which is an extension of the rear axle. The steering wheel and rod protruding through the driver's seat are laughable and tend to confirm rumors that early toy designers never saw a real car! Everyone has to start somewhere!

No standards would be set for right- or left-hand drive for many years to come.

310.
MARX
Armored Tank

1921. USA
7″ long
Litho Tin

A no-frills pull toy made to sell for 10¢ brings laughter to the serious business of war!

Pressed from such lightweight tin as to be almost weightless, the toy has amazingly survived various wars!

311.
MARX
'Armored Trucking Co.'
Truck

1927. USA
10″ long
Litho Tin
Windup

Armored trucks were developed to transport money without losing it en route.

The manufacturer has achieved a feeling of quality in this attractive, lightweight toy that sold for 25¢, using lithography to imitate steel plates with rivets used on imitate real money transporters.

312.
MARX
Mack Dump Truck

1926–7. USA
13½" long
Litho Tin
Windup

An impressive size makes up for the simplicity of this toy which sold for 47¢ at Sears, Roebuck stores and 50¢ elsewhere. A hand lever operates the dump bed. Marx produced the identical truck in a smaller size which sold for exactly half the price.

314.
MARX
Carrier with Three Racers

1930. USA
22¾" long
Litho Tin
Windup

An original and impressive toy, it sold complete for $1.00 in 1930. The Mack cab and three racers each have windup 'motors'. The removable carrier has fold-up support wheels so it can stand alone.

Showing its versatility, Marx sold the racers separately for 25¢ after first fitting them with drivers. The separate racers were also available with fly-wheel 'motors' and could be used as part of a garage set.

313.
MARX
Royal Coupe

c. 1930. USA
9" long
Litho Tin
Windup

A sports coupe with an exaggerated motor ornament suggesting a flamboyant car of the classic period, still wears the 25¢ price sticker from McCrory's on its roof.

315.
MARX
Three-Piece Auto Set

1930. USA
Pumps 9½"
long
Car 8" long
Light 7" high
Litho Tin

Marx strove for value for money and produced many multi-piece tin toys in the dollar range.

This set required batteries, which were supplied with the toy. The bulbs on the pumps and street signal light up, the headlights on the car work, and a windup 'motor' moves it away after a fillup. Lots of action for $1.00.

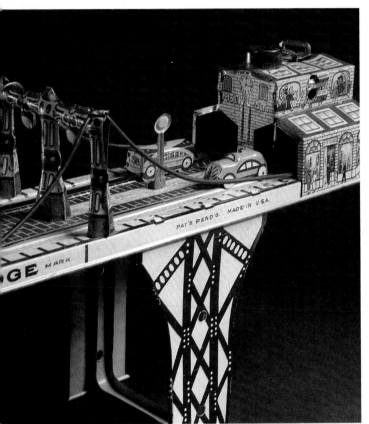

316.
MARX
Busy Bridge

c. 1930. USA
24″ long
Litho Tin

Next to London Bridge, now moved to Lake Havasu in Arizona, the best known American bridge is the Brooklyn Bridge. Marx was a master of American tin lithography. Its toys related to events and people in everyday life.

By 1928, the number of Marx toys relating to transportation was phenomenal! The company's smallest cars traverse the bridge. The same scale cars, trucks and ambulances were found in grab machines and Cracker Jack boxes. (See fig. 357).

318. ↘
NONPAREIL
Police Patrol

Early 1920s.
USA
9½″ long
Litho Tin

Military Ambulance

1919.
6¼″ long
Litho Tin
Windup

Delivery Truck

Mid-1920s.
10¼″ long
Litho Tin
Windup

I am frequently asked if there are any parts missing on some Nonpareil toys (by adults not children). The American firm with a French name stretched the size of its toys without added parts to make them appear good value for money, leaving the rest to the imagination.

A bit of history is recalled by the military ambulance with its First World War lady in uniform at the wheel. The army ambulance and police patrol wholesaled for around 7¢ each.

Nonpareil toys display a considerable amount of slot and tab construction usually associated with foreign tin toys. The folded tin tailgate with bin sides is unusual. It tilts to open. Here, again, is an empty driver's compartment, designed to be bare.

319.
STRAUSS
No. 72 Water Sprinkler
Truck
No. 73 Standard Oil Truck

1925. USA
Both 10½″ long
Litho Tin
Windup

Modifications to the tank and changes in decoration create two models with entirely different duties. The tanks are not fillable. Packed in colorfully illustrated boxes, interesting enough to collect for themselves, the toys sold for 75¢ each.

These trucks are marked with the manufacturer's name.

← **317.**
MARX
Coupe

Early 1930s.
USA
11½″ long
Litho Tin
Windup

This sporty coupe has all the extras that would make a real car most attractive. These features include landaulet bars on the hardtop, a golf bag compartment, a folding luggage rack and long hood for that big motor. A composite of many makes, the toy came in offbeat color combinations not likely to be found on a real model.

→ **320.**
MAKER UNKNOWN
American Railway Express

Mid-1920s. USA
10″ long
Litho Tin
Windup

A hinged roof lifts to accommodate small packages. Railway express trucks traveled to the train station to bring back trunks and large packages. The trucks with mesh grille sides were once a familiar sight in every large American town.

→ **321.**
UPTON
Boy & Co. Wrecker

c. 1926. USA
8½″ long
Litho Tin

Constructed from extremely lightweight stamped tin, every economy was used in manufacture to produce a really cheap toy. A bent wire crank handle elevates the hook . . . nothing more than a Christmas tree ornament hook. The crane swivels on the chassis to provide the only activity besides the wheels. Still, it is a 10¢ charmer, flimsy or not.

323.

This German bisque head tomboy with a composition body and glass eyes is 40 inches tall. Her favorite toys include a straw-filled, mohair Teddy Bear, a tin circus truck and biscuit tin bus.

Circus animals were generally moved by train and enclosed transport trucks to lessen travel time and exposure to cold and drafts which could prove devastating. Sometimes, local trucks were hired to move cages. On the whole, real automotive circus cage trucks were unpopular in the 1920s and 1930s. Parades utilized wheeled cages drawn by animals, as slow-moving trucks were prone to overheating. Walking animals also provided a dramatic preview. Since toys were copied from the real thing, similarly few circus trucks were made. Understandably the ones found today are scarce.

STRAUSS	1926. USA
Big Show Circus Truck	9″ long
	Litho Tin
	Windup

This truck has an interesting interaction of moving wheels and jumping lion with tamer.

MAKER UNKNOWN	1920s. Dutch
Biscuit Box Bus	16½″ long
	Litho Tin

Made for the Dutch market, the roof is hinged. One of many interesting cookie and confection tin containers also produced in Great Britain for world-wide export.

English biscuit tins were sold world-wide as Christmastime gifts. Developed to protect the contents for shipping, the tins served as decorative repositories for other items when empty. A practical second use for automotive tins were their play value. The best-known biscuit tins were used by Thomas Huntley's firm Huntley & Palmer, a world-famous business originating in the 1830s. Thomas and his brother, Joseph, a tinsmith, introduced the first transfer printed tin boxes in 1868. They were a revolutionary change from the paper labels which were originally pasted on the tins and were lost or damaged due to dampness. Automotive biscuit tins in truck, bus and circus wagons were ideal forms for advertising. Rising costs after 1930 reduced the tins to simple box forms with lithographed designs.

| Teddy Bear | c. 1908 |
| | 17″ high |

Yellow mohair, straw stuffed, slender jointed arms and legs, elongated torso and irregular face with pointed nose. Named after President Theodore Roosevelt in 1902, no toy is more American. A 1908 catalog showed this bear and stated they 'were all the rage, the best plaything ever invented, and a sensible toy'. Truer words were never spoken!

322.	Late 1890s.
WEEDEN	USA
Steam Automobile	8½″ long
	Painted Tin
	Steam operated

A runabout model is driven by a miniature live steam engine located in the rear compartment with access to the boiler located under the removable seat. A closed-sided body is a protective measure against little fingers.

Over 50 American automobile manufacturers were listed in business before 1900. This list did not include the many individuals who made experimental steam cars at this time. Included on the list were the Grout, Lane, Stanley and Locomobile steamers, none of which resemble the toy.

Generally speaking, most early runabouts were short-bodied affairs and more open than the Weeden toy. The crudely designed body was probably secondary to the importance of its live steam operation. It sold for $1.00.

Flaking paint due to heat is the penalty paid for operating any painted, live steam toy.

Racers

Speedster bodies were available from specialty firms for Model Ts, making it possible to convert the Ford into a dirt-track racer. The number of Model Ts produced and sold in 1923 came to an astounding 1,788,477. This included a great number of bare chassis for truck and utility bodies as well as speedster conversions. Often the Ford dealer provided the sales and installation of special non-factory bodies, but soon a whole separate industry of small body shops appeared to transform all sorts of cars and trucks to individual tastes and customer needs.

These merchants were the forerunners of speed and body shops which today sell custom accessories and speed equipment to car hobbyists.

Bodies that could be adapted to either a Ford or Chevrolet chassis were sold in the early 1920s by the American Auto Top Company of Delphi, Indiana, and the Central Auto Supply in Louisville, Kentucky. These bodies were not always intended for racing but were a form of the earliest sports car.

324.   c. 1925. USA
BUFFALO   25½″ long
'Silver Bullet' Racer   Litho Tin

A spiral spring is pulled from the tail of this torpedo-shaped racer and released for motion.

An inexpensive toy when new, the tin was 'stretched', and the toy appeared sensational value for a little boy who liked his racers BIG!

325.   1930. USA
CHAMPION   8½″ long
Racer   Cast Iron

Some of the newer devices and accessories incorporated into the designs of speed racers included bumpers and guards against crashes.

The great number of deaths and injuries as cars increased in number necessitated these safety factors.

Toy manufacturers were quick to copy the newest designs and add a few of their own, like Champion's elongated version.

196

326.
GILBERT
Stutz Racer

1914. USA
9½″ long
Litho Tin
Windup

The real 1914 Stutz Bearcat is the best known of all speedsters. Winning races made it popular despite its high price and 4-cylinder motor. In 1916, the Stutz raced in sixteen events and failed to gain a place only once, creating a sensation in the racing world. It achieved recognition for speed as well as durability and became the Mercer car's only rival.

Gilbert's toy version of the popular Stutz racer is operated by a strong patent spring attachment which is wound by a front crank. Like the real car, the toy carries the same bright yellow color with black trim. Mail order houses sold the toy for 59¢ and exaggerated the actual length by as much as an inch in their catalogs.

328.
HUBLEY
Auto Racer

1927–8. USA
9¾″ long
Cast Iron &
Aluminum

Only the rear section is aluminum, while the rest of the body is constructed of cast iron. The aluminum is given a high polish to resemble a real racer. Nickel-plated steel disc wheels reflect another fad of this period.

Helmets and goggles were used to keep hair and dirt from the driver's face.

327.
HUBLEY
'Red Devil' Racer #5

1927–8. USA
9¾″ long
Cast Iron &
aluminum

Hubley carried its racer with an opening hood for eight years but made variations using different materials to lessen the weight for shipping. No explanation was given in the original catalogs but various style wheels and a marked difference in shipping weights made the purpose apparent.

A clicker which simulates a running motor was an added feature on spoked wheels of nickel-plated steel. It could *not* be installed on a solid iron wheel. A cast aluminum rear section and cast aluminum motor lightened the toy, while the cast iron hood served to give the toy stability and the feel of strength demanded by buyers. The cast iron driver is fastened in during the assembly to avoid its loss.

329.
HUBLEY
'Auto Racer'

1927–8. USA
9½″ long
Cast Iron

Hubley was just beginning to experiment with the use of aluminum castings for parts. While searching for buyer approval of the new material it was careful to retain the completely cast iron racer shown. Smaller wheels account for the ¼″ shortened length. To draw attention to itself Hubley advertised 'Raise the hood to see the Motor' and sold far more racers than its now-famous Packard sedan with a separate hood and motor. (See figs. 27 and 28.)

330.
HUBLEY
Racer

1931. USA
10¾″ long
Cast Iron

Hubley patented the exhaust flame feature in 1931, the same year the toy was released. The 'flames' move up and down on alternate sides to copy exhaust from early racers.

Racing cars were recently granted a classification for competition in the Antique Automobile Club of America. Their importance in automotive history is finally being recognized. The competitive achievements of racers and their drivers were well known to most boys. Racing drivers were generally regarded as daredevils, and some were. They contributed to the development of the automobile by testing engines, tires, and fuel, which in turn contributed to the high performance of automobiles. Boys loved toy racers. With one in hand, they could set their own records.

331.
JONES & BIXLER (Kenton after 1913)
'Peerless' Racer

c. 1908. USA
Large: 7¾" long
Small: 5¾" long
Cast Iron

Barney Oldfield was a household word in the 1900s when this toy Peerless was made and sold. Modifications and changes were constant on the real monstrously sized car. The toy does not depict an exact model of the Green Dragon or the Peerless entered in the first Gordon-Bennett race, but instead captures the essence of both these mighty racers of the period.

Kenton favored products of its Ohio neighbors, such as Peerless.

332.

Dirt-track races were a regular Saturday night feature outside small towns and at county fairgrounds throughout the United States during the late 1920s.

Oval tracks had long straightaways and curves which were sometimes banked. Higher speeds could be maintained on banked curves. In the early days, spectators lined the speedway, cheering their favorites to victory. If a racer crashed it was likely to plow into the crowds. This eventually led to the building of closed tracks and grandstand seats, giving spectators a better view and racing promoters better control of the crowds.

KENTON	1925. USA
(*Top*) Sport Racer	8¾″ long
	Cast Iron

Early racing cars were big, clumsy looking machines. To increase their power and speed, it was necessary to make the engine bigger.

HUBLEY	1929. USA
(*Center*) 'Golden Arrow'	6¾″ long
Racer	Cast Iron

Hubley's version of the streamlined, low-to-the-ground Golden Arrow was made in several sizes and carried for seven years.

Hubley popularized cast iron toy racers and manufactured and sold a large variety of types and sizes through 1941. Unlike racers that competed against each other, the Golden Arrow was specially designed to race against time and compete for a world speed record.

KENTON	1927. USA
(*Front*) Track Racer	6⅞″ long
	Cast Iron

The #8 track racer is smaller and trimmer as a result of technical advances in engines and bodies of the late 1920s. A narrow driver's compartment is accessible with added doors and a step.

When our driver gets down to the serious business of racing, he will assume a typical hunched-over racing posture and place his cap backward on his head so it will not catch the wind.

No. 1440 Racer

Length 8 inches, width 3 inches, height 2 inches.
Color: Assorted red, silver and blue. Driver's head and number high lighted with gold bronze. White rubber wheels with red centers on the blue and silver toys, blue centers on the red toys.
Packed 6 in box, 3 dozen in case.
Case net weight 36 lbs., case gross weight 42 lbs.
Case measurements: 11x12x20 inches.

A catalog shows the only racer offered by Arcade, 1935–1936.

333.　　　　　　　　　1927. USA
KINGSBURY　　　　　　　19″ long
'Mystery Sunbeam' Racer　　Pressed Steel

At Daytona Beach, Florida, with Major
H. O. D. Seagrave at the wheel, the Sunbeam
raised the world's land speed record to 203.79
miles per hour on March 29, 1927. Dunlop
produced special tires to withstand the speed
and several safety devices were added to
protect the driver. The original racing car is
preserved and exhibited at the National
Motor Museum in Beaulieu, England. It
measures 25 ft. long and 8 ft. wide.

Toy racers appeared regularly in the
Kingsbury toy line. An original tag with facts
concerning the Sunbeam's fame still remains
with this toy. Kingsbury held exclusive rights
to reproduce the toy version of this racer
which won the speed record in three
successive years. Price: $3.00, 50¢ extra west
of Mississippi.

334.　　　　　　　　　1929. USA
KINGSBURY　　　　　　　21″ long
'Golden Arrow' Racer　　Pressed Steel

This racer captured a new world's land speed
record at 231.44 miles per hour at Daytona
Beach, Florida on March 11, 1929. Kingsbury
promptly produced an exact model of the
winner driven by Major H. O. D. Seagrave.

The real racer was built in London and is
housed today at the National Motor Museum
in Beaulieu, England. It is interesting that the
world's faster driver in 1929, Sir Henry
Seagrave (he was knighted in 1927 for other
achievements), was also a collector and
designer of toy trains.

Our example of the Golden Arrow is not
gold but pink! It has also done a lot of racing.
A $3 toy in 1929, the cost was 10% higher
west of the Mississippi.

336. → 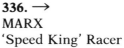   1929. USA
MARX   16″ long
'Speed King' Racer   Litho Tin
       Windup

Early racing drivers liked to brag that their cars could strike lightning. To a small boy, this torpedo-shaped windup racer would have conjured up the image of a rocket that could possibly do just that!

335.   c. 1915. USA
STRUCTO   12½″ long
'Auto Builder #8'   Pressed Steel

The racer is copied from the fabled 1914 cut-down Stutz Bearcat speedster with a cylindrical fuel tank mounted directly behind the driver's compartment, a low-slung chassis, double bucket seats, and little else except a long hood. A big, slow-turning engine, a T- head, 4-cylinder, Wisconsin unit gained the buyers' respect with racing successes and endurance records.

A box containing all parts necessary to build the green enameled 2-seat speedster was priced at $5.00.

A powerful, quality, gear-driven clockwork mechanism could make construction an educational exercise – another sales point. The fact that the racer could also be disassembled undoubtedly contributed to its scarcity. Structo advertised its toys, 'Make Men of Boys!'

337. →   c. 1929. USA
VINDEX   11″ long
Racer   Cast Iron

Tires, brakes and clutches were tested by racers, leading to the development of better cars for the roads. The high mortality rate of businesses in 1929 kept survivors on their toes striving for better products and better cars.

Vindex toys were overpriced. This racer, for instance, was $1.50 wholesale plus shipping. Hubley's #5 racer (see fig. 327, one with spoke wheels), a comparable toy if not better, was ony 67¢. Toys were a sideline for Vindex, who picked the worst possible time to enter the market in the late 1920s.

The racer is also found with pressed steel spoke wheels and black rubber tires exactly like those on Hubley's racers. Wheels and tires were often purchased from specialty manufacturers. In business only a couple of years, Vindex toys are rare, due to the small numbers found today.

338. ←   c. 1905. USA
WILKINS   10″ long
Automobile Racer   Pressed Steel

In 1902, divided front seats and engines under the hood made their appearance. The radiator was placed in front of the engine on American cars the following year. Wilkins' racer represents a stripped down runabout, modified for racing.

339. ↗   1912. USA
WILKINS   9¼″ long
Auto Racer   Pressed Steel

Wilkins successfully sold this toy through 1919, when it was offered for 89¢.

The policeman with a movable stop and go sign was made in 1914 by the Bradford Company of Brooklyn, New York, and is 6½″ high.

340.   c. 1932. USA
WILLIAMS   8½″ long
Racer   Cast Iron

All engine and just enough space for the driver, this racer is designed close to the ground for a low center of gravity, an aid for making fast turns!

This is one of Williams' larger toys. It specialized in N.D.Q. (nickel, dime and quarter) toys, which included a sizeable line of toys with interchangeable bodies.

Friction & Flywheel

In searching for reasons to explain the success of flywheel and friction toy automobiles and trucks, it can only be assumed that it was due to their availability at a very prosperous time in the American economy. Also, they were different. Typical of the American preference for rugged toys, their size and weight added to the illusion of durability. This was a prime consideration for parents concerned with keeping their children occupied and getting good value for their money.

Webster's Dictionary defines friction as the act of rubbing the surface of one body against another. The word *friction* used in the context of spinning flywheel-type motors manufactured from the turn of the century through the mid-1930s is a misnomer. In spite of this, many toys were described as 'friction' and 'friction type' by jobbers and wholesalers in their catalogs and sales brochures. Thus, it has become a generic term in use since the 1880s. Foreign imports were called 'momentum toys' in catalog listings, another generic term for flywheel-driven toys. The name 'hill climbers' was also used in conjunction with early friction toys for their ability to climb uphill once they were set in motion. However, owners of friction toys would most likely question the validity of this claim. The best thing that can be said about the toys is that they do *not* go lickety-split downhill! Their weighty mechanisms create a drag which acts as a safety factor.

Manufacturers of American friction toys became an inbred society by the early 1920s, when designers and chief employees of companies joined competitors or formed their own businesses in competition with former employers. In some instances, a manufacturer would sell out only to start anew with the same toy designs, as in the case of D. P. Clark, who was involved with several friction toy firms and was sued for infringements on patents he had sold with a company but then continued to use.

Aside from the animosity this aroused within the trade, it created an industry where the outward physical appearance of toys resembled each other down to the same color paints and designs. This has caused much confusion to antique toy collectors intent on identifying the toys by manufacturer. Recently a successful in-depth study of patents issued was concluded by collector Raymond Spong. Attribution is based on the type of mechanism used, often just a small detail.

There are changes in design for which no patents appear to exist. Here, we must rely on the most minute details and an experienced eye. I have found that a good portion of these variations is attributable to the Dayton Friction Toy Company in the late 1920s and early 1930s.

Friction toys had been around for a long time without any great improvement of action or design when they began to lose public favor in the depressed years of the late 1920s. While other established toy manufacturers were able to adapt to smaller toys, friction makers were unable to make the transition. The Turner and Dayton companies tried retailing directly to the public through mail order, but the public would not spend $2 to $6 for toys during a depression. History would eventually prove that the bulk of the market was in N.D.Q. toys, the only affordable playthings for many families forced to make sweeping changes due to financial reverses.

→ 341.	c. 1902. USA
CLARK	6" & 7" long
Electric Runabouts	Cast Iron. Steel & Wood

Women were happy to surrender the horse and buggy for automobiles. When not driving, they were happy passengers despite the 'back seat driver' stories circulated by men.

Most highly favored were the electric cars. From 1896 to 1928, 54 different makes were manufactured. No cranking and noiseless operation were the biggest selling points. Women felt they were also easier to drive. However, the electric cars were limited to flat, level land and distances not exceeding a battery charge. They were mostly found in cities and towns that met these requirements. Automobiles gave women a new-found freedom. For those who lived in the country, there was no longer the trouble of hitching the horse to the buggy.

Here, a pair of wood- and steel-bodied 'electrics' with cast iron buggy tops are steered by cast iron ladies, accompanied by interested children. Cast iron flywheels seen between the wheels help propel the toys.

The wheels on the larger car can be set to run in circles. The rear wheels are engaged with the flywheel axle by pressing the toy to the floor. Movement results when the toy is pushed forward. This innovation allowed the front wheels to be freed for steering. It also allowed separation of the wheels, which was important for a more realistic automobile design. The smaller counterpart on the right rides on fixed close- coupled wheels.

The outline of these toys is strictly American; a transitional design taken from buggies.

342.
CLARK
Touring Car

1904. USA
8½″ long
Pressed Steel

A hood and secure seating are refinements on 1904 Clark automobiles in an endeavor to copy real cars, although the close-coupled wheels used by the manufacturer to execute friction action are unrealistic.

Hand striping, usually applied by young, inexperienced laborers, was aimed to copy real cars. Precision machine striping was still a long way off.

The words 'hill climber' were commonly used in advertising by all of the manufacturers. Clark slyly used the term to his advantage by stamping it on the underside of his toys for a time, thus making it appear exclusively his own.

Patent #593,174, issued on November 2, 1897 to Israel Donald Boyer and his wife, Edith, was the basis for the first American automotive friction toys. Often, this date is found stamped on the underside of Clark toys and does not necessarily refer to the actual age of the toy, as the practice was continued for some time following its issue.

343.
CLARK
Touring Car

1905. USA
12½″ long
Pressed Steel &
Wood

Special care has been given to this almost-perfect example of a hand-painted car. The hood and lamps are shaped from solid pieces of wood.

Most interesting is the painted tin driver which is original to the toy and appears to be of German manufacture. Friction car manufacturers preferred drivers in a contrasting material, such as cast iron or painted tin. The weight of steel did not lend itself to the satisfactory formation of figures with pronounced details. The price of the toy was $1.48 from the Boston Store, Chicago.

344.
CLARK
Fire Engine with Hose Reel

1905. USA
10¾″ long
Pressed Steel &
Wood

The childish rendition of early automotive toy designers is evident in this toy, where the driver sits perched in space without protection and the steering wheel turns nothing at all.

The wheels are stamped from steel. One rear wheel is pressed with gear teeth on the inner rim. A gear on the flywheel axle meshes with that wheel for a firm grip.

Featured in the Boston Store Christmas catalog in 1905 for 49¢, the hose reel winds automatically when the truck is in motion.

345.
DAYTON
Touring Car

c. 1908. USA
13¼" long
Pressed Steel

Friction-driven pressed steel toys by Dayton were sturdily built and designed to take punishment. Many of these early toys have held up better than ones produced much later. Durability was never a problem.

Prior to the First World War, manufacturers of automotive friction toys avoided the use of windshields and, in some cases, steering wheels. Collectors have preferred to add appropriate looking parts for appearance's sake.

The steering wheel and figures are standard on this toy, which appears to have been copied from a 7-passenger Stoddard-Dayton tourer made in Dayton, Ohio, from 1904 through 1913. One of the great American cars of its day, it was manufactured by the Dayton Motor Car Company.

346.
DAYTON
Closed Limousine

1919. USA
13¼" long
Pressed Steel

The sharp, straight lines of this automobile give it an armored car look appropriate to its First World War era. Sold by Sears, Roebuck for $1.39, it was also available with a lever spring-wound mechanism for the same price.

The limousine was outdated just a few years later when curved fenders and well-rounded metal edges gained in popularity.

347.
DAYTON
Dump Truck

Mid-1920s. USA
20¼″ long
Pressed Steel

The all-time favorite truck for all automotive toy manufacturers was a model with a dump bed. Dayton's version of the 5-ton truck was propelled by a flat iron wheel encased in a pressed steel housing which did little to propel the toy forward, despite its maker's claim. The wheels are formed from two stamped steel halves.

A couple of years later, the company introduced its 'GYRO MOTORS' which were set in a horizontal position still using models from its regular line. In addition, 1926 cars and trucks sported rubber tires.

348.
MASON & PARKER
Fire Engine

Patented
December 12,
1905. USA
10″ long
Pressed Steel &
Wood

So many similarities exist between this toy designed by Homer N. Parker and one produced in the Wilkins-Kingsbury line for over forty years that I would venture to speculate that Kingsbury acquired the rights to the design, discarding the flywheel mechanism and adding its sealed clockwork

mechanism. The Kingsbury version of the toy appeared about 1906.

A Wilkins driver fitted on a Mason & Parker toy is not so unusual, since these drivers were found on other manufacturers' toys for many years following 1905.

By way of comparison with the Wilkins fire engine (fig. 240), it is apparent that the seat and sheet metal parts connecting the wood pumper were designed by the same person or copied by Wilkins, raising questions of who, what, where, and when? In Raymond A. Spong's *Flywheel Powered Toys*, he points out that Kingsbury was granted a patent

on the very same day as Parker for an inertia-wheeled toy using a slightly different arrangement to transfer power to the running wheels. More speculation is raised by the fact that the two men were from the same general area.

349.
MASON & PARKER
Aerial Fire Truck #80

1906. USA
16½″ long
Pressed Steel & Wood.
Cast Iron wheels

A flywheel-driven toy with a mechanism

complex enough to patent yet simple in theory provides the energy which gives movement to this toy. A cast iron flywheel, once spinning, transfers energy to gears connected to the wheels.

Not visible are wood ladders which can be raised with a hand-held winch located behind the driver. Soft primary colors and stencil trim impart a primitive feeling to this toy which was made for only a brief period.

Wheels can be positioned to run in a circle by moving flat steel straps fastened to the underside of the truck bed. Removable steps hook over the sides of the bed.

350.
REPUBLIC
Fire Engine

Early 1920s.
USA
12½" long
Pressed Steel

Republic toys can be identified by the date Nov.1, 1921, stamped on the cover of the friction mechanism. The fillerboard of Republic trucks was designed to conceal the mechanism mounted between the rear wheels. Fillerboard is that section of metal between the back edge of the running boards and the lower edge of the truck body.

351.
MASON & PARKER
Auto Dray #82

1906. USA
12" long
Pressed Steel & Wood

The truck is operated by chain drive, a system whereby the final drive is conveyed from the countershaft to the wheels by chains. Real chain-drive vehicles are found as late as 1914.

Steel cross-straps fastened to the bottom side of the wooden bed can be pivoted to make the truck run in a circle.

352.
SCHEIBLE
Fire Engine

c. 1917. USA
11¾″ long
Pressed Steel

Pressed from sheet metal and hand-decorated, this friction pumper is totally out of proportion compared with its real-life look-alike fire engine.

Propelled by a friction 'motor' which was difficult to use, this method of propulsion was not sound in principle for use by children. It takes the grip and strength of Arnold Schwarzenegger to get the toy rolling!

353.
TURNER
Racer with Track

c. 1915. USA
Car 8″ long
Pressed Steel

The front crank winds an extra-heavy spring connected to a gear between the rear wheels to propel this inertia flywheel-driven racer. An oval and tilted track cradles the wheels.

This substantially built toy using stamped-steel wheels was marketed during an exciting time when racing was making history and important news for little boys.

From a technical standpoint, the mechanism is a hybrid . . . a cross between a windup and friction toy.

A sign of prosperity in the mid-1920s is reflected in the cost of this toy. Shown in a dealer's 1926 Turner catalog, it wholesaled for eleven dollars plus shipping from Dayton, Ohio. The real Lincoln was a quality car preferred by owners with chauffeurs.

No. 566
LINCOLN SEDAN

Dimensions:	27″ Long. 11″ High. 10″ Wide.	Materials:	Heavy Sheet Auto Steel.
		Construction:	Electric welded and securely cleated with heavy lugs.
Equipment:	Turner Motor. Rubber Tires.	Packing:	One in a Corrugated Carton ⅓ doz. to a Case.
		Weight:	10 lbs. per Toy. 46 lbs. per Case.
Finish:	Light Green and Gold.		

Penny Toys

Penny toys have been collected since they were first introduced. An article in *The New Illustrated Magazine* published in 1899 states that penny toys have been produced and collected since 1851! The article reveals that the penny toys most in demand in 1899 were mechanical ones or toys with movement. Not much has changed. Penny toy automobiles with tiny windup 'motors' are actively sought but are scarce – all are precious collectibles and record the evolution of automotive design.

Jobbers imported them from Germany by the gross, with the greatest number making their way into this country to homes of Pennsylvania German immigrants. They were used to decorate what is known as a 'Putz' or Christmas Garden, the scenes created beneath a Christmas tree at holiday time. The tree itself was first popularized in Germany and brought to America by German immigrants.

At the turn of the century, penny toys were sold by street hawkers outside theaters and markets. 'Penny Toys' was a misnomer once they left Germany. They cost some 2¢ in London and sometimes as much as 10¢ with a 'mechanical motor' in the U.S. From the earliest transitional automobile, one step from a carriage, to an up-to-date car of 1917, it is apparent some manufacturers kept the penny toy line as long as possible before the First World War interrupted imports.

Originally designed to utilize scraps of tin, the toys were at first assembled by families wishing to earn extra money. This cottage industry was discontinued when penny toys became big business. The undersides of some penny toys reveal the recycled use of misprinted or scrap tin.

354.

c. 1900–1917

The penny toy cars and trucks pictured are only a sampling of the vast number and various designs made. German manufacturers represented are:

G. G. Kellermann
J. Philip Meier
Joh. Distler

Better tin penny toys sold from 89¢ to $1.30 a gross wholesale in 1909. Any machine-manufactured tin toy under 5″ long, selling for 10¢ and under and made before 1930 is generally regarded today as a penny toy by collectors and dealers.

Penny toys also include games, dolls, marbles, miniatures, books and other small toys, such as play wrist watches or pocket watches, whistles, rattles, and tiny boxes, sets of tools and puzzles. These little toys made of paper, composition, wire and cast metal, are not to be overlooked as many are intriguing collectibles.

It is a tribute to their makers and keepers that they have survived to again give the pleasure for which they were initially intended.

An American firm, the Kirchhof Patent Company, produced many tin penny toys resembling German ones. A tin propeller that moved up a spiral rod, clickers and other small automotive tin toys were made by them in the early 1900s.

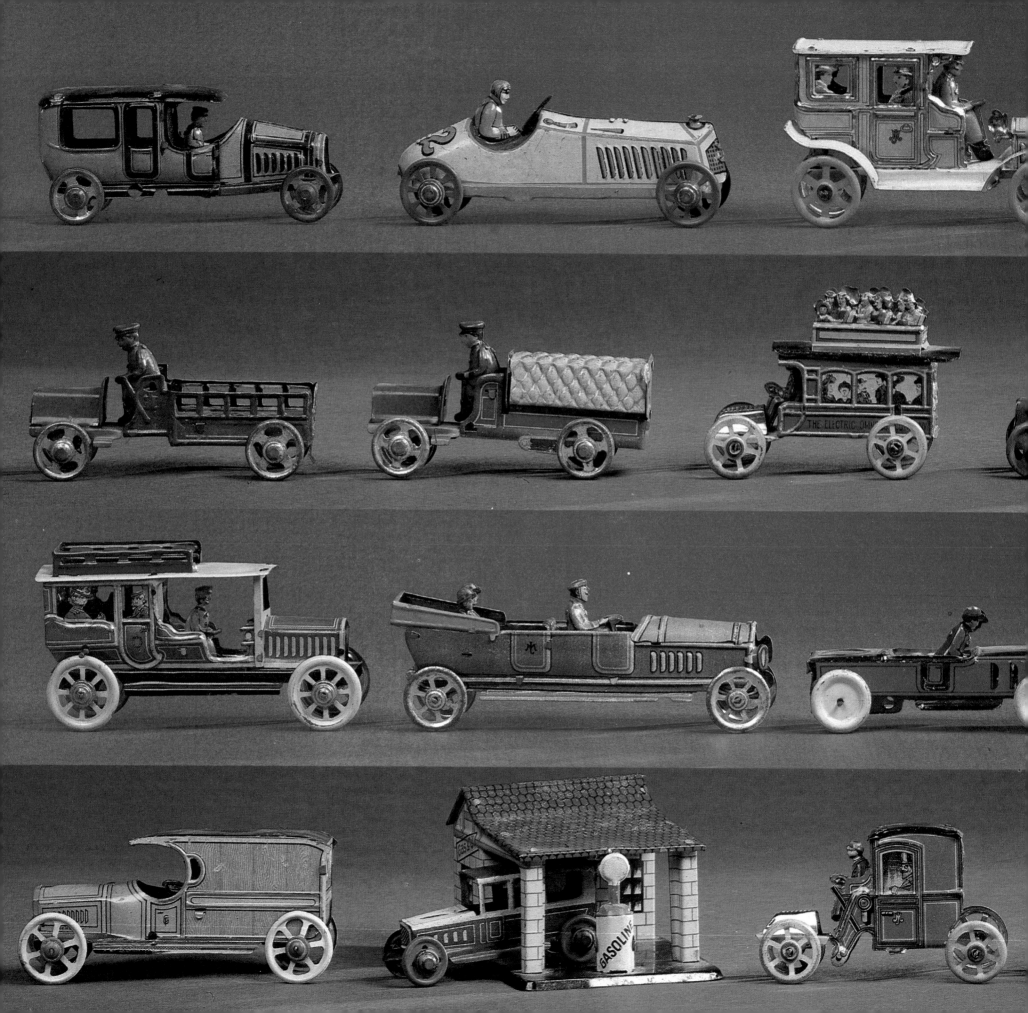

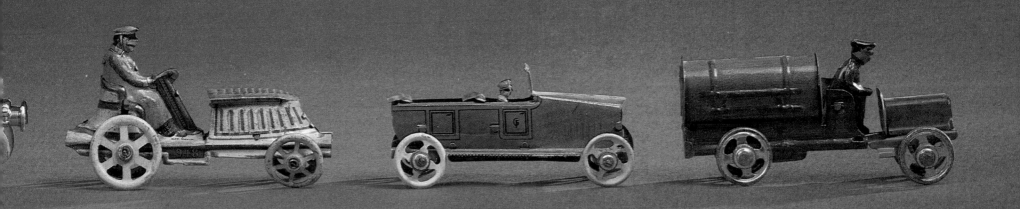

355. c. 1914. France
MAKER UNKNOWN Car 4" long
Touring Car Tin

Penny toys were useful accessories for playtime. They added realism to scenes and were cheap gifts for a youngster enthralled with the new method of transportation.

Arnold's clockwork German Santa Claus penny toy is of exceptionally high quality for a toy of its size. A tail-first airplane on the pylon occupies air space and adds interest to a toy automobile collector's shelves; a reminder that many a real car and airplane have competed in races through the years.

356. ↗ 1930. Germany
EINFALT 5"–6" long
Cars–Limousines–Delivery Litho Tin.
Vans

With a low price of 5¢ each retail, these lithographed tin toys were sold during the Depression for a share of the only market that

was strong. The price doubled with the addition of a windup. They were also boxed as a set. Collectors regard these as oversize penny toys.

357. → 1920s & 1930s.
MARX, CHEIN and Germany &
Maker Unknown U.S.A.
Penny toy premiums Cars 1" to 2⅛" long
  Litho Tin

Tiny toys formed from one piece of cut and folded lithographed tin were made for inclusion in Cracker Jack boxes, grab machines and for use on larger toys and games.

These can be rightfully termed penny toys but only if you were successful on the first try at the grab machine. The charge was 1¢ per try. Cracker Jacks were 5¢ a box in the mid-1920s.

In America before 1917, it was possible to buy small boxes of candy for 1¢ which included a toy! Toys included were tiny dolls, clickers, whistles, puzzles, marbles as well as the folded tin toys shown. Sometimes, the box itself was printed to act as an extra plaything. One company printed a train engine on one box and cars on others. The empty boxes could be collected and lined up to form a circus train. Some boxes were printed with toy eye glasses which could be cut from the box when it was opened flat. Nothing wasted, and all for a penny.

Small cast iron collectibles

N.D.Q. Toys

Named 'Midgets' by Hubley, and 'Assortments' by Arcade, these small toys were popular during the late 1920s and early 1930s and sold for a nickel, dime or quarter. Not surprisingly, they were called 'N.D.Q. toys' by hardware dealers and other counter salesmen. N.D.Q. toys were generally wholesaled by the gross or in boxed assortments.

These toys are often found with decals of shoe companies on the roofs or sides. They were giveaways offered with the purchase of childrens' shoes when kids went back to school at the end of summer.

Striking similarities exist between the toy Dent dream car and the real car originated by an Englishman, Sir Dennistoun Burney, a dirigible designer. It is believed the lines of the Burney also suggested the body later used on the first Volkswagen Beetle prototype in 1936.

358.   USA
                           Cast Iron
                           Small
                           Collectibles

1st row, left to right;
1933 Plymouth, ARCADE 4¾″ long.
1930 Lifesaver Truck. HUBLEY 4¼″ long.
1926 Pickup Truck. WILLIAMS 4¾″ long.

2nd row, right to left
1932 Delivery Van. HUBLEY 4½″ long.
c. 1925 Coupe. DENT 5″ long.
1930 Milk Truck. HUBLEY 3¾″ long.

3rd row, left to right:
1930 Dream Car. WILLIAMS 4⅞″ long.
c. 1920 Taxi. WILLIAMS 5¼″ long.
1930 Moving Van. WILLIAMS 4¾″ long.

4th row, left to right:
1930 Tank Truck. HUBLEY 5¾″ long
1930 Delivery Truck. KILGORE 6″ long.
1932 Railway Express. HUBLEY 5″ long.

359.
Clockwise from left:
c. 1906 DENT
c. 1906 DENT
c. 1900 KENTON
c. 1903 HARRIS

Early 1900s.
USA
6″ long
4¼″ long
4″ long
4″ long
Cast Iron

Four early tiller cars create a traffic jam. In 1900, the first New York automobile show opened in the old Madison Square Garden. Wheel steering was introduced this year for the first time on some models. A speedometer was placed on the market, even though most cars traveling through cities were limited to about 12 miles per hour. Anything faster was considered breakneck speed for these oldtimers, and was only possible downhill! When in 1905 motorists were confronted with the first speed traps, they were as irate as drivers today.

The larger Dent car was 89¢ in 1906. The high wheel Kenton has an open 'turtle' deck to reduce weight, a consideration with toy manufacturers as early as 1900. The tillers pivot to enable the cars to run in circles.

360. →
ARCADE
Model A Assortment

1928 USA
5″ to 5½″ long
Cast Iron

Boxed sets were a big part of Arcade's business between 1928 and 1934. It appeared to be a method whereby farm and automotive toys could be repackaged and repriced as assortments. Each box contained a double-page flyer listing other current toys available.

These Fords appear never to have been played with. Only the box is suffering from old age. The Model A set must have been a favorite. It is listed for five continuous years.

The Ford Company constantly added new innovations to its cars to stimulate sales and publicity. The big news in 1928 was shatter-proof glass, which was to become standard equipment on all Model As. It was also a simple, trouble-free and economical car, the main reason for its popularity. Top speed was usually 65 miles per hour with fuel consumption about 25 miles to the gallon.

No. 2000X Pontiac Wrecker

Length 4¼ inches, width 1⅝ inches, height 1¾ inches.
Color: Assorted red, blue and green. Nickeled radiator, hood center, lights and bumper, and nickeled steel wrecker hook. White rubber wheels with red centers on blue and green toys, blue centers on red toy.
Packed 1 dozen in box, 1 gross in case.
Case net weight 72 lbs., case gross weight 78 lbs.
Case measurements: 10x14x15 inches.

No. 1350Y Yellow Cab

Length 4¼ inches, width 1⅝ inches, height 1½ inches.
Color: Yellow, with "Yellow Cab" stencilled in black on the top. Nickeled radiator, lights, bumper and hood center. White rubber wheels with black centers.
Packed 1 dozen in box, 1 gross in case.
Case net weight 68 lbs., case gross weight 74 lbs.
Case measurements: 10x14x15 inches.

No. 1350X Pontiac Sedan

Length 4¼ inches, width 1⅝ inches, height 1½ inches.
Color: Assorted blue, green, orchid and red. Nickeled radiator, hood center, lights and bumper, white rubber wheels with red centers on blue and green toys, blue centers on orchid and red toys.
Packed 1 dozen in box, 1 gross in case.
Case net weight 68 lbs., case gross weight 74 lbs.
Case measurements: 10x14x15 inches.

No. 2780X Pontiac Stake Truck

Length 4¼ inches, width 1⅝ inches, height 1½ inches.
Color: Assorted red, green and blue. Nickeled radiator, lights and bumper. White rubber wheels with red centers on blue and green toys, blue centers on red toy.
Packed 1 dozen in box, 1 gross in case.
Case net weight 70 lbs., case gross weight 76 lbs.
Case measurements: 10x14x15 inches.

No. 1450X Racer

Length 5¾ inches, width 2 inches, height 1⅜ inches.
Color: Assorted silver, green, red and blue. White rubber wheels with red centers on blue, green and silver toys, blue centers on red toy.
Packed 1 dozen in box, 1 gross in case.
Case net weight 70 lbs., case gross weight 76 lbs.
Case measurements: 11x12x17 inches.

No. 1460X DeSoto Sedan

Length 4 inches, width 1⅝ inches, height 1⅜ inches.
Color: Assorted red, green, blue and gray. White rubber wheels with red centers on blue, green and gray toys, blue centers on red toy.
Packed 1 dozen in box, 1 gross in case.
Case net weight 60 lbs., case gross weight 66 lbs.
Case measurements: 10x14x15 inches.

Toys that retailed for 10¢ each were dubbed 'The 10 Line' by Arcade. The line copied different models of popular makes of cars and trucks, but price was the single most important factor for the success of the toys.

Pontiac cars were completely restyled in 1935 with 'Silver Streak' radiators and 'suicide' doors which hinged from the rear. Pontiac reversed the hinges on the doors in 1936, but the toys remained the same as those shown in this illustration from a 1936 catalog.

The popularity of the little DeSoto soon ended, but a few of the Pontiac toys were continued by the manufacturer through 1940.

225

Glass

361. c. 1913. USA
VAIL BROS. 3½″ long
Candy Container Glass

This electric automobile still holds its treasure of original candy pellets.

362. → 1912–1942
Made by American glass 3″ to 4¾″ long
companies
Candy Containers and
Bottles

Glass candy container automotive toys were low cost novelties sold as souvenirs and small gifts mainly through 5 and 10 cent stores. Regarded as trinkets and ornamental toys, they were saved as decorative objects when empty.

A few automobiles have been found with paper advertising labels attached to them, proving their use as free giveaways. The large variety of cars, trucks and related glass items makes them ideal collectibles.

Sold for 10¢ to 12¢, the assortment shown includes a yellow taxi of the early 1920s; perfume bottles of the early 1940s; Amos and Andy of about 1930; and a wonderful tin top jitney bus with tin wheels of 1912 vintage.

227

Wood

→
364. 1919. USA
CASS 14¾" long
Stake Truck Painted Wood
Clockwork

A simple design made to appeal to the younger child where correctly defined details are not required, this truck is painted in one of the most popular colors. The color red denotes the heart in some cultures and has long been a predominent color used on children's toys to capture attention. It is also said that the color red creates excitement.

Movable front wheels of cast iron are controlled with the steering wheel.

363. 1908. USA
ARCADE 8½" long
Runabout Auto Wood, Pressed
Steel, Cast Iron

Possibly the first automobile produced by Arcade, the runabout combines several materials. The nickeled driver was adapted from Arcade's horse-drawn circus wagon and thus has hands positioned upward to receive horses' reins. This circus wagon and driver lasted well into the 1930s, but the 25¢ runabout was closed out after a few years.

Proper scale did not seem of importance to early toy manufacturers. Real cars on the road in the early 1900s were so varied and new, standard designs were not yet established. Local blacksmiths and wagon shops were turning out experimental bodies, often to customers' specifications. The first Model T, produced late in 1908, used standardized body styles for the first time.

→
365. 1919. USA
CASS 16" long
Stake Truck Painted Wood

A pre-First World War type truck is updated with smaller wheels to lower the body and make it appear more modern.

It carries a 1925 Racer by Birchcraft that operates with a rubber band 'spring'. A painted black tack holds the rear spare and suffices for a radiator cap!

Both toys were intended for the very young.

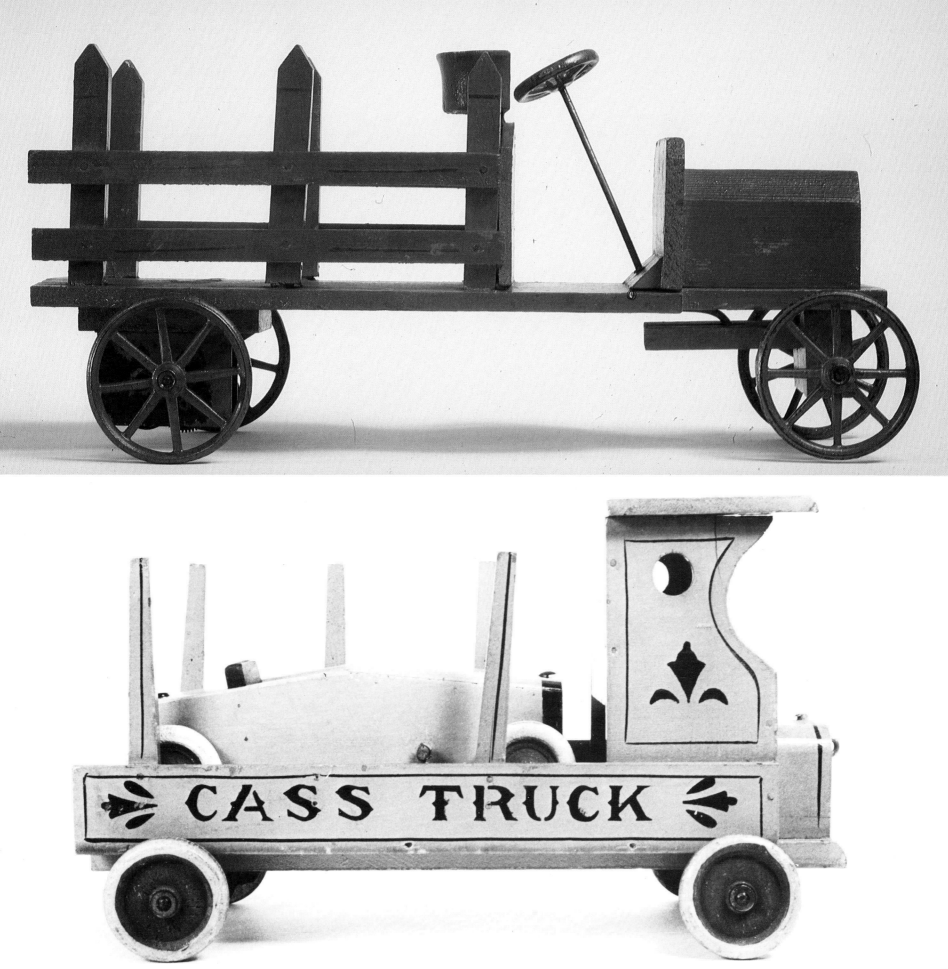

→

367. 1925
MAKER UNKNOWN 11¾″ long
'Speedy Felix' Automobile Painted wood
Leatherette ears

A patented toy, Felix the Cat drives a speedster created by Pat Sullivan for King Features. Felix was a comic strip character who also appeared in comic short movies. The George Borgfeldt Company retained an exclusive right to Felix toys and commissioned their manufacture under the private label 'Nifty'. The identity of the manufacturer was kept secret but it is known there were many working under the 'Nifty' label for Borgfeldt, both in America and in Germany in the 1920s.

366. 1918. USA
OROTECH 13½″ long
Army Truck Wood, metal
trim

A wartime toy born out of desperation and the only materials available at the time.

A twist of wire serves as the steering wheel while a wood cigar box body is decorated with paper. A former employee of the company told me the shortage was so severe in 1918 that the materials were first assembled and *then* the toy was designed.

Something like putting the cart before the horse!

A deluxe version had a simple canvas roof with wire bow supports.

The trucks were sold through 1920, possibly to utilize materials on hand while gearing up for new designs. A pathetic-looking reminder of difficult times.

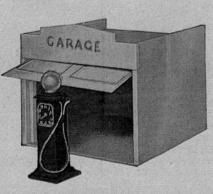

No. 905 Garage and Gas Pump

Length 8 inches, width 6¾ inches, height 6¼ inches.
Made of wood, finished in white with green trim.
Steel door on front is overhead type, easily opened and closed.
One cast iron pump finished in red, 4¼ inches high.
Packed 1 in box, 1 dozen in case.
Case net weight 19 lbs., case gross weight 24 lbs.
Case measurements: 15x16x18 inches.

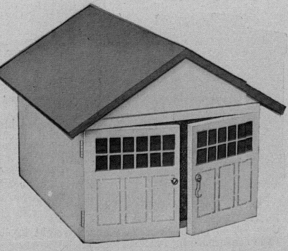

No. 907 Wood Garage

Length 14 inches, width 11¼ inches, height 8¾ inches.
Color: Cream color with green trimmings and green roof.
Mechanical: Doors open on hinges, and lock. Large enough to hold two Arcade automobiles.
Packed ½ dozen to case.
Case net weight 23 lbs., case gross weight 30 lbs.
Case measurements: 30x16x22 inches.

A newly styled garage and globe-top gas pump copied the changes made in their real counterparts in the mid-1930s. Arcade promoted the use of toy garages for store displays.

A buyer could purchase the gas pump alone for 10¢.

Arcade's 1936 wholesale catalog offered four different toy garages scaled for use with its cars and trucks. The No. 907 shown here was typical of a garage in a suburban neighborhood.

Paper

← **368.**
DENT
Cast Aluminum Toys

c. 1929–30. USA
3¼″–6″ long.
Aluminum

'Polished aluminum toys, lightweight and indestructible', is the catalog description. They were, but unfortunately they didn't sell well. In addition, the cost of raw materials was exceptionally high in 1929–30; and casting with aluminum was not a common procedure, proving to be more difficult than expected. Buffing and polishing by hand added to labor costs, making the line a financial disaster. The above assorted toys in the Gottschalk Junk Yard still wear their original shine. The trim is always red.

In 1930, the hook and ladder truck and dump truck retailed for 25¢, the same price as their cast iron counterparts with pressed steel wheels.

Production problems and high material costs plagued attempts to successfully market cast aluminum toys. The lessened weight was meant to lure retailers with prospects of lower shipping costs. However, public acceptance was lacking; and the line soon disappeared from Dent's offerings. Very few of these toys have surfaced, and when they do, they do not fit into specific collections. Nevertheless, they are interesting toys that document a time in Dent history.

The Freidag Manufacturing Company also tried marketing cast aluminum toys without success.

369.
MAKER UNKNOWN
Child's Halloween Mask.

c. 1908
Lithographed
cardboard

For children who wanted to masquerade as a chauffeur.

→
370.

For the collector, there is an amazing array of trinkets and ephemera waiting to be collected. It's all a matter of taste.

Shown here are a book, game, puzzle and card made for children – examples of the variety of automobilia which can be gathered for fun and pleasure.

The early 1900s paper on cardboard auto is a candy container. It is 5½″ long.

In addition to the Tom Swift books, adventure, mystery and humor can be found in *The Automobile Girls* by Laura Dent Crane, The *Motor Boys* by Clarence Young and *The Motor Girls* by Margaret Penrose. Written in the early 1900s, these children's books remained popular through the 1930s. The common threads that tie the books together are motoring trips leading to adventures in which the car always plays an important part in the story. Embossed pictures in color on the bindings give the books special appeal.

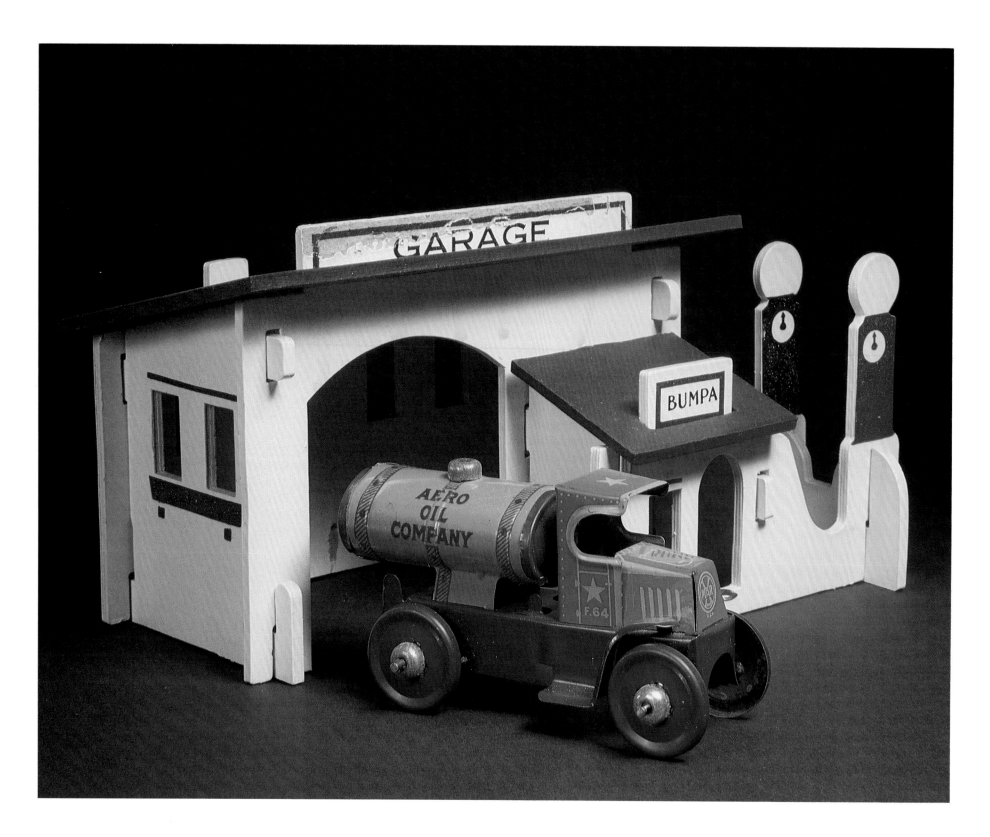

371.
MILTON BRADLEY
'Bumpalow' Garage

1931. USA
Box 11½″ long
Painted
cardboard

MARX
'Aero' Gas Truck

Made by a famous manufacturer of games,

USA
5½″ long
Litho Tin

cards and puzzles, the garage is easily assembled by even the smallest child. The completed garage is unique in that it is made from thick, painted cardboard rather than printed paper.

Games

372.
JEANETTE
'Brownie Auto Race'

1920s. USA
10⅝" Dia.
Litho Steel

Spinning arrow race game with cast lead racers, each marked with names of early racing cars – Stutz, Maxwell, Dodge etc.

Parlor games kept children occupied before the advent of television. Games were designed to amuse, teach and give companionship when played with one or more persons. They helped develop skills in the arts, sciences and mathematics as well as the winning strategy. Automotive themes were used in various card games. Indeed, the game of Touring was one of the best-selling card games ever made.

Advertising Premium Toys

Advertising giveaways were toys that were handed out free. Premiums usually required a nominal payment along with box tops or sometimes just box tops alone. Toys were offered by magazines in exchange for subscriptions. Sometimes, a nominal payment was charged in addition, depending upon the value of the toy.

Automotive advertising toys are the least familiar objects among free giveaways, as they appear to have been made in comparatively small numbers. This is hardly surprising as it was much easier to pack and handle flat items, such as calendars and little tin trays, than something on wheels. Advertisers were also happier with less easily destructible gifts, which would remind the recipient of the kind advertiser! Still a few automotive toys were produced, like the Star shoes racer which was given free with a pair of shoes, a small tin 1938 Ford bank with a dealers ad on the roof, and other small automobile and truck toys embellished with decals encouraging return visits to an automobile agency or repair shop. They have survived to remind us that nothing is free anymore!

→
374.   c. 1924 USA
BUDDY L   24" long
International Harvester   Pressed Steel
Truck

Sold only through International Harvester dealers, this Buddy L express truck was a promotional toy made by special arrangement with the manufacturer.

373.   1924. USA
ARCADE   10¾" long
Red Baby Dump Truck   Cast Iron

Arcade's first Red Baby truck was produced in 1924 a few years after International Harvester's success with the real ones. One reason for this delay could have been their limited appeal in large cities where they would not have had the impact felt in rural and farm areas. Taxis and Ford automobiles were Arcade's prime automotive products until this time.

The very first Arcade Red Baby truck is illustrated in Arcade's catalog with spoke wheels and the name was stamped on the toy. Disc wheels were a popular option on real cars and available along with rubber tires on the toys. By offering options for toys, it was comparable to the adult buyer ordering his car. A child could select the make, model, color and wheels for his toy. By bolting down the bed of the truck with the tailgate cast in an open position, the toy was easily converted to a stationary bed model. Once on the market, the Red Baby was a very successful toy, suitable for playing outside in the sand box or indoors.

International Harvester trucks were also sold through the Arcade catalog. Thousands of toys sold through the I-H agencies, which numbered 15,000 in 1922. The company also provided the toy trucks in advertising flyers to dealers.

Toy Dump Truck

Children get hours of pleasure playing with a dump truck in the sand pile. Looks like your Red Baby; good advertising for your business.

This toy dump truck is 10¾ inches in length, 4¼ inches in height, 3½ inches in width, and finished in the same bright red color as shown in the lower illustration. The ratchet and crank are finished in nickel. They operate a rope and pulley and elevate the dump bed. Rubber tires can be furnished in place of the cast tires which are painted white, as shown in the following illustration.

Packed one each in a paper box, one dozen to a case. Case gross shipping weight 55 pounds. A freight allowance of 60 cents is made on shipments of two dozen or more. Can be sold at retail $1.00 to $1.25. Prices:

	Iron Wheels		Disk Wheels, Rubber Tires	
1 and 2 dozen	$8.40 a dozen		1 and 2 dozen	$9.65 a dozen
3 to 5	8.25		3 to 5	9.50
6 to 12	8.00		6 to 12	9.25

f.o.b. Freeport, Illinois

An additional 10 per cent is added for less than case lots.

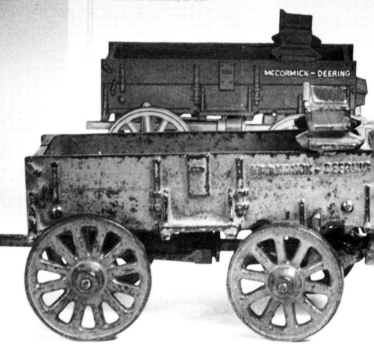

ARCADE   1925–30. USA
375. McCormick-Deering   Cast Iron
Tractor
376. McCormick-Deering
Weber Wagon
377. McCormick-Deering
Plow

Pages from an original International
Harvester flyer for dealers show toys offered
through farm machinery showrooms, a sales
tactic indirectly aimed at the adult who
would bring children to the showroom.

International Harvester was created in
1902 by the merger of the McCormick
Company, Deering, Plano, Milwaukee,
Warder, Glessner and Bushnell companies. It
retained the use of the McCormick-Deering
name on its farm equipment and
machinery.

In the late twenties, *Farm Mechanics
Magazine* offered a free toy for every three-
year subscription of $1.00. The Weber wagon
required two subscriptions.

→
378.   c. 1930. USA
AMERICAN NATIONAL   27″ long
Richfield Oil Co.   11″ high
Tank Truck   Pressed Steel

Produced under the 'Giant' brand label,
this indoor-outdoor Mack truck is rarely
found today because of its limited
production.

The outstanding features of the toy are
its superior design and extra-large size;
furthermore, it carries early advertising of
the Atlantic-Richfield Company, now
known as ARCO.

Toy Wagon

individual boxes, one dozen to a case. Shipping
horses, approximately 35 pounds.

individual boxes, two to a box, one dozen
ng weight of case, approximately 30 pounds.
wagon $1.10, horses $0.40, complete $1.50.

Prices

ns without horses

... dozen $8.40 a dozen
5 dozen   8.25
zen, or more   8.00
f two)   3.50
report, Illinois
per cent is added for less than case lots.

Something to Go with the Miniature Tractor

These toy plows are exact miniatures of the McCormick-
Deering tractor plows used on farms all over the world.
They can be sold at retail for 50 cents, particularly making
an ideal combination with the toy tractor.

McCormick-Deering toy plows are made of cast iron,
furnished with a hook for attaching to the tractor. Painted
bright red, with yellow wheels, and silver colored moldboard
shares, and coulters. "McCormick-Deering" is cast into one
of the handles—good advertising for dealers selling plows.
Being 7 inches long, 3½ inches wide, and 2½ inches high, their

size is in proportion to the McCormick-Deering miniature
tractor.

Packed in individual boxes, three dozen to a case. Shipping weight per case, 56 pounds.

Prices

1 and 2 dozen   - $3.50 a dozen
3 to 11 "   3.25
12 dozen, or more -   3.00

f.o.b. Freeport, Illinois.

An additional 10 per cent is added for less than case lot shipments.

Actual Size, Painted Red and Yellow with Silver Moldboard and Coulters.

↓ **379**

A page from a rare 1927 Chevrolet dealers' advertising notebook, provided by Chevrolet Motors, answers the question about Arcade toys which appeared with dealers advertising.

From the information provided, it is safe to assume that Arcade received advance drawings of new models in order to release the toys at the same time as the real cars were introduced.

Although Arcade was not the first toy manufacturer to produce custom toys for commercial advertising, it was one of the first to make them in cast iron. Most notable are its 1921 Yellow Taxis, 1933 Pierce Silver Arrow sedans, and World's Fair buses of 1933 and 1940 (see figs. 384 & 385).

Wood Miniatures of Car Models

There isn't a father or mother in your community who wouldn't delight in bringing home to their youngsters one of these miniatures of Chevrolet models. You can distribute them in various ways—at your showroom, at lodge banquets, at fairs, picnics and numerous other events—and build up for yourself a tremendous amount of good will.

Get your name into the homes of your neighborhood—reach the pocket nerve of your prospects by appealing to the sentiment of their children! Order a trial quantity of these sturdy, wooden miniature Chevrolets today! And distribute them to the best advantage! Then observe the increased popularity that you and your firm will enjoy. These wood miniatures of Chevrolets are furnished in five models—Coupe, Coach, Sedan, Landau and One-ton Truck. They can be supplied with or without dealer imprint, as desired. When imprinted, dealer's name and address is in embossed gold lettering, on the panel of truck body and side apron of passenger cars. Minimum order accepted is one hundred of any one model. Deliveries in from 14 to 21 days. Order direct from Birchcraft, Inc., Waukesha, Wisconsin, attaching check to order. Specify method of shipment. If you want your miniatures imprinted, be sure to accompany order with copy for imprint. Prices are as follows:

	Imprinted:	
100	....	$ 12.00
250	....	28.50
500	....	56.00
1000	....	110.00
	Not imprinted:	
100	....	$ 11.00
250	....	27.50
500	....	53.50
1000	....	105.00

All prices f. o. b. Waukesha, Wis.

↑ **380 & 381.**
ARCADE
Chevrolet Sedan & Coupe

1927. USA
8¼″ long
Cast Iron

Arcade worked with the advertising department at Chevrolet Motors to produce a wonderful set of toys which could be used in Chevy's advertising promotions. Car dealers ordered toys as giveaways to parents who would visit their showrooms for a trial ride in the real cars.

The advertising business was always a large part of Arcade's success. Starting with its first automotive toy, the Yellow Taxi, cooperation with the real manufacturers helped sell a lot of toys and created faithful likenesses of forthcoming models.

The sedan is a typical example of an advertising order. The coupe, devoid of advertising, was sold through the Arcade catalog to toy stores.

Spare tires bear paper labels with the Chevy logo, and radiators have the bowtie trademark stamp. 1928 issues can be identified by color. Red, green, blue and yellow were used that year. The '27 Chevys were discontinued in 1929.

Miniatures of Chevrolet Models
(*Cast Iron Toys*)

At the dealer banquets, held throughout the country this year, we gave to each dealer in attendance a miniature "Improved" Chevrolet Coupe, exactly 1/15th the size of the Coupe itself. Dealers everywhere were so impressed with them that we have been deluged with letters asking where they could be secured and at what prices. Arrangements have, therefore, been made with the manufacturers, the Arcade Manufacturing Company, Freeport, Illinois, to supply the "Improved" Sedan and Coupe, and the One-ton Truck with cab and stake body. Distribution in any one of a hundred different ways means good will for you and good advertising. If you doubt this, order a case and offer them to the first dozen people

who come into your showroom. There will not be one but who will enthusiastically accept. The Sedan and Coupe are 1/15th size, that is, they are 1/15th the size of a real car, the proportions being correct throughout; the Truck, 1/20th. Each model is finished in correct color combinations, the same as the cars they represent, the Truck having a black chassis and cab and a gray stake body. The Sedan and

Coupe come regularly with disc wheels, tires nickeled; the Truck, imitation wood wheels with white enameled tires. Real rubber tires, if ordered, can be furnished at extra cost as noted below.

PRICES

The Sedan and Coupe are packed one dozen to the case and priced at $7.20 per dozen, f. o. b. Freeport, Illinois. If less than a case is wanted, the price is $1.00 each.

The Truck is packed one dozen to the case and is priced at $6.00 per dozen, f. o. b. Freeport, Illinois, and if less than a case is wanted, at $.75 each. If rubber tires are wanted, the Sedan or Coupe are $8.95 per dozen; the Truck, $7.50 per dozen. In less than case lots, Sedan or Coupe, $1.15; Truck, $.85 each.

WHERE TO ORDER

Place your order direct for the quantity desired, if possible in even case lots, with the Arcade Manufacturing Company, Freeport, Illinois, enclosing check with order, payable to the Arcade Manufacturing Company. Shipment will be made to you direct within from three to ten days from time your order is received. Be sure and specify whether shipment is to be made by express or freight.

382.
ARCADE
White Moving Van

Late 1928. USA
13½″ long
Cast Iron

The White Company, designed its 1928 moving vans to carry heavier loads with expanded space over the cab. The extra window post was used as a brace. Pictures of the real van show the windshield sloped forward from the top, just the opposite direction from the toy. Often toy makers were forced to make changes to avoid production problems.

383.
ARCADE
White Delivery Truck

1931. USA
8½″ long
Cast Iron

Carried without advertising in the 1931 Arcade jobbers' catalog, regular colors were red, green and blue. White trucks were the creation of three brothers, sons of Thomas H.

Large, smooth side panels are an ideal billboard for advertisements. This toy bears the name of a Washington, D.C. moving company, a custom order available direct from Arcade.

An eighteenth-century cast iron chair by Stevens awaits loading along with a late 1920s Kilgore table and stove.

White, founder of The White Sewing Machine Co. of Cleveland, Ohio. The brothers made delivery vans for the commercial trade as early as 1900. From the beginning, White trucks were a moving force in the development of automotive progress. A 'Peerless Laundry and Cleaners' sign stamped on this truck is clear evidence that Arcade's advertising promotional sales were a continuous sideline from their start in the 1920s. (See fig. 173.)

384.
ARCADE
'Century of Progress' Buses

1933–4. USA
14½″, 12″,
10½″, 7⅝″, 6″
long
Cast Iron

Arcade's proximity to the site of the Century of Progress fair was its entree to manufacture the souvenir toys. The fleet of real two-piece buses was especially designed to carry fair visitors. These toys were faithful copies used as advertising for Greyhound and General Motors. A range of sizes afforded a selection priced from 25¢ to $1.00 for the four largest sets. The smallest bus is cast in one piece and does not appear in Arcade's catalogs or advertising. It was probably produced as a premium or giveaway on special order.

The toys were sold in Arcade's special booth at the fair and were listed in their wholesale catalogs as well. Children unable to attend the fair could still own the revolutionary new trailer buses since toy shops stocked them, with the words 'Greyhound Lines' to distinguish them from the souvenirs. The buses proved to be a bonanza for Arcade, selling in large numbers and helping the company through a critical financial period.

Stores in and around the hotels and fairgrounds also made the toy buses available to visitors through announcements in newspapers and flyers, an indication of the immense demand for them.

The cast iron building is a still bank.

385.
ARCADE
New York World's Fair Bus

1939. USA
10½" long
Cast Iron

A New York World's Fair license was required to manufacture toys depicting the Greyhound buses used within the fair area. Arcade's experience and success with toys from the Chicago Fair of 1933 was probably helpful in its advance planning for New York.

The real Greyhound was designed especially for quick hops on and off from both sides of the bus.

Two smaller sizes of the Greyhound bus were sold along with a Greyhound tractor which pulled open trailers for passengers who wanted to sightsee as well as ride. These were sold at the fair, and at toy stores throughout the New York area.

Greyhound Lines

1939 NEW YORK WORLD'S FAIR BUS

↑**386.**
DENT
'Freeman's Dairy Truck'

c. 1930. USA
5¾" long
Cast Iron

In the 1930s milk came from trucks. Freeman's Dairy serviced the Lehigh County area in Pennsylvania, one of the biggest dairy regions of the state.

The red truck with cast iron wheels was a giveaway for premium customers. It is also found with other company names.

387.
EBERL
'Hochschild, Kohn & Co.'
Delivery Van

1907. Germany
7" long
Litho Tin
Windup

The Hochschild Kohn department store opened its first store in November, 1897. Deliveries were made by horse and wagon. When motorized delivery was instituted around 1906, purchases made in the morning were delivered in the afternoon. The tin wind-up truck carrying the store's colors was featured during their tenth year in business. Reportedly given away free with an Easter suit, remaining trucks were a featured item sold in the toy department. A Tootsietoy delivery van in the same colors was handed out by the store's Santa Claus in later years.

Eberl made the same truck for other companies, including the C. F. Hovey Co. of Boston, Massachusetts, Gibson's Chocolates of Providence, Rhode Island, and Gately, and Fitzgerald & Co.

388. c. 1910.
EBERL Germany
'Bamberger's' Delivery Truck 7½" long
Litho Tin,
Windup

Louis Bamberger established the store in 1892, expanding all the time. In 1928 it was sold to R. H. Macy but continued under the same management.

The Newark, New Jersey department store truck has a roof rack and fenders, and was produced with and without a driver.

Delivery trucks with store names are sought after as advertising items and are not as common as one would suspect. Obtainable only with sizable purchases from the respective stores for a limited period, or as a premium from the department store, they were made and issued in few numbers, making them scarce toys today.

389. c. 1912.
TIPP AND EBERL Germany
Strawbridge & Clothier 7½" long
Delivery Truck Litho Tin
Windup

Similarities in many tin toys have given birth to speculation concerning the possibility of joint but unacknowledged business ventures within the early toy industry. Rarely is evidence produced to substantiate these suppositions, but in this instance there is clear proof.

This store delivery van is marked with a large early Tipp emblem on the radiator and a small Hans Eberl trademark on the rear section. The truck style dates from around the time Tipp was forming its company, and it is entirely possible it was not in full operation when the Philadelphia department store placed its order. Eberl was probably the manufacturer, but as Tipp held the toy contract its insignia was in a prominent position.

The windup truck copies Strawbridge and Clothier's real delivery trucks complete with the store emblem. The open section on the right side allows the driver to step out for deliveries.

390.
FISCHER
Advertising Limousine

c. 1913. Germany
8¼" long
Litho Tin
Windup

When toy automobiles are used for advertising, the best surface for promotion is the roof. Where the customer desired a lower profile, a manufacturer would use the underside of the car. Tin penny toys given away by the Chicago Theatre Concessions Company to stimulate attendance on slow nights, had the German toys printed on the underside and merely initialed on the top side.

This windup limousine has a sparkler mechanism built into the back of the toy to add the illusion of backfire.

Peppy slogans were once popular with American stores. Fischer made this toy, printed with ads, for several other stores. The toys were ordered through the Borgfeldt Company office in New York, Borgfeldt's salesmen using this sideline as a way of expanding their sales without offending regular toy customers.

One such ad on an identical toy reads:

'Every car will steer you to
Steers
Gay & Eden Sts.
Furniture and floor coverings'

248

Hessmobile Racer.

Given, post-paid, to any Companion subscriber for one new subscription and 15 cents extra. Price $1.00, post-paid.

This is a perfect imitation of a high-powered French racing motor car, with the driver and his assistant in position. The propelling power is supplied by a motor the friction momentum secured the This ther long

391. 1911. Germany
HESS Litho Tin
Hessmobile Racer

Shown with the advertisement clipped from an October, 1911 *Youth's Companion*, the Hessmobile racer was one of the magazine's most sought after premiums.

The racer had great appeal with its colorful lithography, trim appearance, and start-stop device for the flywheel motor, that winds from the crank. A crank is used to get the flywheel spinning and when pressed to start the lever puts the spinning gear in contact with the wheels. Lightweight foreign tin toys worked nicely with flywheels.

A popular toy which appeared both here and abroad from 1908 through 1915.

392 & 393. Early 1930s. USA
LINDSTROM Cab 3″ long
Advertising Trucks Trailers 3½″ long
Litho Tin

These small clockwork trucks carried advertising for various major companies of the day. By adding advertising to their toy lines, companies found a way to increase business. Here are but a few of the dozen or more products promoted on these trailers.

249

Marx produced the little lithographed tin Bamberger's truck in the late 1920s. It reportedly was handed out free by the store Santa Claus.

The 1917 Star Brand Shoes racer and Moxie toys were given away free, unassembled and folded flat in an envelope.

For publicity reasons, the 1928 lithographed tin Model A Ford car was distributed just *before* the real car was released in December, 1927. Upton Machinery made the cheap toy assembled with slots and tabs.

A pair of paper-on-wood 'flats' were made by Birchcraft in 1921, the last year for the Dodge name until it returned on trucks in 1929. From 1922 to 1928, most Dodge trucks were sold under the Graham Brothers name.

Birchcraft made wood advertising flats for funeral parlors, using a hearse, limousines, and moving company vans. These were giveaways for adults – a nice souvenir!

The pressed steel car with a roof sign advertises singer Sophie Tucker's radio show for Roi-Tan Cigars on its back.

Arcade produced the cast iron, 1936 bus with a local Pennsylvania company name on the roof. It is 7¾″ long.

The real 1917 Moxiemobile was built on a Dort automobile chassis. A life-like horse provided seating for the Moxie salesman. The company used a variety of unique machines incorporating a horse for the purpose of selling, advertising and delivery through the 1930s.

395.	c. 1928. USA
MARX	13″ long
'Lincoln Transfer'	Litho Tin
	Windup

Marx combined two effective advertising gimmicks, a popular windup Mack truck with large, bold lettering. The Mack was always a favorite plaything of little boys. This one has space for the child's own toys. The moving company's name was intended to be remembered by the child and parent due to its highly visible ad. If anyone was doing business in 1928, it was the movers!

Marx produced other toys with ads. All came directly from its production stock with a few exceptions. Like other toy companies in the thirties, Marx was not opposed to the advertising sideline.

Metalcraft
Identification guide for dating trucks

Changes in real truck design were reflected in toys and in the absence of other material provide the best guide for dating. However, Metalcraft factory workers report that earlier dies were not discarded when improvements were added. Orders were dictated by taste, price and the requirements of buyers. Dies and patterns were kept and replaced only when they were worn out. Thus, a 1930 style truck could have been merchandised for five years.

1928
First trucks produced. Separate windshield posts, straight radiator, 'White' script logo on radiator shell, polished steel wheels.

1929
Single-piece cab door with integral windshield posts, all-steel wheels.

1930
Same as 1929. Front bumper added.

1931–2
Same as 1930. Demountable B. F. Goodrich black rubber tires.

1933
Redesigned massive V-shaped radiator grille, battery-operated headlights, new four-louver hood.

1935
Streamlined restyling with heart-shaped radiator grille.

396.   1928. USA
METALCRAFT   11" long
'Coca-Cola' Bottling Truck   Pressed Steel

Metalcraft produced three models of the popular Coca-Cola truck, each time updating the chassis and cab and using the same body. The trucks were promoted through the mid-1930s. The ten little glass bottles with their distinctive shape were subcontracted to Libbey-Owens Glass Company and to be more realistic were filled with a dark liquid resembling Coca-Cola. Most bottles have emptied from evaporation over the years even though their caps may not have been removed.

The Coca-Cola Company sponsored premium days in various large cities to promote its cola for 5¢ a bottle. With the purchase of a 6-pack, the beverage company representative dispensed a coupon redeemable against a Metalcraft truck when accompanied with a 49¢ payment.

The most successful promotional truck in its line, the 'Coke' truck was the forerunner of a series of advertising vehicles, although it was not Metalcraft's first.

253

397.
METALCRAFT
Towing Truck

1928. USA
11½ long
overall
Pressed Steel

Metalcraft trucks were styled on the 1928 trucks of the White Motor Corporation of Cleveland, Ohio. This towing truck, one of the first in its line, shows the simplicity of the initial offerings. All metal wheels, separate windshield posts that become an integral part of the body in later models, and a plain-looking wrecking crane show a complete departure from other manufacturers' toy trucks, which were becoming more intricate in design. The competition was also more expensive, which probably accounts for the initial success of Metalcraft trucks. Ranging in price from 29¢ to 49¢, premium specials offered by stores were well-made and good value.

The White Company's script logo is found pressed into the top of the toy radiator.

398.
METALCRAFT
'Kroger' Truck

1929. USA
11⅛" long
Pressed Steel

The Kroger Stores, a grocery chain, gave its customers a store coupon which was punched once by the cashier for each 25¢ spent in the store. When the card was completely punched, a toy truck could be redeemed for the card plus 49¢. The same offer was made by The Jewel Tea Company and other merchants, usually a few months before Christmas. Announcements were made over the radio and store clerks would arrange a special display at the main entrance.

The Kroger truck came packed in a box printed with grocery shelf items which could be cut-out and folded into tiny boxes for stocking the van. The boxes were name-brand products.

Separate windshield posts were eliminated this year. The new design was stronger and eliminated a production process.

399.
METALCRAFT
Machinery Carrier
with 'Baby Ruth' Steam
Shovel

1930–31. USA
14½″ long closed
Pressed Steel
7″ long

In 1931, Metalcraft used the slogan 'Designed and priced for 1931 conditions', showing the company was aware of the prevailing business climate at the time.

Metalcraft toys have long been underrated and if nothing else are noteworthy for surviving a turbulent business period. The Machinery hauler and its companion steam shovel are among the best Metalcraft toys. They are well made, colorful and original in design.

Metalcraft introduced the machinery carrier late in 1930.

400.
METALCRAFT
'Goodrich-Silvertown Tires'
Wrecker

1931–32 USA
12″ long
Pressed Steel

The black rubber tires were demountable when new. Age has petrified them, and they are too brittle for removal today. The bed of the truck has three open slots to support the spares in an upright position.

401.
METALCRAFT
'Sunshine Biscuits' Truck

1933. USA
12½″ long
Pressed Steel

The Sunshine truck was another of Metalcraft's new body designs manufactured specifically to display special advertising. The cardboard box it came in was printed with miniature cut-out boxes of Loose-Wiles products.

Toys containing advertising of national brands like this truck have wide appeal. Advertising collectors sometimes collect everything bearing the logo or adverts of a single company. Others only collect items that were nationally recognized brands. Though made in large numbers, this toy is relatively scarce because of its desirability.

403.
METALCRAFT
'Shell Oil' Truck

1933. USA ↘
12½″ long
Pressed Steel

Names on the Shell oil barrels illustrate the company's widespread distribution to the aircraft industry, marine suppliers and factories.

An early employee of Metalcraft recalls an attempt to sell the newly-designed truck directly to Shell for premiums without success. Ultimately it was sold through jobbers for the first time in 1933 along with the Goodrich, the Sunshine and the Coca-Cola bottling trucks. The newest improved models featuring battery operated lights sold for 80¢ each retail. The 'business leader' trucks were still available for custom orders.

402.
METALCRAFT
'Krug's' Bakery Truck

1933. USA
12½" long
Pressed Steel

Bakeries that sold their goods door to door like Krug's favored premiums for encouraging repeat business. The bakery truck is an example of a simple advertisement applied with stencil.

Metalcraft trucks were welded exceptionally well. Rarely are the toys found in a collapsed condition or with missing wheels. The only weakness is the radiator, which is separate and applied with tabs, and the battery levers which are just heavy bent wire. It takes a strong blow to dislodge both parts, something which little boys manage quite well.

Rust is the toy collector's enemy. Though finished with baked enamel, neglected Metalcrafts are prone to rust like any discarded toy. However, collectors will tolerate a limited amount as long as the advertising sections are not greatly affected.

404.
METALCRAFT
'Smile' Truck

1933. USA
12½" long
Pressed Steel

An express truck like the real ones that delivered a citrus-flavored drink of the 1920s and 1930s.

Headlamps are operated with the lever mounted on the side and batteries fitted under the cab. Some Metalcraft trucks in this period were fitted with an S-hook accessory which hung from the door to carry a spare tire.

405.
METALCRAFT
'Bunte' Truck

1933. USA
12½" long
Pressed Steel

A stationary bed holds candy from a company that is still in business and was well known in the 1930s.

Metalcraft made trucks for beer, pretzel, and chocolate companies. These advertising toys represented companies in the food, beverage and candy lines more than any other businesses.

407.
METALCRAFT
Acme Stores Truck

1935. USA
13" long
Pressed Steel

Count Alexis de Sakhnoffsky, a youthful Russian, was already an important influence in automotive designing circles abroad when he was commissioned by the White Motor Company of Cleveland, Ohio, to completely redesign their trucks for 1935.

Metalcraft immediately adopted the idea of a new, revised design for their latest toy. The undulating curves on the body and heart-shaped radiator with recessed battery-operated lights were meant to suggest or copy Sakhnoffsky's style, though in fact the toy differed from his design.

formed in the early thirties under the aegis of President Franklin D. Roosevelt's New Deal. Its purpose was to enforce codes for fair competition in business and industry. The NRA was abolished in 1935 when the Supreme Court ruled it unconstitutional.

In the beginning, manufacturers used these paper stickers on goods as proof of their patriotism and support of President Roosevelt's plan.

The original sticker also dates the truck, sometimes referred to by toy collectors as a 'pickle' truck, as that was Heinz's most famous food product in the Thirties along with ketchup. The body of the truck was specially designed to copy the company's real delivery trucks. It has a large stamped steel tailgate and also holds more advertising than any previous Metalcraft models.

This was Metalcraft's most successful 1933 toy. It sold by the thousands.

406.
METALCRAFT
'Heinz' Truck

1933. USA
12″ long
Pressed Steel

This truck bears a paper NRA sticker pasted on its roof. The National Recovery Administration was a government agency

→
408.
STRAUSS

Delivery Van with
Advertising

c. 1913. USA
9¼″ long

Lithographed
Sheet Tin

European Toys

German goods became unpopular in America during the post-First World War period, due in part to the formation of manufacturers associations which worked to keep foreign competition out. One such group was the Toy Manufacturers of the U.S.A., whose logo of Uncle Sam's top hat filled with American toys conveyed its patriotic message.

It was an ideal time for Americans to try to restrain competitive imports. An embargo on German goods during the war period, and the post-war baby boom had created a lucrative market for toys. Meanwhile, Germany was experiencing a shortage of materials, labor problems, high shipping costs and taxes levied to aid recovery from the huge losses suffered in the war. When Toy Manufacturers of the U.S.A. lobbied for high tariffs to be imposed on imported toys, it added to Germany's woes.

It has long been suspected that German factories secretly continued to supply parts to some American toy makers. Reports in the newspapers of American toy manufacturers visiting Germany heighten this suspicion. More incriminating are the various parts found on some American toys of definitely European construction and appearance, especially figures and wheels on some tin toys. On the other hand it could be argued that these parts were designed by Europeans living and working in the States and using methods perfected in Germany. Many early American toy manufacturers were of German descent, and hired German immigrants.

In 1904, America's toy purchases from Germany were almost equal the United State's entire production of toys. In 1914, Germany supplied 85% of all toy imports, being equal to 56% of total U.S. toy production. By 1923, German imports formed 88% of total toy imports, but were only 13% of the total U.S. production.

The success of the post-war American campaign was further confirmed when in 1925, the U.S. Vice Consul of Germany reported a grave crisis in the German toy industry. The export of toys from Germany had declined at an alarming rate and unemployment was increasingly serious.

Some 9,000 workers were normally employed full time. Now, 2,000 were working, with 5,000 just part-time. The state was paying subsidies to the unemployed workers without relief in sight. Similar conditions existed throughout Germany and not just in Nuremburg.

The United States and Japan had gained a foothold in the toy industry that would prevail for the next few years. Business interests and protect their investments and were successful in imposing duty rates on imports. The 'Buy American' theme continued.

With the Great Depression, the demand for toys, American and foreign, would diminish and only the most stalwart firms would survive. After the Second World War, the toy world, in common with everything else, had changed completely. Plastic outmoded tin and new machinery and manufacturing methods were needed. Many companies did not attempt such reorganization and disappeared completely.

409.
BING
Racers

1904. Germany
11½", 8½" long
Painted Tin
Clockwork

One of the few European luxury toys distributed in the United States in 1904. Found listed in Smith Hardware's wholesale catalog, the racers are the *only* toy automobile listed that year. It is possible they were carried on a trial basis, for next year's catalog does not list a single toy car.

Quality toys, the heavily enameled cars with brass clockworks and nickeled trim, were made when pride in workmanship was valued.

The racing number plates are replacements.

410 & 411.
BING
Model T Fords

1923. Germany
6½″ long
Painted and
Litho Tin
Windup

Bing's Fords are the most accurate models ever produced in tin. The lady drivers are surely a result of Henry Ford's world-wide sales promotions directed at women. He even published a booklet in 1912 stressing the advantages of his cars for women.

Perfectionists will find variations on the toys. The Ford logo is found on the running boards of some cars and is missing on others. Notice the tire treads printed on some toys but missing on the touring car shown. Often, the license plate is left blank. A toymaker once told me when the machines broke down, the toy design changed for that day. Collectors love the little Fords no matter how they appear!

Restyled black-radiator Fords (brass radiators ended in 1916) for 1923 are identified by their rectangular rear windows, 'turtle' rear decks, and separate high cowls. (A cowl being the piece of metal that joins at the windshield section with the hood.) Bing added color to Ford toys in 1924.

Fords were already legends when Bing brought out its line of tin models. The lightweight tin worked exceptionally well, with windup motors contributing to their success.

412.

(*Center top*)
STRAUSS
'YELL-O-TAXI'

Mid 1920s. USA
8¼" long
Litho Tin
Windup

(*Left top*)
BING
Yellow Taxi with Disc
Wheels

c. 1914 Germany
7⅛" long
Litho Tin
Windup

(*Front left*)
BING
Brown and Yellow Taxi

1922. Germany
8¼" long
Litho Tin
Windup

(*Front right*)
BING
Yellow Taxi with Meter

1924. Germany
9" long
Litho Tin
Windup

In the 1920s a profusion of foreign tin taxis flooded toy stores for a share of this popular market. Eight to nine inch long yellow taxis sold well in both cast iron and tin. An American taxi by Strauss shares the photo with three from Bing to show Yellow Taxis made specifically for the American market.

Yellow Cabs operated in almost every major city in America using various makes of cars, but always decorated in the company colors as a means of identification. In some cities, taxis were sometimes the only means of transportation.

413.
BRENNER
Touring Car with Garage

1919. England
Car 11″ long
Garage 12″ deep
Litho Tin
Clockwork

The boxy-shaped tourer and matching garage are rare because larger tin garages were sold in limited numbers for single automobiles. The lithographed finish on the toys is reminiscent of those wonderful old English biscuit boxes that are so collectible today.

The license number, B.M. 5090, records the maker's initials and the city of Manchester, along with a stock number. The clockwork spring under the hood is wound by the front crank with transmission to the rear axle. Front cranks were outdated on real cars of this type in America by the end of the First World War.

The steering wheel placement at dead center is suitable for little drivers who may grow up thinking their half of the road is in the middle!

414.
BUB
Mercedes Limousine

c. 1930.
Germany
13½″ long
Litho Tin
Clockwork

Sold complete with the paper trunk on the luggage rack, the limousine has all the accoutrements of a luxury to – opening doors, a glass folding windshield, and detailed tin upholstery for seats. The crackle paint finish is the work of Mother Nature.

A 1910 German windup tin aeronautical toy shares airspace.

415.
KARL BUB
Roadster and Gasoline
Station

1931–2.
Germany
14" long 19"
long Litho Tin

The famed American toy store, F. A. O. Schwarz, started in Baltimore in 1862, and later opened for the sale of toys in New York City. It soon became known as a source for the finest toys sold in America. Its buyers specialized in the more expensive foreign-made toys, some exclusive only to Schwarz.

Both toys shown were featured at Schwarz for the Christmas season of 1932; the car was featured on the catalog cover, along with an oil cart and pump by Doll (see fig. 424).

Day or night service is available with the electric lights on this service station. A unique gas pump actually works. Nothing is spared to make this $10 station one of the best built and expensive stations of its day.

A fine looking roadster with the lines and long wheel base of a classic car of the period was imported and mated with the station. It has a gas tank with filler cap and drain for use with the gas pump, a turn signal that works when the wheel is turned, a rumble seat that opens, and a strong clockwork mechanism. 'Only $2.25', states the catalog.

The car is listed in a 1931 Bub catalog.

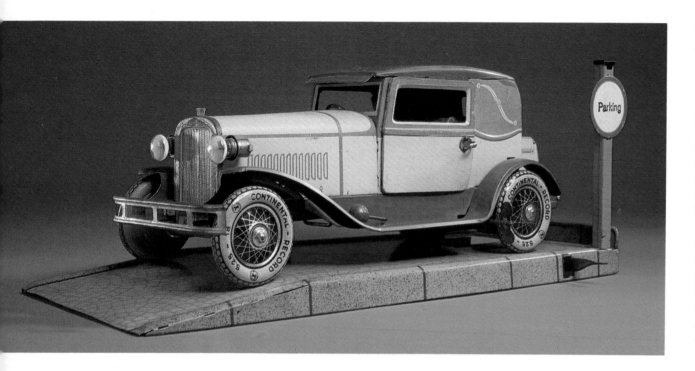

416.
BUB
Sedan with Parking Place

c. 1931.
Germany
12″ long
Litho Tin

A handsome two-door sedan with its own parking space was imported for sale by F. A. O. Schwarz. This automobile was also featured in its 1932 Christmas catalog. When a trigger at the curb on the runway is pressed, the windup car is released, and battery-operated lights automatically go on. $2.50 in 1932.

German manufacturers Bub, Gunthermann, and Distler made lithographed vehicles and toys that were similar in appearance and vied for a share of the decreasing market for imported toys in 1932. One concession they did *not* make was the placement of drivers. All were situated on the right hand side of the car, in accordance with European style.

417.
CARETTE
Closed Limousine

c. 1908.
Germany
10″ long
Litho Tin
Clockwork

Toy historians rely on manufacturers' catalogs for positive identification. Foreign catalogs are hard to come by in their country of origin, let alone after they have crossed an ocean. In recent years, a prominent collector has identified this car as one by the fascinating toymaker, Carette, based on construction similarities and figures which appear identical to those in cars definitely attributed to Carette. We have learned that in America such similarities are not always the basis for positive identification but for the time being, this car can be credited to Carette. One thing is certain: if and when the maker is positively identified, he will receive my applause for his original and charming contribution.

Isinglass windows, in hinged doors, have yellowed from age. A dignified looking lady with a 'fur' neck scarf occupies the rear seat. An English bulldog surveys tin tires in the light of a French street lamp.

The real, large, deluxe cars matching this toy were very expensive and affordable only by the rich who could also support a chauffeur. Early taxis were often such luxury motorcars fitted out for hire. Single, brass carbide lamps made night driving possible in the early 1900s . . . not safe, just possible.

→
418.
CITROEN
B14 Citroen Sedan
LENCI 'The Kid' Doll

1927. France
21″ long
Painted Tin

Andre Citroen made his basic sedan in the largest size possible for an indoor toy. Unlike the large American pressed steel and baked enamel trucks, this car was not made for rough outdoor play.

The delightful Citroen displays tin seats with channel upholstery and is propelled by an electric motor. Of special interest is the fact that Andre Citroen used his toys as a publicity aid. He manufactured the toys at the same time as his real cars with the idea that children growing up with the toys would immediately associate the name of Citroen with cars.

With the addition of a taxi meter and yellow and black colors, the sedan was manufactured as a taxi. Doors open, windows slide open, and headlights work. The Citroen was popular with Paris taxi drivers as a fast, light car in the 1920s.

Lenci of Italy made the sportily clad pressed felt doll during the 1920s. The company copied famous personalities of the period that appealed to the adult consumer. The doll copies Jackie Coogan dressed as a street lad for his movie role in *The Kid*. (Early 1920s.)

419.
DISTLER
'What's Wrong Car'

1930. Germany
7⅝" long
Litho Tin
Windup

A windup with clever action stalls the car periodically while the motor shakes the car from side to side before moving on again, much like a troublesome real car with dirt in the fuel line.

The maker knew the buyers' thoughts when 'What's Wrong Car' was printed on the hood.

→
421.
DISTLER
Two-door Limousine

1932. Germany
12½" long
Litho Tin
Windup

This closed limousine with all the latest features was an exclusive import by F. A. O. Schwarz for its 1932 Christmas season.

Built-in trunks were a streamlining feature that year. The tin balloon tires were introduced almost ten years earlier (1923) on some toys.

A unique feature on this toy is the gas tank, which can be filled and drained – with water, we hope!

420.
DISTLER
Taxi Limousine

1930s. Germany
10½" long
Litho Tin
Windup

A lighted interior silhouettes two men against frosted glass windows. Wearing formal top hats with cigars in hand, the men bow back and forth to each other when the car is in motion. Americans identify the figures as two Alphonse and Gaston comic strip characters who were forever bowing to each other.

A rear stop light and headlights operate with batteries and a lever visible at the hood. The roof lifts up for access to the interior bulb used to light the passenger compartment.

Two words are printed on the back of the toy. A third is scratched off with a pin. It reads, 'Made in –'. An example of someone expressing his sentiments during the Second World War.

423.
DOLL
Live Steam Touring Car

1922. Germany
19″ long
Painted Tin

A sophisticated toy which was outrageously high priced when new. Live steam vehicles were not a financial success due to the lack of control once the toy was set in motion and the dangers associated with steam in general. (The author was once presented with the parts of an exploded car when the owner could not bear to throw the mess away. It gets one thinking about the actual event!)

Several live steam Doll cars have surfaced in American estates, though there is no evidence to show they were actually sold in the USA. We can only assume they were gifts from abroad.

The hood is hinged and lifts to open from both sides. The radiator and lamps are separate parts and removable for access to the live steam engine. Although the windshield framework is intact, but the windshield itself awaits replacement. Despite its luxury class, the fold-down windshields used by Doll for its cars were not real glass but isinglass. Ironically, the burn-proof celluloid-like substance was probably a safety measure!

Very few of these toys survive intact.

← 422.
DOLL
Touring Car

1922. Germany
16″ long
Painted Tin
Clockwork

Toy collectors are inclined to identify every car with a V-shaped radiator as a Mercedes. No wonder. When the Mercedes made its appearance in 1901, it rendered most other motorcars obsolete.

The V-radiator design is first credited to Métallurgique in 1907. The radiator became the Belgian-made car's trademark. By 1914, a great number of cars copied the radiator design and from 1919 to 1923 there was hardly a German car without the V-radiator.

The tourer has a folding isinglass windshield, disc wheels with rubber tires, pressed metal seats, opening doors and quality construction which compares in every way to the fine toys of Marklin and Bing.

The substitute driver is not original but almost the same age and size. He suitably fills a void while seated on a projecting pin in the driver's seat.

Proper identification of a Mercedes is made by the three-pointed star trademark, registered in 1909 but not found on this Doll car.

424.
DOLL
Oil Tank Cart and Gas
Pump

1930. Germany
Cart 6½″ × 6½″
× 4½″
Pump 8″ high
Tin and Glass

In the pre-Second World War period, curbside gas pumps at the local filling station were far from automatic. The early pumps held only five gallons. Before filling up with petrol, it was necessary to hand pump the five gallons into the top glass container of the pump where gravity could aid its flow into the car's tank.

A perfect reproduction of the real oil carts found at service stations in the early 1930s; the side compartment opens to reveal three glass 'quart' bottles which are fillable from the pump when water is used.

A gasoline pump that works when filled with water must have thrilled many a boy. The pump has a valve at the back and the liquid first rises in the glass meter before it flows out the hose. A pan was provided for filling and draining the pump.

These are wonderful miniatures that were made long before real glass was banned from toy production in the United States. They cost $4.75 for the pair.

425. c. 1907.
EBERL Germany
EBO Express 7¾″ long
  Litho Tin
  Windup

Self-advertising is effected with Hans Eberl's company logo and tradename 'EBO' which was used on other toys as well. The rear doors open to hold small objects. The earliest Eberl delivery trucks use the same wheels and hub caps, but are minus fenders.

→
427. 1912. Germany
FISCHER 11″ long
Taxi Litho Tin
  Windup

A street of paper-on-wood houses form the background for this taxi. A fold-down landaulet roof works with the aid of hinged metal straps. A metal panel spans the folding top with its front roof. A taxi meter can be raised and lowered.

 Vertical body striping was popular on taxis and luxury-priced private cars from around 1910 to 1915. It was a means of customizing a car and added to the cost. Going one step better were some owners who ordered large bare outer body areas upholstered with real woven cane cloth or painted with the simulated woven cane pattern. A tedious and costly process, such specialty painting work has all but disappeared on real cars. Only on very rare occasions will a newly-restored, majestic car appear at a national antique car meet sporting these special decorations. When it does, all eyes are on it!

426. c. 1907.
EBERL Germany
Red Cross Truck 7¾″ long
  Litho Tin
  Windup

Peacetime ambulance colors of grey with red and white are used on an EBO Express body to create a variation.

 The tab and slot construction of German tin trucks makes the country of origin easily identifiable.

428.
FISCHER
Limousine

Early 1920s.
Germany
11½″ long
Litho Tin
Windup

By 1920, mass-production techniques had been perfected by German toy makers. It was during this period that competition forced manufacturers to become more inventive and build extras into toys to make them stand out from the mass. Curved roofs and curved lines in opening doors, folding windshields and miniature separate lamps appeared. The newest disc wheels replaced spoke wheels.

On real cars, some discs were not true disc wheels, but covers installed over conventional wire spoke wheels.

429.
FISCHER
Motorcycle

Mid-1920s.
Germany
7″ long
Litho Tin
Windup

In the 1920s motorcycles were better received in Europe than in America. Americans confined their use mostly to police and postal services. As toys were copied from actual vehicles on the road, few motorcycles other than those used for these services were copied by American toymakers, although the motorcycles with civilians astride them were of interest and reasonably salable in the States. Tandem riders give this windup motorcycle the one detail that makes it an exciting toy.

Fischer toys are unpretentious and original designs. They have an undeniable charm.

430.
FISCHER
Automatic Dump Truck

Mid-1920s.
Germany
10¼″ long
Litho Tin
Windup

This truck displays Fischer's trademark. It uses the identical stop-start action for triggering the dump that is found on the 'Nifty Dump', a toy Fischer made for Borgfeldt. Action begins when the toy is placed on the floor. The driver is at lunch!

↓ **431.**
(*Left to right:*)
Dating from just after the First World War to the mid-thirties

TIPP	8″ long	Germany
LEHMANN	9″ long	Litho Tin
LEVY	6¾″ long	Windups
KOHNSTAM	8″ long	
GUNTHERMANN	7″ long	
FISCHER	7″ long	

A group of motorcyclists display the various styles and individual character that emerge from different toymakers. Fischer had a flair for the unusual, which is clearly seen in the integral helmeted duo astride one motorcycle.

Gunthermann's cycle uses one piece of tin rolled over to make up a tire, an unusual construction for a wheel. A flint and an abrasive wheel work to simulate motor sparks.

Lehmann's nattily dressed sports figure is on a beautifully made motorcycle whose fine detail comes closest to the real machine.

Tipp made a series of wonderful lithographed motorcycles, but none are so great as those with sidecars where lady passengers braved the elements and stares of onlookers in the 1930s. This was not as common a sight in real life as the toy would have you believe.

→
433.   1927. Germany
KOHNSTAM   9½" long
Six-Cylinder Limousine   Litho Tin

Designed as an instructive toy, with moving pistons and a reverse, neutral and forward gearshift, the car was introduced in 1927 in two sizes. It was sold through the early 1930s.

The largest car shown here has opening rear doors and sold for $1.39. A smaller, four-cylinder model, 8" long, has two speeds and sold for 95¢ postpaid from Montgomery Ward's mail order house in 1930.

Although the name Moko is on the toy, there are similarities in construction and appearance to the work and design of H. Fischer, who I suspect was the real maker of this toy. Moses Kohnstam is known to have commissioned toys from Fischer and was a jobber for many other manufacturers as well. Fischer's cover of anonymity has been blown in the past few years. He produced toys under contract with a 'no name' identity, which meant that the Fischer name could not appear on toys or in advertising.

→
434.   1913–20s
GREPPERT & KELCH   Germany
Open Tourer and Runabout   Both 5¼" long
                Litho Tin
                Windup

MAKER UNKNOWN   c. 1908.
'Motor' Truck   Germany
                4¾" long
                Litho Tin
                Windup

Here are examples of small cars available in the early 1900s. The toys borrow features from American, German and French cars on the road in their day. When disc wheels became a popular addition to real cars, G & K updated their models by replacing spoke wheels with disc type ones.

Bright lithography and fancy roof trim give the small truck special charm. The toy promotes its windup motor in a unique manner.

432.   1927. Germany
FISCHER   10½" long
Hi-Way Henry   overall
                Litho Tin
                Windup

George Borgfeldt, a New York City toy distributor contracted with H. Fischer to manufacture patented and copyrighted comic strip character toys. These were made under a 'no name' identity and trademarked simply 'Nifty'.

Some of the other comic toys controlled by Borgfeldt were Felix the Cat, Toonerville Trolley, Creeping Buttercup, and Maggie and Jiggs. Borgfeldt also distributed erratic action cars and trucks designed by Fischer exclusively for the New York firm.

Hi-Way Henry is taken from Oscar Hitt's Summer and Spring comic strip. It depicts a family on the move, living out of their battered car.

In movement, the car shakes and shudders and rears up and down while Henry, the dog, bobs in and out of his radiator house. The clothes line sways while the fat lady passenger listens to the radio through earphones with an aerial fastened to the clothesline.

Hi-Way Henry made its bow in January of 1927. The retail price was one dollar. Finding this toy complete, working, and with original parts is a challenge. The new-from-the-box one shown is considered by comic collectors as one of the ultimately desirable toys.

437.
GREPPERT & KELCH
Garage set
Mercedes Limousine
and Raceabout

1927. Germany
7½″ wide × 6½″
deep
Cars 6¼″ long
Litho Tin
Windup

The real Mercedes car originally appeared in 1901. It made its name first in racing, establishing a reputation for a fine, powerful motor. The designer, Frenchman Emil Jellinek, was a racing driver working for Daimler at the time. He encouraged Daimler to manufacture the car to his specifications and contracted for the first series, which he planned to sell as Daimler's French agent.

German sabre-rattling in Europe at this time made Jellinek insist on a less-Germanic name for his design, thus the car was named after his daughter, Mercedes.

An attractive pair of windup toy Mercedes automobiles leave their companion garage. An unusual feature is the clock which folds for storage. The inspiration for these toys came from a rich, two-car owner who kept one closed car for use with a chauffeur and a racy model for quick spins when alone.

Garages

From the turn of the century through the period prior to the First World War, automobiles were housed in barns, stables, carriage houses, sheds or at the owner's place of business, such as a factory or mill. Later, special buildings were designed to hold automobiles, equipment, tools, and if the family was rich, quarters for the chauffeur.

It was not unusual for extremely wealthy families to own a fleet of cars. They built special garages to house them, including space for a repair shop and living quarters for one or more chauffeurs. In 1928, when millionaire socialite Payne Whitney died in New York, his estate disclosed 29 automobiles! Four were Rolls Royces.

For the average family, a single garage with a minimum amount of storage space was a luxury in the 1920s. The more affluent upper middle class families built two-car garages. The style of such separate garages has not changed much from those years.

↖
435.

BING
Fire House with Engines

c. 1910. Germany
7⅞" wide × 6½" deep
Litho Tin
Windup

GEORGE KELLERMANN
Garage with Dump Truck

1920s. Germany
2¾" wide × 5" deep
Litho Tin

BING
Garage with Sedan and Tourer

c. 1925. Germany
7¾" wide × 6⅜" deep
Litho Tin

HULL CO.
U.S. Gas Pump

1917. USA
7 1/16" high
Litho Tin

↑
436.

LEHMANN
Double Garage
'Galop' Racer
and Sedan

1927. Germany
6½" wide × 6" deep
Cars 5½" long
Litho Tin
Windup

BING
Garage, Raceabout
and Limousine
with Chauffeurs

c. 1912. Germany
7¾" wide × 6⅜" deep
Cars 5½" long
Litho Tin
Windup

BING
Single Garage with
Limousine

1913. Germany
4½" wide × 6⅜" deep
Litho Tin
Windup

← 438.
438.
GUNTHERMANN
Four-passenger Touring Car

c. 1904. Germany
11″ long
Litho Tin
Clockwork

Motoring was all the rage among the gentry at the turn of the century and they got dressed in special outfits designed to protect them against dust and rain.

In pleasant weather, open cars were preferred for sightseeing. Still, the passengers wore dusters against dirt and sun. Early big cars were expensive, owned mostly by wealthy people who could afford designer clothes. Closed cars made all the body wrapping unnecessary.

The rear entrance tonneau model holds passengers dressed in matching dusters.

439.
GUNTHERMANN
Coupe Gordon Bennett

1904. Germany
12⅛″ long
5¾″ long
Litho Tin

An American newspaperman, James Gordon Bennett, offered a silver trophy for a race to be contested annually by teams of different nations. The winning nation would hold the race on its soil the following year. The English car won the 1902 race and, fearful of the dangers of racing through the English countryside, England chose Ireland for the 1903 contest.

Colors allocated to competing nations were blue for France, red for the United States, and yellow for Belgium. The decor of the toy shown has special significance. White was Germany's racing color. The green shamrock on the hood stands for Ireland, and a monocle windshield represents a toy produced for the American market. The lines of Germany's entry for 1903, a Mors racer, does not resemble the toy. In creating a marketable product, most toy manufacturers took liberties with the designs of real automobiles they were copying. Nevertheless, the racer has pleasing lines.

This toy was sold through hardware outlets in America in 1904; a common practice since most buyers were men.

A hunched-over driver, the mechanic at his side, peers through the monocle windshield. Racers intended for the European market often came with a horn mounted on the lower right cowl to replace the windshield. All larger size models steer from the right side and perform a figure eight.

The Gordon Bennett racer was sold in several sizes. Larger racers operate by a clockword mechanism. The smaller racer shown is propelled by a flywheel. Gordon Bennett racers are particularly collectible due to their historical significance.

440.
GUNTHERMANN
Three-Seat Limousine

1907. Germany
7½″ long
Litho Tin

A small limousine, with number 10 on the hood, sports miniature lamps, luggage rack, and finely-detailed lithography. Another version was made with passengers in military uniforms.

441.
GUNTHERMANN
Renault Runabout

1907. Germany
7⅛″ long
Painted and
Litho Tin
Windup

A tufted-pattern seat of solid cast metal adds weight and extra workmanship to this toy, and incorporates details which are usually found on the luxury models of Marklin and Bing.

Renault was one of Europe's most prestigious automakers and also one of the earliest manufacturers, dating from 1898. The French company built quiet, reliable and fast cars that were a favorite subject of German toy makers. In 1907 Renault Frères maintained an American branch at Broadway and 57th Street in New York City.

442.
GUNTHERMANN
Taxi

c. 1908. Germany
10″ long
Litho Tin.
Windup

Larger tin cars like this glass windowed taxi were adapted with extras, such as opening doors, glass windows, and a bellows which could emit a horn-like sound. A long-running wind-up motor was an added plus. Small packages and play luggage store nicely in the roof rack.

A special braking system on this toy is operated by a lever with a small wheel attached at its base. Connected to the rear running axle, it is released when the toy is placed on the floor. Often found on Gunthermann toys, the same mechanism was later used on Bub, Fischer and Tipp cars.

443.
GUNTHERMANN
Open Limousine Taxi

c. 1911. Germany
11½″ long
Litho Tin
Windup

Gunthermann extended their product line by producing this toy with the top up, the top down, and in smaller sizes. Glass partition and windshield, opening doors, rubber tires, and separate headlamps help create an impression of quality. Gunthermann added a wood and paper bellows located underneath the toy to create the horn sound, though the actual horn is not in evidence.

This maker had a preference for attached keys on lithographed tin windup and clockwork automobiles, though he used separate keys for his earlier, large and most expensive painted tin models.

445.
GUNTHERMANN
Double-decker Bus

1931. Germany
14″ long
Litho Tin

New York was the first American city to use buses for transporting paying customers in the 1890s. The double-decker buses used along Fifth Avenue in the 1920s were styled after those in use in London.

This bus has London styling with the driver and rear stairs arranged for driving on the left hand side of the road. An F. A. O. Schwarz import, the toy has seats on both decks, a strong clockwork motor, and headlights which operate by batteries. Large double wheels keep the bus steady. A child, happy to own such a big, colorful bus, is not likely to question the name 'General' on the side or the placement of doors.

← 444.
BUB
Limousine

1912. Germany
8½″ long
Litho Tin
Windup

A typical closed limousine with opening doors. This type of toy car was so basic it remained unchanged for many years. Bub produced it in a variety of sizes and colors and optional extras were lights and glass windows.

GUNTHERMANN
Touring Car

c. 1910. Germany
8″ long
Litho Tin

Wire roof braces and flat, stamped, tin, lithographed side lamps are vulnerable parts on a cheap toy. Extending the product line, the manufacturer produced the same model with the top folded down, thus eliminating the roof wires; however, the cheaply made side lamps did not last long either.

The cars drive beneath a rare, clockwork, Hubley elevated railway patented in 1893. The train moves at a high speed on the circular sheet metal track passing under cast iron arches with the aid of a central clockwork motor.

↗ 446.
GUNTHERMANN
Classic Limousine

c. 1932. Germany
18″ long
Litho Tin
Clockwork

The incorporation of all the latest features is typical of a classic 1930s car. A canvas roll-back top, double bumpers, opening doors, 'electric' lights, and an opening trunk, gives importance to a brilliantly colored limousine.

The actual designation 'classic car' refers to cars of specific make and year deemed worthy of the term by the Classic Car Club of America. These cars were mainly luxury cars of their period from 1925 through 1942. The list includes both American and European makes.

447.
HAUSSER
Anti-aircraft Auto Truck

1933. Germany
13½" long
Tin, with figures
by Elastolin

A deluxe, clockwork military toy with an air defense gun which can be elevated to a vertical position by means of a wheel at the side. Shooting rubber plugs for projectiles, the gun uses paper caps as ammunition and revolves on its base at the same time.

The finely detailed, all metal construction vehicle has seats that lift for storage in addition to concealed storage compartments at the side of the car, one of which reveals the stem for winding the spring. The spools on the front and rear were used to transport wire.

There was no need to import paper caps into the United States. They were readily available from sources such as the Kilgore factory in Ohio. Sheets of paper caps were often cut and rolled in the homes of neighborhood families on hand operated rollers as a cottage industry. Together with firecrackers, they were banned from use in most states from the early 1920s. For this reason, toys using explosive paper caps had limited sales in the U.S. and are scarcely found objects today.

Lehmann

The company of Ernst Paul Lehmann was one of the most prolific German manufacturers of lithographed tin toys. His colorful, painted and lithographed tin wind-up toys were among the huge number of imports reaching America before the effects of the First World War broke the German monopoly in the American toy market.

Lehmann toys were unique designs which were patented here and abroad. 95% of the Lehmanns were earmarked for export, though not all for the U.S.

The Lehmann auto vehicles were among the best sellers, intriguing children for several decades with toys of unequalled quality and action.

← 448. 1907. Germany
HESS 10″ long
'Hessmobile' Racer Litho Tin

The flywheel-driven motor is concealed beneath the removeable undulating hood cover. The separate hood and hinged trunk lid increases the liklihood of parts being missing. A substitute driver tends the car, while a German lithographed tin saxaphone player squeeze toy provides entertainment with cymbals and rolling eyes. The black musician was made expressly for export.

449. 1904–14.
LEHMANN Germany
Runabout Cars 4″ long
  Litho Tin

A fleet of runabouts exhibit variations on a very successful model in the Lehmann line of early automobiles. One boy steers a flywheel propelled car of 1904. The small, brightly lithographed tin toys were imported in vast quantities. They were listed for 85¢ to 95¢ a dozen in the pages of Butler Brothers wholesale catalog, probably the largest wholesale firm in America at the time.

← 450.
LEHMANN
'Uhu' Amphibian
Automobile

1907. Germany
9½" long
Litho Tin
Windup

The boat-automobile runs in a circle while the head of the driver swivels too. Paddles on wheels are an ingenious idea that was still imaginary in 1906.

↓ 451.
LEHMANN
'EHE' Truck
'Panne' Tourer
'ITO' Sedan

c. 1911–14.
Germany
6¾" long
6¾" long
6¾" long
Litho Tin
Windup

American toy designs, copied only the simplest automobiles during the first quarter of the twentieth century. For the most part, these toys kept their unadorned, elementary look in direct contrast to German imports which were formed from tin in more intricate ways. The very nature of the lightweight tin coupled with German know-how, resulted in special metal formations which embodied refined workmanship. At the same time, production methods were more advanced, enabling the Germans to produce a cheaper toy.

EHE wholesaled for $2.00 per dozen in 1914. The auto dray can be set to run in circles.

ITO, the limousine with open spoke wheels, was offered for 19¢ by Sears, Roebuck & Co. in 1912.

452.
LEHMANN
'IHI' Meat Van
Mail Van
'AHA' Truck

1908–13.
Germany
6¾" long
5¼" long
5¼"
Litho Tin
Windup

Cloth drop-side curtains were used to protect meat from dust and dirt in the days before refrigerated products in enclosed metal vans. Early vans were used to transport meat short distances.

The yellow truck bears a European postal insignia. Until worldwide travel became known, it is doubtful whether the average U.S. citizen would have been aware of this detail when the toy was sold in America.

The AHA was made with and without a driver. Opening rear doors are a fine detail on a small, inexpensive truck. Lehmann's serious attention to minute details earned it a reputation for excellent value for money in the U.S. and a fair share of the toy market all over the world. Lehmann toys were sold in Mexico, South America, Australia, South Africa, England, and Europe.

454.
LEHMANN
'Tut-Tut'

c. 1905. Germany
7″ long
Litho Tin
Windup

A long time favorite of retailers, the fat man in a nice runabout steers an irregular course while blowing a horn. A pair of paper and wood bellows works the horn 'toot-toot' from which noise the toy got its name. Selling for 39¢ in 1905 through 1912, the toy is not rare; however, collectors have made it a favorite collectible. It was featured in the Christmas 1905 Boston Store catalog (Chicago, Illinois).

LEHMANN
'Baldur' Automobile

1920. Germany
10″ long
Litho Tin
Windup

One of Lehmann's larger automobiles in colors representing a taxi-limousine.

Lehmann proudly marked this car on all four sides *plus* the wheels.

LEHMANN
'Autin' car

c. 1914. Germany
4″ long
Litho Tin
Windup

A boy drives his soapbox delivery cart. A simple toy which sold well.

→ **455.**
LEHMANN
Postal Truck

1933. Germany
7⅛″ long
Litho Tin
Windup

The postal truck bearing the Nazi emblem of Hitler's regime was kept hidden in its box by an American owner during the Second World War. Possession of German toys was considered unpatriotic by many Americans while the war raged in Europe, especially one marked with a Nazi emblem.

In my early collecting days, I was able to acquire many German-made toys with the name of the country deliberately scratched off the toy with a pin, leaving only the words 'Made in'. Japanese toys received equal treatment at the hands of patriots. If you find a toy today in such a condition, you can be sure it was made in one of these two countries.

Lehmann modernized its 1927 delivery van with a change in color and name to Deutsche Reichspost, copying the change on the real post office trucks in 1933.

← **453.**
LEHMANN
'Autobus'

c. 1908. Germany
8″ long
Litho Tin
Windup

The most detailed tin bus of its type, Lehmann's double-decker contains seats on the top deck which are reached by a delicate spiral stairway.

This was certainly the most beautiful tin bus offered by Sears, Roebuck in 1912 for 37¢. An all-time favorite when new, the toy enjoys equal popularity today with collectors.

457.
LE RAPIDE
Auto-Train

Early 1930s.
France
16½″ long
Cast metal

The toy is modeled from a real auto-train using a Hispano-Suiza for the conversion.

456.
RAUH
Horseless Carriage

1904. Germany
4″ long
Litho Tin

Mail order catalogs catered for families in rural areas where automobiles were rarely seen in the early 1900s. Once an automobile ran over one of his chickens, a farmer wanted no part of the new-fangled contraptions!

Sears, Roebuck listed just one toy automobile in its 1904 catalog. It was this flywheel-driven horseless carriage. The toy still carries its original 25¢ price tag. Scaled just a little larger than a penny toy, the price was nonetheless high, but without competition, the toy was a curiosity and saleable. Sears featured the toy for four continuous years.

Sharing space in this paper-on-wood German stable is a French painted tin carriage, predecessor to the car.

The bird waits patiently for the car to be washed!

This train was used primarily to move military troops in Europe.

Famous for early racing successes and royal patronage, the Hispano-Suiza is regarded mainly as a French make, although, as the name suggests, its origins are Spanish and Swiss. Designed by Swiss engineer, Marc Birkigt, a factory was established in Paris in 1911 to assemble Hispano-Suizas, supplying a rich French market until it folded in 1938.

The toy copies the armored plate body fastened with rivets which was used on the real train. Michelin tires were fitted on the wheels.

Monsieur Bibendum, the famous Michelin Tire man, is cast iron and once held the tubing for an air compressor. An example of early automotive advertising, he represents a stack of pneumatic tyres. Bibendum supposedly ate nails, glass and horseshoes without the slightest risk to his health!

459. ↘
RISSMAN
'Topsy Turvy Tom'

1926–7.
Germany
10″ long
Litho Tin
Windup

The roll-over car is lithographed in bright patches of color. It copies one actually used by clowns to entertain circus viewers between high wire acts. The #13 on the radiator emphasizes the sort of luck associated with clowns.

The intriguing windup mechanism was a complex contraption devised to confuse the best of boy mechanics. The biggest wonder is that it still operates. When running, the car rolls over and over.

The trademark on this toy is a puzzle. It combines the well-known Hans Eberl clown in a circle but with the RI-CO mark of William Rissmann. Both manufacturers were Nuremberg makers of stamped metal toys dating from the early 1900s. It is possible the two companies combined forces during this period.

RI-CO is not to be confused with the Spanish firm of the same name. Topsy Turvy Tom is clearly stamped 'Made in Germany'.

458.
STOCK
Three-Wheel Runabout

c. 1908.
Germany
4¾″ long
Litho Tin
Windup

Women were highly visible drivers in the early 1900s. They chose small, light cars or battery-operated ones which were easily started.

Lightness was the aim of three-wheel cars, where a steering lever guides the vehicle with ease. No reverse was necessary, as the cars turned in a small radius. Quick, economical transportation for short distances made three wheelers popular for a while. No need for a garage either, since these cars could be parked under the house or in a shed. In 1906, one manufacturer advertised that the crate which held his car was suitable for use as a garage!

Stock made some charming and colorful windup tin toys, ranging from penny toys with advertising to little automobiles like the one shown. Most were original designs. The runabout sold in the United States for less than 50¢.

461.

MAKER UNKNOWN

Wagonette

1899. France
12″ long
Handpainted
Tin

I've contended for years that I don't have a favorite toy automobile, but I must admit this one is a close contender. One day, I followed a lead on 'an old toy wagon' offered to me by an antiques dealer by phone. I was told the toy could be seen in her shop, which was thirty-eight miles from my home. When I arrived, I was handed the most awful mess you've ever seen. With the wheels barely peeping through, the entire 'wagon' was enveloped with hundreds of yards of package wrapping string; so much, in fact, that our attempts to cut it away with an old dull pair of scissors proved futile. Since the cost of the toy seemed reasonable, I paid for my purchase with the feeling one gets with the buying of a grab bag and hurried home. Tired from the long trip, I placed the huge bundle of string aside for a rainy day when my patience might permit the unraveling.

That day came. At last, tired of trying to peer through the mass of string and cord, I started cutting away at the ball, which measured well over two feet in diameter. The whole time, I was muttering to myself about such a crazy way of saving string. At one point, the mass gave away enough for me to place a finger through an opening. Convinced I had felt a steering wheel was enough to spur me on. When at last the toy was completely uncovered, I was amazed to behold a perfectly beautiful French painted tin depot wagon from the turn of the century.

Note the lily pad step and oddball color combination of red, brown and black. The flooring is painted to resemble woodgraining. A dotted swiss fabric surrey roof cover was copied from a picture of the identical toy in a French catalog, dated 1899. The frilly ruffles are different from the straight fringe found on American surrey tops.

Real depot wagons were used to transport hotel guests to and from the station in the summertime. They were popular through the early 1900s period.

At the turn of the century, toy manufacturers were converting their production of horse-drawn vehicles to motorized toys. This changeover is known as the transitional period. The Wagonette is a perfect example of this period. It also has that unmistakable stamp of fine French workmanship.

P.S. The antiques dealer explained that the toy was formerly owned by a gentleman whose hobby was saving string, starting all of the balls around some object. One ball almost three feet in diameter was sold to a restaurant that planned to place it on display. It was believed to have a large antique wire mouse trap as its center. The former owner in his late eighties was moved to a rest home and is probably still at work wrapping string around things!

460.

TIPP

Open Bus

Mid 1920s.
Germany
11″ long.

Parlour Coach

10¾″ long
Litho Tin
Windup

Tipp offered buses in different versions to cater for a variety of tastes.

294

462.
MAKER UNKNOWN
Motor Hansom
with Dolls

Late 1890s.
France
13″ long
Painted Tin
Clockwork

There were no toys made in America to equal this large French automobile. The bisque-head dolls are an original part of the toy. Their tin torsos fasten them permanently to plush velvet seats.

Expensive when new, due to high tariffs imposed on luxury imports, this type of toy was imported into America in insignificant numbers. They were sold only through exclusive shops in major cities or brought home from Europe as gifts by affluent travelers.

The French excelled in the production of automata, toys which would simulate real-life movements. Bisque heads are used to reinforce the impression of reality. All the charm a French toy can muster is conveyed in this car, whose driver can steer both right and left.

Early electric cars had motors in the rear. The steering wheel was in use in Europe long before America.

463.
MAKER UNKNOWN
Horseless Carriage

c. 1898. France
10″ long
Painted Tin
Clockwork

A French chauffeur inspects a beautiful automobile of delicate and graceful form with tufted silk seats. Propelled by a quality clockwork motor, the vehicle is suitable for holding dolls, making the toy especially appealing to girls as well as boys.

464.
MAKER UNKNOWN
Early Runabout

c. 1900. France
6¼″ long
Painted Tin
Pull Toy

Early French tin automobiles are constructed with soldered seams. They have a delicate look which is even more pronounced when fragile dolls are placed in the driver's seat. The bisque-head chauffeur with driver's cap is an original part of the toy and is rarely found intact as shown.

Large rear wheels indicate a transitional period vehicle.

465.
MAKER PROBABLY
JOUETS DE PARIS
Touring Car

Early 1900s.
France
12″ long
Wood Body
Clockwork

An intriguing Renault, whose tonneau-style body combines wood, tin, and tufted pink silk upholstery. The lamps are castings and the front wheels can be set to run in circles. Despite the potpourri of materials used to produce this clockwork car, it is well made and pleasing to the eye.

A special feature of better early French-made vehicles is the enormous amount of handwork necessary for assembly, installing upholstery, and hand painting when compared with the metal stamped parts found on German cars.

A wonderful 9½″ high clown with dancing puppets was made to be sold in the New Orleans French Quarter around 1913. Representing a Mardi Gras reveler in costume, the head of the clown is painted composition. His tin body holds a windup motor which provides the up and down movement for the articulated lithographed tin boy and girl. Once again, bearing in mind the variety of different substances used, it would be difficult to classify the toy by material. Lead and wood (though not visible) is also used.

466.
**MAKER PROBABLY
JOUETS DE PARIS**
Deluxe Limousine

c. 1908. France
15″ long
Painted Tin
Clockwork

Bent wire work, delicately pierced tin and molded edging help identify this car as distinctly French. Seldom is a car this size and age found with all its parts intact, a tribute to the care it has received.

Like most French cars of quality, the rear seat is upholstered and the windows are glass. It was designed as a toy for the wealthy, as was the real car.

The limousine tours Philadelphia with City Hall in sight.

467.
MAKER UNKNOWN
Roly-Poly Chauffeur

1914. Germany
3¾″ high
Composition
and Papier
Maché

Papier maché dates back to the time of ancient Egypt. It was first used to line and decorate coffins of the Pharoahs. The raw material was taken from papyrus pith by Egyptians, Greeks and Romans to make paper. Centuries later, it is still in use worldwide.

Papier mache toys and dolls faded from use when labor costs started to outweigh this substitute for conventional materials.

Roly-Polys were popular from the early 1900s to the mid-1920s. Rarely are they seen with a driver's cap and goggles. Ours wears a silly grin and does his driving on tin wheels. He sold for 45¢.

469.
MAKER UNKNOWN
Cloverleaf roadster

Mid-1930s.
Probably
German
13″ long
Litho Tin

This roadster with a windup motor has a unique cloverleaf seating arrangement to accommodate three passengers. Many 'ragtop' owners were extroverts who wished to be seen and noticed. The convertible top is not visible on this toy, although a car of this type and vintage would have had a top of some sort. Many were made to drop into a concealed space. Convertibles and roadsters with fold-down tops evoke a special aura of youth and nostalgia.

Construction appears to be of German manufacture, probably for the English trade.

The license plate bears the initials I.S.

← **468.**
MAKER UNKNOWN
'Jellus Autopolo'

c. 1917.
Germany
6½″ long
Litho Tin
Windup

An unusual toy in subject matter as well as design. Polo played from an automobile is unknown in this country, but must have existed someplace, at some time, in order for a designer to have composed a toy with this theme. I can only imagine the car crashes that resulted from this seemingly impossible game! But then, cars have been used for crazier things.

The windup motor assisted by a pivotal front axle moves the car in a totally erratic fashion as one would imagine. The player's loose arm swings from the rocking motion.

Possibly the prototype action was later copied by Marx for his Whoopee cars of the late 1920s and 1930s.

Restoration & Repair

470.
ARCADE
Mack Tank Truck

1929. USA
12¾″ long
Cast Iron
with Tin Tank

The last all cast iron Mack tank truck was made in 1928 and did not hold water. In 1929, this toy was introduced with a tank that appears to have been adapted from an actual can. Its play value was increased by holding water. Two domes on the tank are dummies while the third has a cap that unscrews for filling. Water is drained by a rubber hose from the rear. In 1930, the toy tank was redesigned with three filler openings and caps.

When I acquired this tanker, it was because of its transitional interest. However, there

was a problem. The tank looked as if it had been run over by a real Mack truck! I was searching for a way to restore and preserve the original part when a friend came up with an offer to help. He would seal the openings and used compressed air to blow the smashed can into shape. To make a long story short, it worked, greatly improving the tank but still leaving serious folds in the tin. I must caution readers at this point that this procedure should not be attempted by anyone but the most experienced. It could be dangerous . . . for you as well as the toy!

'Too much air and we might have an explosion,' my friend warned, so we decided to stop while we still had a whole tank.

A few days later, a friend who collects

advertising stopped by for a friendly chat. He related a story of finding a rare gun powder can which was creased. By filling it with water and freezing it, the can had returned to its original form.

You guessed it. Into the freezer went the tank, cast iron chassis and all, where it remained under watchful eyes for several days. When it came out of the freezer, all that was left to do was connect a hose to the drain hole for melting ice. There will always be a few lines, but we all acquire those with age!

Herewith we present the Mack Tank Truck – rarity superseding its poor condition.

This model was made for only one year – 1929, a year more remembered for its stock market crash.

471.　　　　　　　　　1936. USA
ARCADE　　　　　　　6¼″ long
'Borden's' Milk　　　　Cast Iron
Bottle Truck

The bottle truck was typical of special-bodied trucks built on a 6-cylinder Dodge chassis by private body companies that specialized in advertising oddities.

The bottle was made for other milk companies in addition to Borden and could be custom ordered with personalized names from Arcade.

The one shown here was not a special order but was carried in Arcade's 1936 catalog. The name 'Borden's' is cast on the side. It retailed for 25¢.

Special tires with a deep patterned tread and painted centers were fitted on the original toy. The wooden wheels and rubber tires are necessary substitutes until the correct replacements can be found.

Perfectionists have been known to acquire a toy simply for the wheels. After removing the originals and replacing them with reproductions, they then sell the toy. A scarcity of antique toys will soon eliminate this practice.

I am from the school that frowns on this habit. I would much rather reproduction rubber tires were made to the exact specifications of the original ones. Wheels, if they are excellent new castings can do service until original ones come along. That goes for drivers and figures, as well. As long as there is no effort made to deceive anyone, the toy will give more pleasure if it looks good while waiting for original spare parts.

472 & 473.　　　　　　1923. USA
KENTON　　　　　　　7½″ long
Yellow Taxi　　　　　　Cast Iron

Sloping windshields hinged for ventilation first appeared in 1920. Kenton utilized this newest automotive innovation in its closed cars for 1923.

Overpaint was removed from the taxi to determine its true condition and appearance. Smaller taxis are for some reason, rarer than larger ones and warrant the effort and expense to bring them back to their original state. If the removal reveals no paint whatsoever, then nothing is lost; it can be repainted and you'll be back where you started.

Be ready to expect other revelations, however; repainting sometimes conceals repairs or reproduced toys or parts. The novice should learn to recognize the outlines and forms of reproduced toys and carry a

magnet for checking cast iron toys. Providing the toy is not an original brass pattern, the magnet will help detect epoxy or lead parts.

First and most important, make absolutely certain the toy is worth restoring. The best toy restorers are few and far between. They are also very expensive. Most are toy collectors themselves who prefer to work on better toys. If the toy is worthy of the time and money spent, it also warrants correct restoration, original paint colors, and fine recasting of parts.

Professional toy restorers have both the tools and the knowledge to prepare a rare or scarce toy for posterity. The owner will be proud to display such a toy once it is finished.

When paint is removed from a run-of-the-mill toy to discover bare iron – stop there. Unless you are experienced, do not try paint removal. It is delicate, tedious work best left to the experts. They know when the original coat of paint, if it still exists, has been reached.

Kenton used a type of paint on their early toys that flakes with age. No undercoat was used and though it was described as an enamel, the oils dried with time. For this reason the removal of overpaint on Kenton toys is an even more precarious job because the chemicals used in the process can cause further drying of the original coat of paint.

Careful thought should be given to Kenton toys before attempting any work on them.

→
474.
MAKER UNKNOWN
Live Steam Touring Car

Early 1920s.
12¾″ long
Painted Tin & Brass

By 1922 steam had been used to operate not only over 125 makes of automobile but trucks, buses, a motorcycle and even an airplane. Cars included such makes as Doble, Grout, Locomobile, Ross, Lane, White, Delling, Toledo and Stanley. There were others, but the one that stands foremost in American's minds is the Stanley.

One steam-operated car that received tremendous publicity when it was introduced in 1922 was the Coats. Made only in a touring model, the car was not a successful venture and folded in 1923.

Both the Coats and the Stanley Steamer resembled each other outwardly and closely resemble the steam toy shown here. The steam engines were housed under a conventional hood with a flat radiator. Copying the real cars, the toy piston connects gears driving the rear axle.

This toy was acquired devoid of paint except for a few specks here and there which helped determine the original color and door outlines. One wheel was missing and the fold-down top was smashed. This car was a dilapidated toy whose only future lay in restoration. Until recent years, the restoration of antique toys was unacceptable to toy car collectors but with the scarcity of better toys and the number of collectors on the rise, the restoration procedure is putting more good old toys back into circulation. With them comes a new breed of toy restorers and those who can provide various missing parts. These are now being mass-produced and help to avoid a handmade look on a machine produced toy. Decalcomanias for the most popular makes of toys are also being reproduced.

Antique toy collectors have long known that the new-in-the-box toy seldoms exists. We have inherited playthings from children and with that goes the penalty of a much-used and usually well-loved item, one that could have been passed from generation to generation and most likely from one child to another in the same family. Unlike the family silver and china, toys tend to receive much rougher treatment than other things one inherits.

This steam car was sent to a restorer of toys. The list of estimates reads like one for a real car: clean upholstery, straighten metal, determine colors and striping from chips and make tracings before removal of chips, replace wheel and matching hubcap, order tire, polish brass hood, check engine for working order, etc.

Every effort was made to ensure the car would be returned to its original condition and color. Care was taken not to over-restore. Eighteen months later, the bill arrived. It read like one from Tiffany.

For anyone considering a restoration on any toy, first determine that the toy is worth

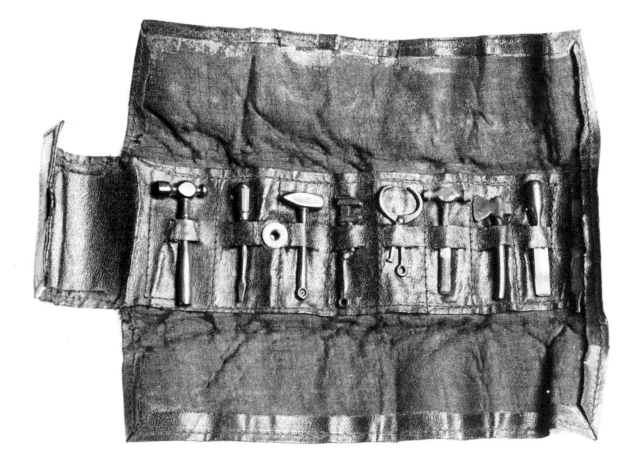

the expense and trouble. Second, get an appraisal before starting work. Last, get a firm commitment on the time required or set a time limit.

→
475.   1925. USA
KENTON   7½" long
Roadster   Cast Iron

Once introduced, this car rolled on and continued in production through the late 1920s. The seat is level with the tops of the doors, perhaps an intentionally comical arrangement. Luckily, Kenton didn't add a roof!

The paint is original. The crazing happened a long time ago, and has the appearance of paint which dried too fast, causing shrinkage. But, who can be certain about 50 year old paint?

Early Kenton automobiles must be cleaned and washed with the utmost care. The paints have a high incidence of not only flaking and peeling, but also color running.

I recall the first 1910 fire patrol I scrubbed clean in my early collecting years. The car was white, but under so much dirt, the white was not discernible to the eye until scrubbed.

I placed the soapy toy in the sink and ran clean water over it to rinse off the soap, looking with horror as the entire toy shed its coat of paint like a snake. The paint went glub-glub down the drain and that was that!

We profit by our mistakes and I have been very cautious when cleaning Kenton toys since that time. However, though I find there is a greater tendency for early red and yellow colors to run, all colors should be checked underneath the toy. It is best not to expose unpainted surfaces to water which cannot be quickly dried. Rust can form or the moisture will lift the remaining paint if the toy is not dried immediately. A convenient tool for drying toys is a small hand-held hair dryer. The heat can be regulated and moisture in crevices quickly dried.

American Manufacturers

US Patent Issue Dates

Where patent numbers are given on a toy or its box, the year of issue can be traced by using the following chart. This is an aid in dating a toy.

Year	Patent Number	Year	Patent Number
1860	26,642	1918	1,251,458
1861	31,005	1919	1,290,027
1862	34,045	1920	1,326,899
1863	37,266	1921	1,364,063
1864	41,047	1922	1,401,948
1865	45,685	1923	1,440,362
1866	51,784	1924	1,478,996
1867	60,658	1925	1,521,590
1868	72,959	1926	1,568,040
1869	85,503	1927	1,612,790
1870	98,460	1928	1,654,521
1871	110,617	1929	1,696,897
1872	122,304	1930	1,742,181
1873	134,504	1931	1,787,424
1874	146,120	1932	1,839,190
1875	158,350	1933	1,892,663
1876	171,641	1934	1,944,449
1877	185,813	1935	1,985,878
1878	198,733	1936	2,026,510
1879	211,078	1937	2,066,309
1880	223,211	1938	2,101,004
1881	236,137	1939	2,142,080
1882	251,685	1940	2,185,170
1883	269,820	1941	2,227,418
1884	291,016	1942	2,268,540
1885	310,163		
1886	333,494		
1887	355,291		
1888	375,720		
1889	395,305		
1890	418,665		
1891	443,987		
1892	466,315		
1893	488,976		
1894	511,744		
1895	531,619		
1896	552,502		
1897	574,369		
1898	596,467		
1899	616,871		
1900	640,167		
1901	664,827		
1902	690,385		
1903	717,521		
1904	748,567		
1905	778,834		
1906	808,618		
1907	839,799		
1908	875,679		
1909	908,436		
1910	945,010		
1911	980,178		
1912	1,013,095		
1913	1,049,326		
1914	1,083,267		
1915	1,123,212		
1916	1,166,419		
1917	1,210,389		

Research into the origins and histories of old toy companies continues to progress. During the past ten years, we have learned more than ever before about the background of these businesses. It is my hope that this research will continue to supplement and perhaps in some cases correct information revealed to date. When the records are complete, it will have been the work of many people. If by this book I have increased the knowledge about toy cars and their makers, then I feel I will have fulfilled my share of the work.

Lillian Gottschalk

ACME TOY WORKS,
Chicago, Illinois
1903–8

The company was founded by Jacob Lauth who produced two patented clockwork toys, a curved dash Oldsmobile and a delivery truck with a canopied roof in pressed steel.

In 1905, he formed J. Lauth & Co. for the production of real automobiles. As Lauth-Juergens Co. he unveiled a demonstration model of his first car, a five-seat tourer, but production of the automobile did not begin until 1907. The partners moved the firm to Fremont, Ohio, in 1910. Operating under the name Lauth-Juergens Motor Car Company it was engaged solely in the production of commercial vehicles.

When Acme was dissolved in 1908, the toy company had not been active for several years.

ALL METAL PRODUCTS COMPANY
WYANDOTTE TOYS
Wyandotte, Michigan
1920–56

When George Stallings and William F. Schmidt joined to form a company, they originally planned to produce parts for automobiles. Instead, they decided there was a market for toy guns and rifles and embarked on toy production by the fall of 1921. Toy guns would dominate Wyandotte output from 1921 to 1929. Other toys, such as pressed steel airplanes, miniature automobiles, racers, mechanical toys, games, targets, pistol holster sets, and musical tops were also produced. Toys for girls included pressed steel dustpans, baskets and trays, as well as other playhouse toys.

Arthur W. Edwards and Harry Tucker became interested in the corporation and after buying into it took an active role in running the company. Edwards became President and General Manager and ran the company until his death in August 1932. Tucker left the company in early 1925. Edwards was succeeded by his son C. Lee Edwards, and Charles A. Brethen, who served as Secretary.

In 1935, Wyandotte claimed to have sold over 5½ million toy guns, which it shipped all over the world. Its large pressed steel automotive toys with baked enamel finish and battery-operated lights were popular sellers during the 1930s.

In April 1947, William A. Wenner, an employee of the company since 1927, was elected to the Presidency.

In 1950, Wyandotte bought the Hafner Manufacturing Company and continued to produce the Hafner line of trains. A year later, C. Lee Edwards, Mary Reberdyand and the estate of Arthur W. Edwards sold their interests to a new group of investors who reorganized the company. The new Directors included Morris Birnbaum, Charles Block, Charles Haskill, Allen Morgan, John D. Scarborough and Jacob Shapiro.

Following the latest reorganization, one plant was moved to Martin's Ferry, Ohio, another to Pequa, Ohio, and another sold to the McCord Corporation for its gasket division.

In 1955, C. Lee Edwards and William Wenner wished to retire and sold their remaining company stock, which they had accepted as part of the 1951 sale. The company was facing serious financial difficulty at this time.

Louis Marx reportedly purchased some of the Wyandotte product lines along with the Hafner dies and sent them to his factory in Mexico; thereby eliminating the possibility of anyone else using the dies in competition with Marx trains.

All Metal Products filed for bankruptcy November 6, 1956.

AMERICAN NATIONAL COMPANY,
Toledo, Ohio
c. 1894
Motto: 'Raise the Kiddies on wheels'.

Manufacturers of coaster wagons, tricycles, toy wheelbarrows, scooters, bicycles and other sidewalk toys, it produced a line of juvenile vehicles of outstanding quality and variety starting about 1912. By the mid-1920s, the line was extensive, and the company owned three factories: the American Metal Wheel Company in Toledo, the National Wheel Company in Perrysburg, Ohio and the Witzler Wood Work Company, also in Perrysburg, where parts were made.

In the late 1920s and early 1930s, the company produced a line of pressed steel toy trucks, including a Bulldog Mack, in competition with Buddy L and Keystone. But the toys were no match for its competitors whose reputations were already long established. These large indoor-outdoor toys with the brand name 'Giant' were phased out in the early 1930s.

Founded by brothers William, Walter and Harry Diemer, the company remained active through the early 1930s.

ANDES FOUNDRY COMPANY
Lancaster, Pennsylvania
1919–29

Eugene B. Andes, a machine designer, founded the company with orders for paper caps from the Kilgore Company of Westerville, Ohio, makers of cap guns and toys. Andes designed and built the machines necessary to produce the caps. Prospering, the company soon moved to larger quarters and eventually started to produce its own line of cap guns with patents on several original designs. To make the cast iron components for the cap pistols, a foundry was rented for company use. In May, 1922, it was completely destroyed by fire, ruining at the same time patterns from other companies which Andes jobbed as fill-ins. Hubley came to its aid and supplied the necessary parts in time for the 4th of July business. When Hubley continued to raise its prices, Andes became annoyed and promptly returned to the foundry business, building a new plant which was operating by 1923. Andes was again given orders from Kilgore and continued to supply the Ohio company with parts and caps.

In 1927, Kilgore approached Andes with a merger offer. The merger combined Andes with Kilgore and the Federal Manufacturing Company. It was agreed that Federal would produce the cap pistols and its own line, and Andes would make the cast iron toys, handing over all the guns and caps to Kilgore, which they did. These three firms became known as 'American Toys'.* Shortly after, more and more cities began to ban the use of home fireworks including the paper caps. This problem, combined with the poor economy, saw orders diminish to virtually nothing. Old established foundries and businesses were closing daily. It was no time to hang on.

Pressed metal and diecast toys made cast iron obsolete. Diecasting provided more detail, was a less costly and more efficient process and cheaper to produce. American Toys closed, and the merger was dissolved in 1929. Andes continued the foundry after reorganizing the company under the name Andes, Incorporated. It made small cast iron parts on orders from other companies, but no more toys. Mr. Andes died in an accident in 1931.

A 1928 photo of the Andes Foundry shows Kilgore's Arctic Ice Cream truck, stake and dump trucks, buses, wagons, airplanes and a Model T on display. Along with sets of five toys per box, most of the toys in the picture had a 50¢ retail market value per item.

ARCADE MANUFACTURING COMPANY
Freeport, Illinois
1868–1946

When the Novelty Iron Works was founded in 1868 by brothers E. H. and Charles Morgan with the backing of J. B. Hazen, it was one of the first industries in the city of Freeport. Primary products of the company were feed grinders, plows and agricultural products for the surrounding farm community.

Water pumps, windmills, iron sections used for store fronts and flooring and box coffee mills were added to the line in 1884. Moving its operations to a new part of Freeport called the Arcade Addition, the company was incorporated and renamed after the section of town in which it was located in 1885.

In 1893, Arcade was again reorganized when

* Andes continued to cast the Kilgore toys with the Kilgore name on them.

L. L. Mun, Sr. and his son bought into the company. Munn, Sr. was made President and continued in that office until his death in 1908 when he was succeeded by E. H. Morgan, who died in 1928. At this time, L. L. Munn, Jr. took over as President and General Manager. Other officers were B. C. Trueblood, son-in-law of E. H. Morgan, who had been associated with Arcade since 1911; Isaac P. Gassman, Munn, Jr.'s son-in-law, who was with the company from 1918 and H. F. Zartman, with the company from 1920.

In 1884 E. H. Morgan conceived the idea of utilizing scrap lumber from the box coffee mills to make toy coffee mills. These were Arcade's first toys and by 1939 the company manufactured over 300 toy items.

During the 1920s, Arcade designed special molding machines to speed up its output and marketed the machines to other companies, as well.

The company slogan 'They Look Real' was adopted in the 1920s, in keeping with its program and policy to adopt the shape and color of articles and vehicles from real life as models for its toys.

Sometime during the 1920s, Arcade became completely mechanized. Toys moved from molding machines to a tumbler where rough edges and sprues were removed. Poorly fitting parts were repaired and parts were plated where required. Moving to an assembly room, the toys were fastened with rivets and then painted either by dipping or spraying. A decal was applied after drying and during the final inspection. Most Arcade toys have the name cast into the toy.

The first cast iron car made by Arcade, the Yellow Cab, was conceived as an addition to Arcade's sideline of toys. It represented only a tiny percentage of the total business at the time. Following the tremendous success of the toy, Arcade quickly recognized the importance of the automobile and concentrated heavily on cars. The company successfully developed what was probably the most important cast iron automotive toy line in America.

Other notable toys by Arcade are farm toys, advertising toys and comic toys (like Andy and Chester Gump), toy banks, trains, doll house furnishings and cast iron penny toys, using many real objects as models.

Arcade was sold to Rockwell Manufacturing Company of Buffalo, N.Y. in 1946. Toy production had ceased in 1942.

GEORGE BORGFELDT & COMPANY
New York, N.Y.
1881–1962

George Borgfeldt formed a partnership with brothers Marcell and Joseph L. Kahle for the purpose of importing as wholesalers. The company obtained exclusive rights for the manufacture of copyrighted toys and subcontracted for their production, using 'Nifty', a smiling moon face, as the company trademark.

Toys and novelties were made to Borgfeldt's

specifications under a 'no name' identity, so that the manufacturer could not mark the toy with its own name or trademark. A few years ago, paper boxes for the cast iron Toonerville Trolley were found stacked in the closed Dent factory. The Dent name was imprinted on the boxes, along with the 'Nifty' trademark. Could they have been rejected by Borgfeldt as a violation of its company policy?

In 1900, Borgfeldt resigned and moved to Europe. His partners continued the diverse business, manufacturing toy candy containers, dolls, cast iron, wood and tin toys, all subcontracted to its order. The Toonerville Trolley and Highway Henry are two famous Borgfeldt toys.

Felix the Cat, Maggie and Jiggs, and Creeping Buttercup were other comic toys ordered and sold by Borgfeldt in the 1920s. Gibbs toys made in Canton, Ohio, used the firm as its New York representative. During the First World War, the company stocked paper novelties, glass candy containers and wooden toys. The firm closed around 1962.

The line of 'Oh Boy' pressed steel cars and trucks was specially fabricated under the control of Borgfeldt & Co.

Borgfeldt represented Margarete Steiff in America.

MILTON BRADLEY COMPANY
Springfield, Massachusetts
1860 to present

The Milton Bradley Company was founded in 1860. It produced a wide range of games and toys, including the Bumpalow Garage.

BUDDY 'L'

Moline Press Steel Company	1910
Moline Pressed Steel Company	1913
Buddy 'L' Manufacturing Company	1930
East Moline Toy Company	1936
Buddy 'L' Wood Products Company, Glens Falls, N.Y.	1944
Buddy L Corporation	1960
	to present

Founded by Fred A. Lundahl, to manufacture stamped steel fenders and parts for International Harvester trucks. Utilizing the scraps of 20-gauge auto body steel left over at the factory, Lundahl made his son Buddy a little doll table and chairs. To distinguish him from all the boys named Buddy in the neighborhood, Lundahl's boy was called Buddy L. He was four years old in 1920 when his father brought home an open bed, open cab, pickup truck he had made in a reduced scale, using the International truck as a model. When Buddy L's friends saw the sturdily built replica of a real truck, they immediately clamored for Mr. Lundahl to make them one. In 1921, Lundahl presented to his son the same truck with a dump bed for extra play value, and the interest it raised in the neighborhood inspired Lundahl to investigate the possibility of merchandising the toy.

After he called on F. A. O. Schwarz in New York and Marshall Field & Company in Chicago, with samples of the trucks and a steam shovel, the stores were enthusiastic enough to place huge orders.

The first Buddy L toys were introduced to the trade in September of 1921, in time for the Christmas season. The truck parts business was continued along with the toys while sales offices were established for the latter. The toy business was an immediate success and soon outgrew the truck parts business, until the factory converted completely to toy production in 1923.

The line of Buddy L cars and trucks continued to grow and prosper. In 1926, there were 29 different toys offered for the season. Cranes, steam rollers, cement mixers, and a tugboat had joined the toy line by the late 1920s. The trucks continued to copy real International Harvester designs and changed their appearance in the early 1930s with new pressed steel wheels and rubber tires. They made the most dramatic change in 1935, when electric headlamps were added to totally redesigned trucks with bright metal radiators. Proving they were strong enough to ride, removable saddle-seats were added to some trucks and a removable handle for steering from the back. Tandem trailers made up the 1935 Buddy L Overland trailer truck, and a six-wheel Railway Express truck with a Wrigley Chewing Gum advertisement on the sides of the trailer was a highlight of the toy line that year.

Hydraulic lifts appeared on some toy trucks throughout the years. When Fred Lundahl died in 1930, J. W. Bettendorf bought control of the company. The company struggled along with newly designed, lower cost toys, but it was continually plagued with financial difficulties, until it was dissolved by court order in June, 1939.

During the Second World War, the supply of metal was requisitioned for defense use, and toy manufacturers looked for ways to supply a market badly in need for toys on the home front. Henry Katz and his partner Milton Klein produced wooden Buddy L automotive toys, including a Town and Country Chrysler station wagon and a DeSoto Yellow Taxi from 1942 to 1946. They operated under the name Buddy 'L' Wood Products Co., in Glens Falls, New York. The public lost interest in the wood toys the moment the war ended.

Toys were manufactured from light-weight steel during the 1950s. The quality and workmanship suffered by comparison with the company's earlier toy products, and the toys failed to sell in appreciable numbers. Again, the company reorganized to form the Buddy L Corporation.

In 1964, the company began the manufacture of pressed steel barbecue grills, which were sold through hardware and chain stores. The company moved its operation from Moline to Neosho, Missouri, in 1969, where it continued the production of Buddy L toys. The barbecue business was sold in 1974.

Buddy L toys of the 1920s were the very first heavy-gauge steel playthings geared for outdoor use that were copies of a real truck. It was the beginning of an industry that was widely copied, providing youngsters with outstanding playthings, of great realism and a long-lasting quality product.

BUFFALO TOY & TOOL WORKS
Buffalo, New York
1924–68

The company was organized in 1924 for the production of tools, dies and metal stampings. Frank R. Labin was named General Manager. During the 1920s and 1930s, Buffalo marketed a line of light-weight, lithographed, pressed steel toys and games. Some were activated by a spiral rod connected to the spring. These included aeronautical toys, carousels and automotive toys. Toy production was halted during the Second World War. Following the war, the company produced a line of housewares without success. Screw machine products were an addition to the industrial metal stampings produced, but changes in the business climate of the 1960s forced Buffalo to close in 1968.

BUTLER BROTHERS
New York City, New York
1876–1950s

Butler Brothers was not a manufacturer but an important wholesale distributor of general merchandise that finally closed in the 1950s. It sold by catalog to merchants only and carried an extensive line of toys as well are other goods. By 1916, its sample houses were located in 33 cities across the United States. The line included toys from most major manufacturers. Much information can be drawn from the books which include drawings and prices. Often the manufacturer's name was given.

CARLISLE & FINCH COMPANY
Cincinnati, Ohio
1893 to present (Produced toys from 1895–1915)

Robert S. Finch and Morton Carlisle formed a partnership in 1893 to purchase the Cincinnati division of the General Electric Company. Later, Carlisle sold his interests to Finch, but the company retained the original name.

From 1896, the company produced a line of electrical novelties, dynamos, motors, gas engines, battery-operated electric railway trolleys, trains, and accessories such as stations with automatic signals. Boats and automobiles were later added to a line of marine lights, marine engines and home electric systems. Robert Finch was interested in automobiles from the start. Around 1900, he built one for his personal use which he drove to work each day. A products catalog issued by the company in 1900 shows the earliest toy automobile made by Knapp Electric, placing Carlisle & Finch in the position of distributors. Electric toys were a main product line in 1896. The company stressed their educational value. Requested by the U.S. Government to step up production of marine lighting and other products in 1915, the toy line was discontinued.

The company is still in business and owned by the Finch family. It manufactures marine searchlights, rotating lighthouse beacons, and lighting apparatus for shipping vessels.

N.D. CASS
Athol, Massachusetts
c. 1894 to present

Makers of wooden toys, including toy trunks, barns, stables, automobiles and trucks, with and without clockworks. The Company also produced dolls and children's furniture and is still a going business.

CHAMPION HARDWARE COMPANY
Geneva, Ohio
1883–1954 (produced toys from 1930–6)

Founded in 1883 in Cleveland, Ohio, by John A. and Ezra Hasenpflug as the Champion Safety Lock Company. Its first product and the basis for the formation of the company, was a special piece of hardware that locked windows in a partly open position.

In 1902, Champion purchased a building in Geneva, Ohio and after remodeling, moved in January 1903. The company took over a nearby three-story building in 1911 and maintained its old quarters as offices. Taking the name Champion Hardware Company about 1911, the company established an iron foundry three years later. It prospered for the next few years, expanding its line to include builders' hardware.

In 1924, the company expanded again by adding a structure which connected the two buildings. This year, the Hasenpflug family sold its interest in Champion and C. I. Chamberlin, a prominent member of the community and first President of the Geneva Chamber of Commerce,* was elected President of Champion Hardware.

In addition to its own needs, Champion produced cast iron parts for other companies. Contract work became a major part of the overall business. In 1930, so much of this outside business ceased that Champion was forced to seek ways to continue in operation. Chamberlin and the company directors made the decision to produce a line of cast iron toys in order to utilize all the facilities. Sales were mainly to chain and variety stores.

By the time cast iron toys lost favor in the marketplace, the hardware business had revived. Champion ceased toy production in 1936 and returned to the production of builders' hardware on a full time basis. The toys had served their purpose in bridging depression years.

Chamberlin, who was responsible for setting the company on a sound financial course, was elected Chairman of the Board in 1944. He was succeeded

* The Geneva Chamber of Commerce was organized in May 1906.

by Thorpe Miller as President, Treasurer and General Manager. Ralph Maynard became Vice-President, Secretary and Sales Manager.

J. Garfield Brown served as Superintendent until 1918. Guy Wellman held this position from about 1920 to 1944. Both men are credited with contributing much to the success of the company.

Champion filled government contracts during the Second World War. It turned to hardware, once again, following the war. Washington Steel Products, a manufacturer of cabinet hardware bought Champion in 1954 and merged the company with its own operation. Washington is no longer in business.

J. CHEIN & COMPANY
New York, N.Y.
Harrison, New Jersey
1903 until 1948
CHEIN INDUSTRIES
Burlington, New Jersey
1948 to present
(produced toys from 1903 to 1979)

Founded by Julius Chein in 1903, the company started by making lithographed, sheet metal, mechanical toys. An embargo on German toys gave Chein an edge on the American market during the period preceding the First World War. Pioneers in the use of tin lithography for toys, the company later moved from its modest loft quarters to a new location in Harrison, New Jersey, where it remained until 1948. Chein's wife's brother, Samuel Hoffman, took an active part in the business.

The company was always interested in volume, and during the 1920s and 1950s, turned out a profusion of mechanical tin toys in both large and smaller sizes. Mechanical ferris wheels, roller coasters, rocket ride toys, tin banks, automobiles and trucks dominated the line. After Chein was killed in 1926 while horseback riding in Central Park, his wife Elizabeth took control of the company, aided by her brother, Samuel Hoffman. When she passed away in the early 1950s, her brother managed the company until his death in 1975. Hoffman's son-in-law Irving H. Sachs is now President of the company, which is a privately owned family corporation, now known as Chein Industries in Burlington, New Jersey. When Chein acquired the quality line of Ramsburg Pantryware in 1977, its housewares line slowly outgrew the toys. Today, Chein does not produce toys except on a contract basis for chain stores and mail order houses. It is now engaged in the production of metal decorated housewares, metal canisters sets and waste paper baskets. Chein produced its last toy in 1979.

D. P. CLARK & COMPANY
Dayton, Ohio
1898–1909
SCHIEBLE TOY & NOVELTY
1909–1931

Founded by David P. Clark for the manufacture of toys designed and patented by Israel Donald Boyer and his wife, Edith. Using sheet steel and wood bodies and flywheel and friction mechanisms, the company produced a series of trains, novelty toys and automotive toys. William E. Schieble became a partner in the firm in the early 1900s, but in 1909 parted with Clark after constant disagreement. Renamed Schieble Toy and Novelty by the remaining owner, the company continued to prosper until the late 1920s. Schieble declared bankruptcy in 1931.

MORTON E. CONVERSE COMPANY
Winchendon, Massachusetts
1878–1934
Mason & Converse
1878–1883

Converse bought out his first partner and replaced him with his son Atherton D. in 1890. The first toys of the company were wood Noah's Arks, rocking horses, doll furniture, and ABC blocks. Tin beach pails and toy drums were its main products for awhile. The company made blackboards and doll trunks that years later would be continued by Mason & Parker. In 1916, Atherton became one of the founders of the Toy Manufacturers of the U.S.A. and served as its first deputy Vice-President.

Toy automobiles were made by the company in 1895, when they copied transportation used at the 1893 Columbian Exposition, where the Converse Company had a big display. The first automobiles to be made by Converse were of a light, pressed steel. These automobiles and trucks (some with clockworks) are highly regarded toys by collectors. Their simple, honest looks are pure American. Converse made its last tin toys in 1934. The toy factories once covered six acres. Known to tourists as 'Toy Town', the complex was once considered to be the largest wood toy factory in the world.

CORCORAN MANUFACTURING COMPANY
Washington, Indiana
Early 1920s to early 1940s

Founded by Louis A. Corcoran and operating in Cincinnati in the mid-1920s, this company produced a type of baby tender and exerciser called 'Not-A-Toy', which sold through toy stores and a N.Y. distributor, Paragon Furniture Company, Inc. After a move to Indianapolis and again to Washington in 1928, the toy division became a part of a larger company which produced infant care equipment. Large pressed steel toy automobiles and toy trains of jumbo proportions were added from 1933 through 1935. Toys are marked Cor-Cor on the wheels.

The company was re-organized several times during the 1930s and ceased toy production about 1936. The factory was destroyed by fire in 1937 and rebuilt at a new location. The name was changed to Corcoran Metal Products. During the early 1940s, the company produced goods for the military and made auto parts. About 1947, the assets were sold and absorbed by McCord Corporation, maker of auto parts. McCord closed about 1981.

DAYTON FRICTION TOY WORKS
Dayton, Ohio
1909–35

Having parted with Schieble, D. P. Clark formed this company and continued to use the patents of his former partner, leading to long and drawn out lawsuits being filed against him by Schieble. Clark won the suits on a technicality. Before Clark died in 1924, he sold out to Nelson Talbot. When Richard B. Munday became head of Dayton in 1926, he patented a horizontal flywheel and called his toys 'Gyro' after the gyroscope. The company closed in 1935.

DAYTON TOY & SPECIALTY COMPANY
Dayton, Ohio
active 1920s

Maker of 'SON-NY' toys – heavy gauge pressed steel toys up to 24″ long. Operational during the 1920s.

DENT HARDWARE COMPANY
Fullerton, Pennsylvania
1895–1973

The company was formed in 1895 by Henry H. Dent, an English immigrant, and four partners. A previous job as bookkeeper with the Allentown Hardware Company, where he became Superintendent in 1894, had given him insights into the possibility of owning his own firm. Incorporated that same year with Dent as President and Henry P. Newhard as Secretary, the company manufactured refrigerator and cold storage hardware and cast iron toys. The first toys are believed to have been cast in 1898. The company continued to prosper and soon gained a reputation for exceptionally fine quality casting.

Automotive toys produced by Dent in the 1920s are considered by some to be the finest old toys available. Dent will best be remembered for its very personal interpretation of toy cast iron Mack trucks. The designs possess an original quality not found in other manufacturers' toys. The company was one of the first to experiment with cast aluminum in the 1920s, though the toys were not successful.

Dent was unable to compete with a failing market in the early 1930s. An inability to make concessions in quality, together with the fast rising costs of retooling for diecast toys, contributed to the company's decision to cease toy manufacture. In 1956, the Dent family parted with the Newhard family. Each organized again. The Dent family formed the Dent Manufacturing Company in Northampton, Pennsylvania, and Dent Hardware continued to function under the Newhards, once again making refrigerator locks, handles and hinges, with Miles Newhard, son of an original founder, in charge. With his death, the third generation did not have the desire to continue, and the business closed November, 1973. The equipment and remaining stock were auctioned off in January, 1974.

JAMES FALLOWS & SONS
Philadelphia, Pennsylvania
1874 to late 1890s

James Fallows began with Francis, Field and Francis, early makers of tin toys and housewares. Later, he joined C. B. Porter & Company, another tinware manufacturer, as a Superintendent. Fallows designed toys and in 1877 received a patent for a process which enabled him to emboss designs on tin using one process. These decorative designs along with the Fallows trademark help identify his toys. The trademark is 'IXL'.

The 1877 patent date is found embossed around the seat hole of his large, circa 1894, tin automobile along with the letters IXL (fig. 309). The business faded just about the time lithographed tin toys were finding favor.

FREIDAG MANUFACTURING COMPANY
Freeport, Illinois
Mid-1920s

This company produced a line of small to medium size automotive toys in cast iron and aluminum for a few years during the mid-1920s. Other products were jacks and hardware. The line was small, the company short-lived.

GIBBS MANUFACTURING COMPANY
Canton, Ohio
1884 to present

During his youth, Lewis E. Gibbs worked for his father, Joshua Gibbs, an inventor and plow maker. Later, he formed a company to manufacture plows of his own design which he patented. In 1863, Lewis, along with a partner, formed the Bucher & Gibbs Plow Company.

In 1881, Lewis left Bucher & Gibbs to establish the Gibbs Lawn Rake Company, along with his sons Elmer W. and Alvin J. In addition to rakes, the company manufactured hardware specialties.

The Gibbs Manufacturing Company was established in 1884. Lewis was President; Elmer, Vice-President; and Alvin, Secretary-Treasurer. A few years later the product line was expanded to include toys and notions. Lewis continued as President until his death in 1914. The business continued with his sons and a son-in-law, Frederick W. Preyer, who had joined the firm in 1910.

Gibbs manufactured patented, mechanical spinning tops, doll-size wood wagons with cast iron wheels, toys combining lithographed paper-on-wood and metal and advertising toys to order. An extensive line of toys priced retail from 1¢ to 35¢ sustained the company through the difficult years of the depression.

Gibbs is still a going concern.

A. C. GILBERT COMPANY
New Haven, Connecticut
1908–66

Alfred Carleton Gilbert was born in 1884 into a family that traced its genealogy to Elizabethan explorer, Sir Humphrey Gilbert. Entering Yale University Medical School in 1904, he supported himself by doing local magic shows. He delayed his graduation from Yale to compete in the 1908 London Olympics and won a gold medal. He never returned to competitive sports.

Returning to Yale University, he organized the Mysto Magic Company around 1908, with John Petrie, a local resident and machinist who had a mutual interest in magic and could manufacture the magic apparatus. John's father was a locksmith and had a workshop behind his home, which John used to manufacture magic equipment. Manufacturing boxed sets for the wholesale and retail trade was a full-scale business by 1909 when Gilbert graduated from Medical School. After graduation, Gilbert and Petrie continued to design new products, and Gilbert handled sales and promotion. Retail outlets were opened in New York and other cities.

In 1911, Gilbert bought out Petrie and re-organized the company, developing Erector sets and other toys for his company. Gilbert introduced the Erector sets at the Toy Fairs in 1913, with instant success. The first construction toys in America with moving parts and motors, they sold for $1.00 to $25.00, eventually winning a gold medal in 1915 at the Panama Pacific Exposition. Over 30 million would be sold in the next 40 years. In time, Gilbert would buy out his competitors, Richter Anchor Block and the American branch of Meccano. The Richter American branch factory in Brooklyn was taken over by the Alien Property Custodian, a U.S. Government agency, at the time of the First World War. Purchasing the building blocks, Gilbert promoted the toy line under his aegis well into the 1920s.

Gilbert is credited with being the first American toy manufacturer to use large scale advertising in national magazines, beginning in 1913.

Upon reorganization in 1916, the company name was changed to the A. C. Gilbert Company and the organization occupied a five-block square in New Haven, Connecticut, known as Erector Square. Gilbert soon held 150 patents for his products.

Pressed steel toy automobiles and trucks began to be produced around 1914. Following the First World War, Gilbert developed and produced a line of scientific toys with educational value.

In 1916, Gilbert was active in the founding of the Toy Manufacturers of America, and served as its first President. This organization was formed to further the interests of American toy manufacturers during an embargo on German toys and other products as a result of the war in Europe.

In 1938, Gilbert purchased the ailing American Flyer Corporation and moved it from Chicago to New Haven. He completely redesigned the products, keeping only the name, and turned the trains into a successful line once again.

Acquired by the Wrather Corporation about 1961, a change in the economic climate forced Gilbert out of business in 1966. The toy trains were sold to Lionel, who absorbed the line to avoid competition. The remaining company assets were dissolved by Walter E. Heller, a factoring concern, to settle remaining accounts and debts.

GIRARD MANUFACTURING COMPANY
Girard, Pennsylvania
1935–75
Girard Model Works, Inc.
1922–35
The Toy Works
1919–22

In June 1906, Frank E. Wood, a pattern maker from Shadeland, Pennsylvania established himself on Pennsylvania Avenue in Girard, Pennsylvania. His first job was making patterns for the Lake Erie Foundry, which was in an adjacent location. Later, Wood specialized in springs.

One of his customers was the C. E. Carter Company which was owned by Nick Carter, brother-in-law to Harry Ives (Ives toys). A small company, Carter rented space from The Erie Wrench and Tool Company and manufactured toys for Ferdinand Strauss. In later years, the roles of Carter and Girard would be reversed when the Carter Company made parts including formed wire for the Girard Model Works, which was now making toys for Strauss.

By 1919, the company, now named The Toy Works, was engaged in the production of toys. Spinning tops, skates, banks and a walking porter pushing a wheelbarrow led the line. After a fire completely destroyed the factory in 1920, it was rebuilt and the name of the company changed to the Girard Model Works.

The company manufactured mechanical tin toys and pressed steel clockwork automobiles and trucks in the 1920s and 1930s. It subcontracted toys to order for Louis Marx and Ferdinand Strauss in the 1920s. The Gerard sales office was in the Fifth Avenue Building, New York City.

Only a few Girard toys are marked. Motto: 'Making childhood's hour happier'.

During the early 1920s, Frank Wood's son, Clarence, incorporated a business he named the C. G. Wood Company to produce formed metal wire. Fred Zeisenheim, Stanley L. Connell along with Frank and Clarence Wood became associated with the newly formed company. Zeisenheim and Connell were also active in the operation of Girard and together formed in 1928 a stock company to purchase the Girard Model Works from Frank Wood. Connell stayed only until January 1929 when he resigned and moved away to seek a more lucrative business.

A few months later, Girard signed a five year contract with Louis Marx making him a commission agent. Previously, Girard had contracted with Marx to produce toys for them under the Marx label. For the next few years, Girard produced toys for Marx with his label as well as its own line and the company prospered. In July 1930, it was reported the company occupied 23 buildings in three adjacent towns. Selling to chain stores and mail-order houses, the Marx-Girard line consisted mainly of toys selling for 10¢ to $1.00.

In 1933, Louis Marx became a major stockholder. Girard broke with Marx when the contract with him expired in 1934. Girard established its own sales organization and opened a New York office. The Girard factory had become important to Marx for the trains which were a large segment of his business. The trains were developed and produced at the Girard Model Works, along with pressed steel toy automobiles and trucks which were capturing a good portion of business at the time. Until now, Marx had not exercised any authority over the company. At this point, however, Marx and other stockholders took legal action to control Girard and Girard declared bankruptcy in March 1934.

The company was reorganized in March 1935 as the Girard Manufacturing Company. Officers were: S. Boyd Gunnison, President; Wayne E. Dickey, Secretary; Archie Marcus, Treasurer; and Louis and his brother, David Marx as Directors. The Girard Company was directed from New York by the Marx Company, which held a controlling interest and was renamed the Girard Manufacturing Company to avoid confusion with other Marx-owned factories clustered in the same area.

During the Second World War, Girard filled contracts for the government war department, producing mechanisms for bomb fuses. Following the war, it returned to the manufacture of metal wire and toys and, like other Marx factories, was one of the last producers of metal toys, finally giving up in 1972. The new Federal safety rules were partly responsible for the changeover to molded plastic toys. Besides the expense, the laws prevented Marx from reviving old toys as he had done in the past. Quaker Oats acquired Marx's interest in Girard when they bought the Marx Company's American and English toy divisions in 1972. Financial difficulties brought on by a downturn in the toy market forced the end of toy production at Girard in 1975. Warehouse stock continued to be sold in 1976 and after Dunbee-Combex bought the remaining assets from Quaker Oats in 1976, every part that could be assembled into a toy was utilized. These last toys, along with old stock, competitors' samples, prototypes and toys from the company archives were placed on the auction block in sales conducted in 1977 by major auction houses both here and abroad.

Collectors experience difficulty in separating Girard and Marx pressed steel toy cars and trucks of the 1920s and 1930s – with good reason. Production methods and materials were identical, for they were produced by the same factory . . . Girard. To confuse matters even further, it was reported the C. G. Wood Company manufactured pressed steel cars and trucks for Girard when orders exceeded production capacity at the Girard plant. One such toy, a battery-operated coupe with lights was also marketed as a fire chief car with a siren and is well-known to car collectors.

HAFNER MANUFACTURING COMPANY
Chicago, Illinois
1900–50

Hafner's initial business in 1900 used the name Toy Auto Company. Seven (possibly more) tin, automotive clockwork toys were produced and sold through 1907. Listed in the 1904 Chicago City Directory as W. F. Hafner Company, the owner joined with the Edmunds-Metzel Company in 1907 to manufacture trains and mechanical toys. The company became American Flyer Manufacturing in 1910.

Hafner resigned in 1914 to start again on his own, naming his newest venture Hafner Manufacturing Company. His son John, just out of the Navy, joined him in 1918. The Hafner Company was sold in 1950 to All Metal Products Company of Wyandotte, Michigan, makers of Wyandotte Toys. In 1955, Louis Marx acquired the Hafner dies when Wyandotte closed.

HARDWARE AND WOODENWARE MANUFACTURING COMPANY
New York
1907–12

The company was reorganized by investors from the National Novelty Corporation, who purchased Grey Iron Casting, Jones and Bixler, Stevens, Kenton and eleven other toy companies, some purchased from the courts when National failed. They planned a similar operation as National, but this, too, was a failure, going bankrupt in 1909 but continuing to operate under a court order until its dispersal by court sale in 1912.

HARRIS TOY COMPANY
Toledo, Ohio
about 1887–1913

This foundry had a long history associated with other products before it began to produce cast iron toys in the 1880s. To supplement its catalog, Harris acted as jobbers for Hubley, Wilkins, and Dent. Financial difficulties in 1912 resulted in the sale of the company in 1913 to a manufacturer of tubing. Harris never returned to toy production.

N. N. HILL BRASS COMPANY
East Hampton, Connecticut
c. 1889–1960s

A branch of the National Novelty Corp., from 1903–07, in 1905, Hill was combined with the Watrous Manufacturing Company, another bell toy manufacturer. They shared a catalog for cast iron and pressed steel bell toys, incorporating a bell into their design.

The 1945 issue of *Toys and Novelties* lists Hill Brass as a manufacturer of the following goods: bell toys, costume bells, vehicle bells, chime toys, infant toys, horse reins, iron toys, metal pull toys, rattles, steel toys, toy telephones, wood pull toys, stick horses, kindergarten toys, school supplies and target games.

HOGE MANUFACTURING COMPANY
Active in the 1920s

This company was a Henry Katz organization. Pressed steel cars and trucks made with this label closely copied the designs of Girard and Marx. Most Hoge toys are marked and differ only from Marx and Girard in decoration and variations in the clockworks. Hoge toys were reportedly manufactured by Girard. Henry Katz was involved in the buying and selling of toy companies while at the same time producing toys with his label.

HUBLEY MANUFACTURING COMPANY
Lancaster, Pennsylvania
1894 to present

Motto: 'They're Different'.

The company was listed for the first time in the 1894 city directory. Founded by John E. Hubley and other investors, a factory was built for the manufacture of electric toy train equipment and parts. When a fire destroyed the original factory, the company purchased the Safety Buggy Company factory building and moved to the site in 1909.

Financial difficulties after the death of John Hartman (former plant manager) and factory manager, David Shank, eventually caused the sale of the company. John H. Hartman and Joseph T. Breneman formed a partnership around 1909 and, joined by other investors, purchased the business. Orders from Butler Brothers, the nation's largest wholesale jobber, helped Hubley to discard the original line and start the manufacture of cast iron toys, hardware, and novelties. The first toys were horse-drawn wagons and fire engines, miniature coal stoves, circus trains and guns. Eventually, automotive toys were added. With the rapid growth of the real automotive industry, Hubley kept pace adding toy autos until they almost dominated the line in the 1930s. In the early years, Hubley produced parts for other companies. Later, it was occupied totally with its own production. One of the few toy companies who did not feel the full effects of the Depression, it recognized the importance of N.D.Q.* toys and quickly converted production to the small toys to supply the 5 & 10¢ stores, the biggest outlets at the time.

Hubley pursued a course of producing toys based on nationally advertised brands and subjects, such as Borden's, Old Dutch, Huber, Packard, Indian, Bell Telephone, General Electric, and Maytag. All these brand names were familiar to Americans in the 1920s. Many are still active, just as Hubley and the companies who gave the toymaker an 'exclusive right' to copy the products had hoped.

Hubley emphasized that the special play features incorporated in its toys had great educational value: dump trucks that dumped, grasshoppers with legs that moved in a realistic manner, and toys that worked, especially those that could be taken apart and reassembled.

Faced with a shortage of raw materials and changing times, Hubley ceased toy production to

* Nickel, dime, quarter.

fill war contracts in 1942. It never returned to cast iron toys again. After the war, Hubley took up some areas of toy production, but these were diecast metal, including kits and plastic toys. Hubley still supplies major chain stores.

In 1955, the name changed from Hubley to Gabriel Industries, and the company became a division of CBS in August, 1978.

IVES CORPORATION
Bridgeport, Connecticut
1868–1932
IVES & BLAKESLEE   1872
IVES, BLAKESLEE & COMPANY   1873
E. R. IVES & COMPANY
Plymouth, Connecticut
1868

The company was known by various names throughout the years following 1873: Ives, Blakeslee & Williams Co.; Ives, Williams & Co.; Ives Mfg. Co.; and finally Ives Corporation.

Edward Riley Ives began business in Plymouth, Connecticut as a basket manufacturer and maker of hot air toys. These were of the type that could be fastened to stove vent pipes or heat flues and worked from the upward surge of hot air.

Edward conducted some of his work at the Blakeslee Carriage Shop in Plymouth. His partner, Cornelius Blakeslee, was his brother-in-law; Ives was married to Jennie Blakeslee.

The company moved to Bridgeport, Connecticut in 1870. This town became an active manufacturing center during the 1880s, when Ives manufactured fine, original toys designed by Secor, Warner, and other inventors in the area. Later, it acquired some small toy companies whose products were compatible with the business. Ives acted as a jobber, adding other makers' toys and novelties to advertising flyers and catalogs.

Edward's son, Harry C. Ives, who was active with his father, took over the firm in 1895 after his father's death. Harry became a founder and officer of the Toy Manufacturers of America.

At one time the largest, most prestigious and versatile toymaker in America, the Ives firm went bankrupt in 1929, a fatality of the depression. The company was dissolved in 1932.

JEANETTE TOY AND NOVELTY COMPANY
Jeanette, Pennsylvania
1898 to present

This factory started making hand blown bottles, later adding food jars. About 1910, it produced glass automobile headlight lenses, converting to a line of lithographed tin toys in the 1920s, including children's tea sets, trays, toys and games, along with a line of glass candy containers. The company is now engaged in the manufacture of industrial glass products.

JONES & BIXLER COMPANY
Freemansburg, Pennsylvania
1899–1914

Founded in 1899, the primary stockholders were Charlie A. Jones and Louis S. Bixler, who had just resigned his position of Superintendent for the William Shimer Company. The Jones and Bixler Manufacturing Company was incorporated in 1901 with L. S. Bixler as Manager. In 1903, it became part of the National Novelty Corporation. That same year, the company introduced cast iron automotive toys called the 'Red Devil Line'. When Kenton became a member of National Novelty, L. S. Bixler was transferred there.

From 1909 through 1913, Jones and Bixler and the Kenton Hardware companies were intertwined through various businesses and their involvement in the toy trust. A 1909 J&B catalog clearly shows a Happy patrol with the Kenton name on it. The 1913 J&B catalog pictures the Kenton factory! During this period and later, Kenton catalogs offered toys from the original J&B line.

KELMET CORPORATION
New York N.Y.
1923 – late 1920s

Kelmet toys had a unique beginning, which has only now come to light. For years, collectors have been unable to trace a company factory for a very good reason – there was none.

The idea for Kelmet was born in the Chicago Merchandise Mart sometime around 1923. Toy companies maintained mid-west offices in the Mart, and salesmen for the various companies used to meet at the local speakeasy (prohibition) at the end of the day to discuss common experiences and exchange views and ideas before heading home for the night. Leading the discussions were explorations for ideas to enhance their incomes.

One night, some salesmen came up with a mutually acceptable and feasible scheme and enthusiastically formed a business arrangement to pursue the idea of adding a large, pressed steel truck to their lines. None were available, so they would design and produce the line themselves . . . possibly in Japan. Since none of the men had a competing toy, they felt certain their employers would not object to this venture as long as it did not affect their regular product line. Buddy L was the hottest toy on the market and the salesmen felt there was room for an equally attractive, quality toy. Playing around with their initials, they came up with the name 'Celmet', and planned to have the toy manufactured in Japan. (The name sounded so much like Cell-mate, they changed it to Kelmet.) Herman L. Trisch, the A. C. Gilbert sales manager for the mid-west region, returned to New Haven, company headquarters, for a business trip and, feeling guilty about forming a partnership for Kelmet, decided to reveal the arrangement to Gilbert so there would be no animosity if he found out on his own. Instead of being angry, Gilbert thought it was a great idea and, seeing an

opportunity to keep his factory busy during the off-season, offered to manufacture the toy for Kelmet. The men accepted his offer.

Kelmet purchased from another toy manufacturing company the right to use the name 'Trumodel' for the toy line. Some parts were subcontracted, and Gilbert assembled the finished product. The toys were well made and unusual and attracted buyers looking for distinctive toys. They were carried by salesmen who were not involved with any of the other large pressed steel lines, like Buddy L.

Using a 1923 model White Truck for the basic vehicle in the line, the toys had every advertising gimmick going for them – a copy of a 1923 White Truck, the line called 'Trumodel', and the further designation of 'Big Boy', the name used by White to describe the real truck. The words 'Steel Engineering' were carried in trade magazine ads as a motto along with 'The White Truck'. Thus, Kelmet's Trumodel line of 'Big Boy' Trucks was launched about 1923. By the late 1920s, the White Trucks changed in appearance, gaining rounded hoods and developing a more modern appearance with lower roofs. Kelmet toys were withdrawn from the market in the late 1920s. As made-to-order goods, there were none of the normal problems associated with closing a large factory.

Gilbert kept some examples of the Kelmet toys in the company museum. These and other examples of Gilbert's products were sold at auction in 1966, when the factory closed. Examples of Kelmet toys are scarce.

Gilbert added the Trumodel name to his 1938 line of HO gauge trains. Construction kits for Montgomery Ward in 1929 and Erector sets made for Sears were also called Trumodel in 1929. He even arranged for Kelmet truck parts to be used in Steel-Tech construction kits.

KENTON HARDWARE COMPANY
Kenton, Ohio
1890–1952

Started as the Kenton Lock Manufacturing Company in May 1890, the business produced refrigerator hardware patented by F. M. Perkins of Cleveland, Ohio.

Toy production began in 1894 with banks, toy stoves and horse-drawn fire equipment. One of its first toys was a single horse road cart.

By 1900, renamed the Kenton Hardware Manufacturing Company, cast iron toys became a major interest of the company. When fire destroyed the factory in 1903, it was immediately rebuilt and back in operation that same year.

Kenton was one of the earliest manufacturers to quickly realize the success of the motoring pioneers and make the transition from horse-drawn toys to automotive toys, eventually becoming one of the largest toy auto manufacturers in the United States.

In 1903, thirty-seven toy manufacturers, including Kenton, joined together to form the National Novelty Corporation of New Jersey (see details later in this section). The Wing Manufacturing Company of Chicago brought with it a selection of housewares and a toy savings bank to be added to the toy line. Louis S. Bixler was made General Agent for the newly-formed company, whose purpose was to eliminate competition.

The operation failed and in 1907 it was sold to the Hardware and Woodenware Manufacturing Company of New York City, another small 'toy trust'. Kenton was in receivership five months later. During this interim period, Bixler was made Superintendent of the iron producing factories.

Re-opened in 1909, the company was under the jurisdiction of the court awaiting a reorganization of liquidation. Kenton was sold by court order in 1912. During this three year period, patterns were sent for production to Jones & Bixler, Stevens and Grey Iron Casting.

The Kenton Hardware Manufacturing Company was sold as a separate unit to the Kenton Hardware Company by the court. Louis S. Bixler became President and General Manager (Louis S. Bixler had gained his first experience as a foundryman at Hubley and later as a foreman for the William Shimer Company). His brother, Willard R., was made Assistant Manager.

Automotive toys dominated the Kenton line from 1920 to 1935. Kenton ceased toy production in 1952. The assets of the company were sold in 1953.

Some of the Kenton designs were acquired by the Littlestown Hardware and Foundry in Littlestown, Pennsylvania, producers of 'Utexiqual' brand cast iron toys. The patterns were cast using newer methods to speed production. Tumbling and baked enamel finishes were circumvented in the interests of speed and economy. The Littlestown Foundry closed in 1982.

KEYSTONE MANUFACTURING COMPANY
Boston, Massachusetts
c. 1920–?

The first toys marketed by the Keystone Company were toy motion picture machines and comedy films suitable for children. Charlie Chaplin, William S. Hart, and Tom Mix films dominated the offerings to be used in conjunction with Keystone Moviegraph machines.

Inspired by the success of Buddy L trucks and looking for ways to expand during a prospering economy, Keystone gained permission from the Packard Motor Company to market trucks copied from Packard and to use the famous radiator design and logo.

Using 22-gauge cold rolled steel, the company produced a 1925 model of the Packard truck and used some new innovations to make the toys stand out from Buddy L. Nickeled hub caps and radiator cap, a transparent celluloid windshield, cranks at the front, optional rubber tires offered for 50¢ extra, headlamps, and the guarantee that a 200-pound man could stand on the toy without harming it were a few of the sales gimmicks used to emphasize the difference. Keystone trucks could

also be steered and had signal arms for 'stop' and 'go'.

Though the trucks remained basically the same in design, new numbers were added to the line through 1928. The depression slowed but did not halt Keystone. In 1934, a line of 'Siren Riding Toys' was produced, fitted with a saddle seat in the bed and handlebars for steering in the front.

In 1936, it featured a 'Ride-Em' mail plane. Just 25″ long, it was big enough and strong enough for a small child. Priced far below the $6.00 to $9.00 the truck once commanded, the mail plane was priced at $2.00.

After the Second World War, Keystone continued in the toy business using some of the patterns and dies purchased from Kingsbury when its toy division closed. The line became more diverse with doll houses, shoo-flys, desk and chair sets. The motion picture projectors, films, screens and accessories continued as the basic product.

Keystone Manufacturing does not exist today under this name.

KILGORE MANUFACTURING COMPANY
Westerville, Ohio
Active 1920s–40s?

Motto: 'Toys that last'.

In 1925, Kilgore announced the purchase of the George D. Wanner Co., Dayton, Ohio, the largest manufacturer of kites in the U.S. 'E-Z-FLY', a tailless kite was then manufactured under the Kilgore name. At the time, the main product in the Kilgore line was cast iron cap guns, cannons and toy paper caps. It was joined with the Andes Foundry Company and the Federal Toy Company to form the American Toy Company in 1928. Cast iron trucks, cars and fire engines became its more popular toys. N.D.Q.* toys packed in boxed sets retailing for 50¢ were a specialty of the company. Its biggest outlet, Butler Brothers, was the largest wholesale jobber in America with branches in major cities. Kilgore survived the depression but later concentrated mostly on producing cap pistols and toy paper caps through 1944.

KINGSBURY MANUFACTURING COMPANY
Keene, New Hampshire
1919–1942
Wilkins Toy Company
1887–1919

Harry Thayer Kingsbury, aided financially by his grandfather, bought the Wilkins Toy Company in 1895. Earlier, he had purchased the Clipper Machine Works, a maker of mowers and reapers, after a fire partially destroyed the factory. Combining the two businesses, Kingsbury continued the use of the Wilkins name, though James S. Wilkins did not have any continued interest with the company.

Fascinated with real automobiles, Harry Kingsbury built one for himself when he was 27 years old. Shortly thereafter, the mechanically

* Nickel, dime, quarter.

inclined Kingsbury added toy automobiles to the company line. In 1910, the automotive toy line was expanded and continued to multiply over the years until it completely dominated production.

The company converted to war production during the First World War, and like many companies who prospered before the war, it returned to its original product line, using pre-war patterns with updated features until new patterns could be produced.

Seizing a good opportunity to make a name change, the Wilkins name was dropped in 1919, and the Kingsbury name, which was already well-known throughout the toy industry, was used instead. Copying lines from famous automobiles and airplanes from real life, the company continued to prosper.

During the 1920s, Kingsbury created the Kingsbury Machine Tool Division after his sons Edward and Chester joined the company. When the company received war contracts during the Second World War, this division was expanded to handle those contracts and the toy production equipment was sold to Keystone of Boston. Kingsbury never returned to toy production.

Today, the Kingsbury Machine Tool Corporation makes the machinery that manufactures products and parts for giants such as: Singer Sewing Machine, General Electric, Xerox, International Business Machines (IBM), and automotive companies.

KINGSTON PRODUCTS CORPORATION
Kokomo, Indiana
1890s to present

In the 1890s, Chicago plumbing contractors, Charles T. Byrne and James F. Ryan formed the Kokomo Brass Works to produce brass castings for the plumbing industry. A short time later, they were joined by J. (Billy) Johnson. The company rapidly expanded to include carburetors, crank cases and marine engine castings of brass and aluminum.

In time other companies were added, though not under the direction of the original company. The companies called themselves, the Seven Allied Industries and comprised the Kokomo Brass Works; Kokomo Electric Company; Byrne, Kingston & Company; Hoosier Iron Works; Kokomo Malleable Works; Kokomo Stamped Metal Company and Kokomo Lithograph Company.

The Kokomo Stamped Metal Company was formed when Conron-McNeil, a manufacturer of roller and ice skates, merged with Liberty Pressed Metal Company. Just before the First World War, Kokomo Stamped Metal became a division of Kingston Products. George Kingston, a major stockholder since 1904, gave the company the name Kingston Products around 1912.

The company was reorganized in 1927 under the direction of J. Paul Johnson, who in the 1960s was to become Chairman of the Board.

The combined facilities of Kingston produced real lawn mowers, toy electric stoves and irons, target rifles, ball bearing skates and other toys bearing the name 'Kokomo Toys' during the 1920s and 1930s.

Boxed sets of automotive toys (racers, trucks, buses and fire engines) that operated along an electrically charged fence were produced and marketed from 1925 through 1931. Toy designer Lee Wooley, an employee of Kingston, designed the driver for the electrically-run racers by copying his own profile from a mirror. They were well made toys but very expensive for the time. The electric toys were discontinued in 1931 but the company continued to manufacture toys.

In 1936, Kingston acquired the H. A. Douglas Manufacturing Company of Bronson, Michigan.

Today, operating as Kingston Products, the company is owned by the Scott & Fetzer Company and makes components for vehicle manufacturers.

KIRCHHOF PATENT COMPANY
Newark, New Jersey
1852–?

The founder, Charles Kirchhof, was born in Germany in 1809. He started in business building weaving looms and special machinery in Chemnitz, Saxony, Germany.

Kirchhof made his way to America in 1850 and after several stints with other New York shops, he opened his own business in 1852. Working through patent lawyers, he developed various patents. Among his best known are machines which print in Braille for the blind and those which produce ticker tape for Wall Street. Kirchhof established a factory in Newark in 1865 to manufacture tin candle holders. His wife, Eugenie, continued the business after his death in 1879; following her death in 1881, the business was acquired by Christoph Reinhardt and his wife.

The Reinhardt family was succeeded in the business by the Dietze family, relatives of Mrs. Reinhardt. Carl H. Dietze and his sons managed the company through the 1930s.

The Kirchhof company manufactured noisemakers, small metal toys, novelties and Christmas decorations. Employees were mostly of German descent and the toys had a definite German influence in appearance.

Kirchhof converted its facilities to subcontract work for the war effort, promising to return to toys after victory. The name of the company continued to reflect its beginnings as a developer of patents through the 1940s.

KNAPP ELECTRIC NOVELTY COMPANY
New York City, N.Y.
1899–?

This company was one of America's earliest manufacturers of toy electric automobiles and electric toys using power furnished by wet cell batteries. Toys were distributed by Carlisle & Finch, manufacturers of toy trains and other electrical novelties.

LINDSTROM TOOL & TOY COMPANY
Bridgeport, Connecticut
Active 1913–1940s

Toy automobiles by this maker first appeared about 1913 and ceased during the First World War. They re-appeared after the war and continued through the 1920s. Constructed of lightweight pressed steel and tin, most are mechanical toys.

A 1934 trade magazine advertisement lists mechanical toys and games.

Following the Second World War, the company resumed toy production. Tops, climbing monkeys and toy phonographs were produced. A best-seller, a Doodlebug automobile, was produced at this time. The windup toy ran in a figure 8, and bounced back and forth when a rubber bumper encircling the toy hit a hard surface. The toy copied the action found on amusement park vehicles.

LOUIS MARX & COMPANY
New York, N.Y.
1919–1979

Louis Marx was born in Brooklyn in 1896, the son of an immigrant German tailor. Bright and ambitious, he finished public schooling when he was fifteen. With an introductory note from a family friend to Ferdinand Strauss, he was hired as an office boy and ran errands for the mechanical toy manufacturer. Strauss was quick to recognize Marx's shrewd business qualities and would describe Marx years later as a 'sixteen year old boy with a mind of forty'.

Marx quickly moved up with Strauss and in 1916, when he was 20 years old, Strauss placed Marx in charge of a factory in East Rutherford, New Jersey. In 1917, Marx started pressuring Strauss to specialize in volume manufacturing and sell the retail toy stores operated by the company. They argued and parted when the directors of the Strauss company opposed his plans. Marx served in the army from 1917 to 1918, rising to the rank of Sergeant before his discharge following the First World War. Years later, this experience would influence Marx to produce a few military toys. Another job selling wood products for a Vermont factory gave him experience he would later put into use with wood toys.

In 1919, Marx opened an office for business with his brother, David. Working on a commission basis, they acted as agents between factories and wholesale jobbers. After studying the toys, Marx proposed ways for the factory to produce the toy cheaper or make them better for the same money. Finding ways to mass produce the toys for less, he then obtained orders from chain stores and subcontracted his orders to small factories.

After several years, Marx soon saved enough money to become a toy manufacturer. Renting space in Erie, Pennsylvania, he bought some old dies from Strauss. These re-issues of old designs were first copied by Strauss from Lehmann toys when the patents expired. They were the Climbing

Monkey and 'Alabama Coon Jigger' (known in England as 'Oh My'). It should be noted here the 'Coon Jigger' was still listed in the 1926 Strauss catalog, though the dies were reportedly sold to Marx in 1921.

Marx did not own his factories in the 1920s, but placed such large orders with Strauss, the Girard Model Works and C. G. Wood that they produced the toys with his name and trademark. Marx continued to subcontract for toys made to his designs by small factories until the poor business climate of the 1930s brought prices down. He then started to acquire factories in England and America.

After Marx acquired the Girard Model Works in 1935, he renamed it the Girard Manufacturing Company to avoid confusion with other Marx factories in the nearby area. Pressed steel automobiles and trucks sold by Marx were manufactured by Girard before 1935. Because of similarities in design and finish, Marx and Girard toys are difficult to identify when they are unmarked. Keeping abreast of the times, Marx was quick to buy other factories when the time was right. Always striving to hold costs down, he bought seconds in tin can stock and other rejected material. Marx was quick to manufacture toys which reflected current events.

In 1928, when most toy companies were struggling to stay alive, Marx revived one of the oldest toys around, the Yo-Yo. It was rumored he sold millions! It was part of his plan to produce and sell in volume, supplying 5 & 10¢ cent stores, chain and novelty stores. The Depression did not affect Marx. By now he was a millionaire. In 1940, his wife died, leaving him with four children. He later remarried, fathering four more children.

War production occupied the Marx factories during the Second World War. Returning to toy production after the war, the firm was producing 12½% of all toys manufactured in the United States by 1950.

In his business dealings, Marx never let anyone forget he was the boss who made all the decisions. He did not spend much money on advertising, nor did he use outside salesmen. He depended, instead, on longtime trusted employees within his organization to handle sales. Quaker Oats, the cereal company who also owned Fisher-Price Toys, bought out Marx in 1972. Times had changed and Quaker Oats was caught in the middle. They could not effectively combine Fisher-Price and Marx, and business was in a serious decline. Marx was sold at a loss in 1976 to Dunbee-Combex, the European toy manufacturer. To raise money and reduce inventory, the new owners arranged a series of auctions to liquidate warehouse lots of new and old toys, including prototypes. The toys dating from 1920–60 were sold in New York, Los Angeles and London and included other makes, such as Lehmann, Lionel and Chein. These were originally purchased by Marx so he could examine the competition. The auction generated a large amount of money but did not revive the ailing company. The Marx division declared bankruptcy in 1979. The remaining assets of the company were sold to satisfy creditors. Louis Marx died in retirement in February 1982 in New York City. He was 86 years old.

MASON & PARKER
Winchendon, Massachusets
1899–1956

Partners Orlando Mason and H. N. Parker began manufacturing pressed steel wheeled goods, sometimes called sidewalk toys or juvenile automobiles, as a specialty, and later branched into pressed steel toys to utilize scrap metal. Like many toy companies, they also produced a line of hardware to generate sales in the off season. Many of its toys, large and small, utilized wood parts. The company joined the National Novelty Corporation in 1903, and when A. O. Speare and Company moved from Gardner, Massachusetts to join them, it stopped making metal toys and specialized in wood products after 1907. The Boy's Tool Chest is especially well known. The firm was later known as Mason & Parker Manufacturing Company and specialized in blackboards, toy trunks, and pool tables. The business closed in 1956.

METALCRAFT CORPORATION
St. Louis, Missouri
1920–1937

The Measuregraph Company made dies, stamps and tools for the U.S. Government during the First World War. During peacetime, there was little demand for such products and it looked for ways to utilize its factory facilities. Reorganizing as Metallic Industries, Inc., with new investors, the company began the manufacture of playground equipment and sidewalk toys for children. Two-child toys were its specialty, such as a teeter-totter called a 'teeter-go-round'.

The initial success of the company earned them a membership in the Toy Manufacturers of America after just one year in business. The company continued in business with about a dozen pieces in the line. These included the Merri-whirl, Row-kar, Taxi-plane, Winsum-coaster, Jackrabbit-racer, and others. However, buyers lost interest in 1927.

Following Charles Lindbergh's successful New York to Paris flight in 1927, toy companies scrambled to produce 'Lindy' airplanes and toys. By now, the company, calling itself Metalcraft, acquired the rights to a pressed steel 'Spirit of St. Louis' airplane in kit form, which was to be sold in boxed sets of various sizes. The basic airplane was one size, but the many different styles of airplanes possible from one kit depended on the selection of parts packed with the kit. The box of numerous parts and bolts could keep an active boy busy for hours.

Metalcraft, now headed by Garvey Lyons, was reorganized again. Stock was issued to finance the group's newest toy venture. To capitalize on the event, the company was forced to act fast to get the toy on the market. The company subcontracted for parts with a Hammond, Indiana factory and assembled the kits in its St. Louis factory to speed up the output. Selling the kits by the thousands, the company made a small fortune.

When sales began to diminish on the 'Lindy' kits, Metalcraft looked for a replacement. In 1928, it began the production of wheeled goods, scooters, wagons and tricycles, the only products with which it was acquainted. The poor business climate at the start of 1928 put the business in a slump and while it continued to push sidewalk toys, the company looked about for a real winner.

Aware that cast iron toys were disappearing from the market due to the rising costs of materials and shipping, Metalcraft recognized a need for a toy with the quality of the very successful Buddy L, but smaller in size and more reasonable in price. Possibly Metalcraft first got the idea for its advertising trucks after orders for premiums from the Jewel Tea Company and Kroger Stores.

Metalcraft produced its first pressed steel trucks in 1928. Entering the toy market at a time when most toy companies were folding called for ingenuity. The stamped steel trucks were well made, durable and designed to carry advertising effectively. Metalcraft hoped to achieve high volume production and keep costs down as a result of promotional arrangements with Krogers, Jewel Tea, and the newest customer, Coco-Cola.

Business was picking up with the little trucks, but Metalcraft continued to push wheeled goods as the main product until 1931, when the advertising toys took off and eventually outgrew the large toys. Metalcraft would try to revive the larger toys periodically for the next six years without notable success. It was the toy truck line that would eventually perpetuate the Metalcraft name.

Outgrowing its initial headquarters, the company moved to 5101 Penrose Street in St. Louis in 1931. Samuel C. McCluney, Jr., son of a Director who was also a minor stock holder of the company, worked in the purchasing department after his arrival in September, 1930. He remembers ordering 20-gauge auto body steel from the American Rolling Mill in Middletown, Ohio, for $35 a ton.

'The tool and die shop turned out everything fast in those days', Mr. McCluney recalled. 'One hundred punch presses were worked by operators earning 40¢ an hour from 1931 to 1934. After the presses, the parts were degreased, dipped in paint and baked. Women worked in the assembly lines for 20¢ an hour. After 1934, wages went up an additional 5¢ an hour for both men and women'. The McCluneys had a personal interest in the company, for if it succeeded as it had twice before, there would be a lot of money to be made.

Former employees of the firm recalled that no advertising was used to sell the trucks except an occasional promotional release for the wheeled goods and announcements from companies promoting the toys strictly as premiums. McCluney contends the toy trucks were intended as a premium item from their inception, and it was this approach that kept Metalcraft afloat in the toy market as long as it did when other companies were collapsing.

Metalcraft premiums were not limited to toy trucks. One big seller was an all-metal folding chair of painted, pressed steel. Popular for drug and grocery chains, the chair was redeemed for a fully punched card plus a 99¢ payment. One of the largest premiums offered by grocery stores was a four-wheel coaster wagon about 32" long by 16" wide. A fully punched card for the purchase of a dog food called 'Doggie Dinner' plus 99¢ additional payment redeemed the child's wagon.

An ambitious salesman named Jacoby . . . no one recalls his first name . . . toured the country selling the premium trucks and keeping the factory busy with his orders alone. It was rumored he earned twice as much as the President. People associated with the company also recall there was never a set plan to update the styling on the trucks. Quite simply, changes took place when the dies wore out.

1935 versions copied the outlandish designs of ultra-streamlined trucks. A heart-shaped radiator and wheel covers distinguish that year's model. Not every model was updated. Earlier trucks could be ordered at any time, as long as the dies were usable or had not been thrown away.

In 1932, Metalcraft claimed to have sold almost a million 'business leaders', as it called its toy trucks. In 1933, Metalcraft gambled on several trucks in a new battery-operated line that it planned to sell to major companies as premiums. The plan backfired when the toys were rejected. Metalcraft then attempted a new move for them, by trying to regain old contacts in the wholesale and jobbers market. To successfully do this and pay middlemen, it was necessary for the company to raise prices. At a time when toy manufacturers were cutting prices, Metalcraft was being forced to raise prices that were originally kept low based on volume production. Toys that once sold for a coupon plus 29¢ to 49¢ were now 80¢ or more.

Metalcraft's success was minimal in its attempt to gain a share of the wholesale and jobbers market. The company struggled along until 1936, selling wherever it could gain a foothold, but sales were small and the company too large. Premium orders were still being filled, but the poor business climate was headed down, not up. Metalcraft had run out of bright ideas and closed for good in 1937.

Although Metalcraft trucks are most notable for having survived a turbulent business period, they are also well made, colorful, interesting and highly collectible toys.

NATIONAL NOVELTY CORPORATION
New Jersey
1903–7

Formed with Nicholas H. Colwell as President, this organization became known as the 'Toy Trust', with 37 toy manufacturers placing their companies under control of the Corporation. Many were well-established companies. Acting as a monopoly, the Trust planned to cut down on competition, cut costs, control prices, and promote American toys, especially cast iron and wood toys.

One of the first plans placed in operation was the interchange of parts and patterns to coincide with the port of delivery for the final goods. If a large, heavy, cast iron order was received in the east for shipment to the mid-west, the western foundry would receive the necessary equipment to fill the order. Orders were received and dispensed from a central Trust office. Parts and raw materials were intermingled and exchanged. Purchases were from the central headquarters.

Most of the Trust's ideas worked in theory, but not in practice. In the end, inept handling of the companies resulted in the resignation in 1905 of Ralph Cooley, one of the Trust's most important directors. Proving to be a disaster, the Trust was dissolved by the court in 1907 and the companies sold. Many were repurchased by the original owners and continued as independent operations. Others, unable to reorganize or find backers, were dissolved.

A few of the former investors in National regrouped with some of the toy manufacturers to give their plan another chance. The newly-organized company was named the Hardware and Woodenware Manufacturing Company.

NEFF-MOON TOY COMPANY
Sandusky, Ohio
Active 1920s

This company made a specialty of producing steel automotive toys with interchangeable bodies. These were packaged in sets of 8 to 10 bodies to be used on a single chassis equipped with a friction motor. It also made single unit automobiles. The company was in business through the mid-1920s.

NONPAREIL TOY & NOVELTY COMPANY
Newark, New Jersey
c. 1919 – late 1940s

Located at 231 Goldsmith Avenue, this company produced a large line of inexpensive, lithographed tin toys, some with windup motors. They were mostly small toys like penny toys, and little prize package toys found in cereal boxes during the 1920s and 1930s. It also produced tambourines, tin drums, toy trucks, trains and wagons. The few pieces found marked are usually toy trucks and wagons.

With a materials shortage and loss of manpower during the Second World War, toy production was practically at a standstill except for a few items like wood checkers and novelties. Nonpareil did subcontract work for the war effort. The company maintained a New York City Office at 215 Fourth Avenue, room 1105.

NORTH & JUDD
New Britain, Connecticut
1812 to present
Produced toys for one year in 1930

This company was founded in 1812 for the manufacture of saddlery parts and other small hardware. During the early 1900s, it added small hardware parts for automobiles that were specially ordered, such as knobs, and door handles. Later, a line of buckles, fasteners and other materials used in the manufacture of clothing was added to the line.

During the Depression, the company continued to do business but on a lesser scale. Looking for a way to compensate for loss in production and take advantage of existing facilities, it produced a small line of cast iron toys which was marketed in 1930. Some were new designs, others copies of sales leaders from competing companies with some variation to make them look different.

North & Judd could not compete in the marketplace with the larger, more established cast iron toy companies. Its toys were too expensive to manufacture. So the toy business was abandoned in 1930 after just one year. It should be noted that the company did not have the capacity to produce large cast iron toys.*

Today, operating as North, Judd and Wilcox in Middletown, Connecticut, it is part of Gulf and Western Industries, a large conglomerate. The company still manufactures small parts and hardware.

RIEMANN, SEABREY COMPANY, INC.
New York, N. Y.

Originally started for the manufacture of toys by George F. Riemann, Jr., the company was located at 229 Broadway.

The National Novelty Corporation acquired the business along with most prominent American toy manufacturers in 1903, and later the firm merged with the Hardware & Woodenware Manufacturing Company.

When Hardware & Woodenware was dissolved, some factories were sold back to the original owners. This resulted in the formation of the Riemann, Seabrey Company. Members holding the company at the time were E. W. Seabrey, Riemann, and Major E. W. Brueninghausen. The company moved several times ending up at Broadway and 24th Street in 1934. Clarence Ely was President that year.

Rudolf Stoltz started working in the toy industry with the L. H. Mace Company in its original quarters at 2nd Avenue and Houston Street, New York City. Stoltz was a salesman and chief toy buyer. He moved to Baker & Bennett in 1909, and then joined Riemann, Seabrey in 1922 as an executive officer. In 1934, Stoltz became Vice-President with complete charge of sales and factory contacts.

*Cast iron toys 6 inches or more in length are considered large toys

This company became an important toy manufacturer's representative in the 1920s, acting as sole selling agents for Mason & Parker, Grey Iron Casting, N. N. Hill Brass, J. & E. Stevens, Kenton, and others.

In 1944, many of Riemann, Seabrey's clients turned to defense work. The company took up the slack by representing factories producing wood and paper products such as games, books, party favors, sand boxes, baseballs, poker tables, etc.

REPUBLIC TOOL PRODUCTS COMPANY
Dayton, Ohio
1922–32

Charles F. Black and Elijah Miller left the Dayton Friction Toy Works and started their own business by opening a machine shop. The men produced friction toys in conjunction with the shop, using a patent obtained by Black on November 1, 1921. This date is found stamped on the friction mechanism cover of 'Republic Toys', as they were known.

Republic discontinued toy production in 1932, but remained in business as a machine shop.

SAMPSON TOYS (brand name)

This company produced tin toys for Butler Brothers, a wholesale jobber, during the 1920s. The identity of the manufacturer is not known.

SCHEIBLE TOY & NOVELTY COMPANY
Dayton, Ohio
1909–31

This was a continuation of D. P. Clark & Company, makers of 'Hill Climber' toys, using friction mechanisms. Closed due to bankruptcy.

WILLIAM SHIMER & SON COMPANY
Freemansburg, Pennsylvania
1875–1913

Shimer manufactured a line of cast iron toys including banks, trains, horse-drawn toys and a few small automobiles about 1909/1910. It closed about 1913.

FERDINAND STRAUSS CORPORATION
New York City, N.Y.
Early 1900s – traced to 1944

Strauss, an Alsatian immigrant, began business as an importer in the early 1900s. He commissioned toys from several German toy makers, such as Walter Stock of Solingen, and printed his name on the items along with that of the manufacturer.

When the war in Europe interrupted the flow of imports in 1914, Strauss, with the aid of investors, started manufacturing tin toys. A major producer of mechanical tin toys, he became known as the 'Founder of the mechanical toy industry in America' during the late teens. He opened four retail toy stores in railroad terminals in New York and operated them simultaneously with his manufacturing business. Strauss toys continued to be sold until about 1927, when he sold part of his manufacturing interests but continued to remain active in the toy business.

The company is listed in 1944 trade directories as manufacturers of gliders, mechanical toys and pop guns.

STRUCTO MANUFACTURING COMPANY
Freeport, Illinois
1908–75

Structo was founded in 1908 by Louis and Edward Strohacker and C. C. Thompson of Lowell, Massachusetts, for the purpose of manufacturing Erector Construction Kits.

In 1911, Structo was sued by the English company Meccano, another producer of perforated strip erector type sets, for infringement on its patent rights. Meccano sold toys in the U.S. The case was in and out of the courts for several years; the courts finally ruled in favor of Structo. Shortly thereafter, Meccano bought the patent rights and dies from Structo, and consequently merged with A. C. Gilbert to sell the Erector sets in the US.

In 1919, Structo resurfaced with a newly designed Stutz Bearcat automobile copied from the car which started skyrocketing to fame that year. A year later, a truck was introduced, followed by the #8 racer. The company had a good selection of construction kits and ready-built automotive toys by 1922, when it added the DeLuxe Auto #12. Actually, all of the automobiles were copies of real Stutz cars. Structo sold both construction kits and ready-built automotive toys, ranging from three to eleven dollars.

In order to become more competitive during the depressed business climate of the late 1920s, Structo designed a line of large stamped steel toys called 'push toys'. Unlike the complicated mechanisms found in Stutz cars, these were devoid of windup or clockwork 'motors'. A new business arrangement made A. C. Gilbert its distributor and Structo toys were then partnered with American Flyer trains.

The Strohackers sold a major portion of the business in 1935 to J. G. Gokey and divested themselves of the balance of their stock in 1946.

Fred Ertl, a farm toy manufacturer in Dyersville, Iowa, acquired the remaining toy patents and designs from Gokey's estate following his death in 1975.

THE STURDY CORPORATION
STURDITOYS
Providence, Rhode Island (General sales offices)
Factory in Pawtucket, Rhode Island
active c. 1929–33

Originally, this company was the manufacturer of Prairie window ventilators, Lloyd Automatic Bowling Alleys and pressed steel products. Large pressed steel trucks were manufactured from about 1929 through 1932, and apparently discontinued in 1933. From 1930 through 1932, Victor C. Wetzel served as President and Charles I. Bigney as Treasurer.

A September 1930–31 advertisement lists nineteen models available from $2.75 to $8.50, reduced from a former price schedule of $5.00 to $15.00 retail. Except for the styling of the trucks, features copied the qualities of better known lines such as Buddy 'L' and Keystone, but did not feature a specific make.

TOY MANUFACTURERS OF THE UNITED STATES OF AMERICA, INC.
1916 to present

Founded in 1916. The founder and first President was Alfred Carlton Gilbert. Other officers were Harry C. Ives, Vice President; Atherton D. Converse, 2nd Vice President; Leo Schlesinger, Treasurer; Fletcher D. Dodge, Executive Secretary. Dodge was hired for the job and served for 15 years. The first location was the Flatiron Building in New York City. The association later moved to the Fifth Avenue Building. The organization was founded at a time when resentment over foreign imports was building up in the United States as a result of the war raging in Europe. Eventually, all large toy manufacturers would become active members, some making friendships which lasted throughout their lifetimes. Meetings were often held in resorts as social events with wives and families in attendance. A requirement for membership was two years of continuous production for an established toy manufacturer. This organization was to become a very influential group, sponsoring well-organized and publicized Toy Fairs, where members rented space to show buyers their newest products for the season. To encourage large attendance, the organizers of the Fair encouraged manufacturers to unveil a 'lead' toy or a main feature for the upcoming season.

An annual selling event of the toy industry since 1902, the fairs were offered under the auspices of the Toy Manufacturers of the U.S.A. after its formation in 1916.

The organization explained its function in a 1944 issue of the trade magazine, *Toys and Novelties*. 'A program to protect the industry against external competition; to improve competitive practices and to increase and expand the market for toys. A non-profit organization which promotes the welfare of the entire industry. Membership is a practical "Who's Who" of toy manufacturers.'

Exhibits were held in permanent sales rooms in the Fifth Avenue Building and other buildings near Madison Square. Temporary displays were arranged at the McAlpin Hotel.

The Toy Manufacturers organization issued a directory giving names and locations of exhibitors in the various buildings and sponsored the event for two weeks each spring. Organization members proclaimed their aim: 'The one and only purpose of a Toy Fair is to decrease the cost of buying and selling'.

JOHN C. TURNER COMPANY
Wapakoneta, Ohio
1915 – traced to the late 1940s

Turner, a former worker and inventor with D. P. Clark, then later with Scheible, started his own company in 1915. His first toys were pull toys. He produced his first friction toys about 1917. After a short stint in war production, Turner returned to friction toys. Most were automotive. The company later moved to Wapakoneta, Ohio.

Turner patented a flywheel in 1925 constructed of laminated discs, which could be assembled for perfect balance. This wheel is an aid in identification of Turner toys.

In the late 1920s, when the demand for friction toys dwindled at an alarming rate, Turner started to sell toys direct to the public through mail order advertisements in magazines. Turner favored automotive toys and issued entire catalogs devoted to them.

Riding out several near business failures, Turner converted to war production during the Second World War. In a 1944 buyers guide, *Toys and Novelties*, he promised to return with a line of Turner Steel Toys when 'Victory is won!' The name changed to John C. Turner Corporation and a New York City office was maintained with Blake and Conroy at 1107 Broadway.

UPTON MACHINERY
St. Joseph, Missouri
Active late 1920s.

Toys were a sideline for Upton, who made a cheap line of tin trucks and cars during the late 1920s. Produced from lithographed, pressed tin, using tab and slot construction, some of the automotive toys were produced as promotional items. The line was mostly 10¢ and 15¢ toys.

VINDEX
National Sewing Machine Company,
Belvidere, Illinois
c. 1928–31

Cast iron toys were a sideline with this sewing machine manufacturer, which entered the market with an expensive product at the very height of the Depression and soon failed. Automobiles, airplanes, farm and construction machinery as well as motorcycles filled its 1930 catalog, though it has never been established if all of the models shown were actually produced. However, the toys that have surfaced are quality toys and well made.

Vindex had a predilection for producing toys copied from companies with only modest reputations such as P & H (Pawling & Harnischfeger), Buffalo-Springfield, Belvidere, Bates and Autocar. It seems the company strived to be different from the competition, at least in its designs. This probably accounts for its financial problems. The automotive toys, priced from $1.00 to $3.00 apiece retail, were a commercial disaster at a time when the market for toys selling for over 25¢ was fiercely competitive, and sales for higher priced cast iron toys were almost dormant.

Farm Mechanics Magazine offered Vindex farm toys and machinery as premiums to readers for securing subscriptions to the magazine. This helped sustain Vindex toys for awhile. The farm toys distributed by the magazine surface more often than other items in the Vindex line. Still, all are scarce.

WEEDEN MANUFACTURING COMPANY
New Bedford, Massachusetts
1883–1939

William N. Weeden was born in 1839. As an apprentice with James T. Almy, he learned the trade of watch and jewelry manufacture. Later he moved to Boston and opened a small shop. Here he made stencils and dies and repaired watches for about twelve years.

Some written histories report that Weeden accepted an order from Benedict and Burnham Company to develop a pocket watch and spent some years here and abroad promoting the watch and seeking ways to perfect it. However, a search through the records of the National Watch and Clock Association, and its museum archives failed to turn up any trace of Weeden, though he may have had some minor role which was not recorded.

In the summer of 1882, Weeden returned to his native New Bedford and established himself at Grinnell's Foundry, where he manufactured the tools, dies and machinery necessary to start his own business. Moving to a factory building on Water Street, he began the manufacture of a tin pocket match box with the word 'Matches' on the lid in luminous letters. Other products included tin mechanical banks, a pocket watch case that enclosed a music mechanism and magic lanterns.

In 1884, Weeden invented an inexpensive, workable toy steam engine under an arrangement with Perry Mason and Company, publishers of *Youth's Companion Magazine*. The toy was for use as a premium to get boys interested in selling subscriptions to the magazine. The upright engine, patented in 1885, was a total success and used by the magazine for many years.

A stock company was formed in 1887 with J. Arthur Beauvais as President and Charles E. Barney as Treasurer. Directors were Beauvais, Barney, George S. Homer and Edward S. Brown. Financial difficulties in 1889 led to the reorganization of the company. All previous products of the company, with the exception of the toy steam engines, were dropped from production. There were about 24 models of the steam engine. The company moved to a new location and William S. Richie, former President of the New Bedford Board of Commerce, was made President.

In the ensuing years, the company produced live steam boats, trains, a fire engine with a working pumper, an automobile, and accessories to be used with toy steam engines. Reportedly the company

produced 100 different toys by 1922. Weeden toys were offered as premiums by *The Ladies Home Journal* and *New Styles Magazine*, following the success of *Youth's Companion*.

By the late 1920s, Weeden sales had slipped drastically as a result of the Depression. The company was sold in the early 1930s to the Pairpoint Company, makers of silverplated household and tableware items, including specialty glass. Pairpoint was a well-established New Bedford Company. They were unable to turn Weeden around and closed its doors in 1939.

National Playthings, manufacturers of educational toys and a division of National Fireworks, Inc., of West Hanover, Massachusetts continued to produce electrically operated Weeden steam engines through the forties.

WILKINS TOY COMPANY
Keene, New Hampshire
1890–1919
(also see Kingsbury) continued as Kingsbury until 1942

Founded by James S. Wilkins, the earliest Wilkins catalogs included toys manufactured by other toy manufacturers, an indication it acted as a jobber. Toy trains, horse-drawn carriages, carts, and wagons of cast iron, and some pressed steel parts comprised the Wilkins line. Toy automobiles appeared after 1895, when the company was purchased by Harry Thayer Kingsbury. The Wilkins name continued in use until the end of the First World War.

A. C. WILLIAMS COMPANY
Ravenna, Ohio
1886 – to present
J. W. WILLIAMS COMPANY 1844–86

The original company was known as the J. W. Williams Company. Established in 1844 in Chagrin Falls, Ohio, it produced chain pump reels, spouts, and plow points for the local farming communities. When a wagonload of these goods was completed, John Williams would drive through the country trading his products for scrap iron and farm produce which he both used and sold. From this meager beginning, Williams progressed to manufacturing wagon axles, wheel hubs, and a few polished sad irons. When his son, Adam Clark Williams joined the foundry, a line of pruning tools was added to the line.

A. C. Williams bought the business from his father in 1886. Twice during his ownership, the foundry was completely destroyed by fire. Due to a lack of fire protection in Chagrin Falls and relatively poor shipping facilities, Williams moved the foundry to its present location. The newly built plant opened in 1893. By this time, the products previously manufactured were no longer marketable, except for toy sad irons carried by salesmen. From these successful play irons, Williams moved into the toy business. For the next 30 years, horse-drawn, automobile, tractor and

airplane toys were sold. Extending through this period were toy banks of every description.

During the First World War, the hardware line was reintroduced and toys and banks discontinued while the company produced castings for other companies. Most were items related to war production. Immediately following the war, A. C. Williams, prompted by the illness of his wife and a decision by his son, John, moved to California. Williams' son-in-law, J. H. Bigalow, was made President of the company. Clyde A. Heisler, son-in-law of Bigalow, became an officer of the company.

A. C. Williams toys were sold through Woolworth's, McCrory's and Kresge's stores. The toys were mainly small, 10¢ toys that supplied a huge market through the chain stores. Very few Williams toys are marked and very little catalog material exists today to identify the toys. Still, by making comparisons, their identity is revealed. All have become collectors' items. The automobiles and tractors often used wheels purchased from the Ohio Company and tires from the Johnson Rubber Company of Middlefield, Ohio. The last toy automobiles and trucks were made in 1938, when the hardware line also came to a halt.

Gradual changes were taking place in the toy industry after 1938. Stampings, plastics and rubber were making great inroads, and reducing the demand for cast iron toys. Heisler, now Vice-President, was concerned over considerable unused foundry capacity and pushed for jobbing production of castings for other manufacturers.

The Second World War brought about even more changes to machine tool castings when Williams converted to war production. The company exists today as a corporation with eight divisions producing castings in grey and ductile iron, steel, magnesium and aluminum. These castings are utilized in the oil fields, aircraft and industrial manufacture.

Everything related to the former toy business, including samples and printed material, was dispersed by auction a few years ago.

European Manufacturers

BING BROTHERS (GEBRUDER BING)
Nuremberg, Germany
1866–1933

Brothers Ignaz and Adolf Bing were retailers before starting toy production in 1866. After being one of the largest toy manufacturers in the world in the first quarter of the twentieth century, political developments in Germany and a world-wide depression forced the closing of the toy interests in 1933. A family member, John Bing, established a Bing import showroom in New York City around 1924. Karl Bub acquired some of the company interests along with production equipment in 1936. The Bing Company was noted for lithographed tin toys worked by either clockwork mechanism or steam.

BING CORPORATION
New York City, USA
1924–33

Established about 1924, the company moved to 33 East 17th Street, Union Square, New York, in 1925. Products offered were: Bing's flying airplanes, sailing Zeppelins, Ford automobiles, buses, steam engines, mechanical and electric trains, mechanical boats, Fordson type tractors. An off-shoot of Gebruder Bing, Nuremberg and headed by John Bing, the Bing Corporation bought toys from the German company. It closed at the same time as its German source.

J. G. BRENNER & CO.
Manchester, England

Trademark 'Brenco'. Makers of lithographed tin mechanical cars and toys.

KARL BUB
Nuremberg, Germany
1851–1966

Founded in 1851 by Karl Bub, the management and the toys produced underwent many changes during the 1920s. Bub supplied F. A. O. Schwarz, the leading New York toy store, with many exclusive imports in the 1920s and 1930s. Bub also produced toys in joint ventures with other toy companies. The toys may be marked 'KBN'. Production ended in 1966.

GEORGES CARETTE
Nuremberg, Germany
1886–1917

A Frenchman living and working in Germany, Carette first began by manufacturing scientific toys. His lithographed clockwork automobiles were produced from the early 1900s through 1914. At the outbreak of the First World War, Carette was forced to leave Germany. His catalogs show a vast array of highly collectible lithographed toys.

ANDRÉ CITROEN
Paris, France
1919 to present
Toy manufacture ended in 1935.

Citroen started a firm to manufacture gears in 1913 after a stint as chief engineer for Mors, an automobile manufacturer who became famous in the early 1900s through racing successes. With the financial backing of Jules Salomon, Citroen produced his first car in 1919, and expanded steadily eventually to become, with Peugeot and Renault, one of the 'big three' car firms of France.

Citroen's toy cars first appeared in 1923 as exact models of the real thing and were intended as a form of advertising. The popularity of the toys stimulated the production of many different models.

Citroen toy cars and trucks are marked with a stencil on the underside.

The changing business climate in France forced Citroen to abandon the toy business in order to concentrate his energies on the real cars. His financial difficulties continued, and he was forced to sell to Michelin in early 1935.

JOHANN DISTLER
Nuremberg, Germany
c. 1900–1968

Founded before 1900, Mr. Braun and Mr. Mayer joined Johann Distler as partners about 1917 and gained ownership of the firm upon Distler's death in 1923. Forced to flee the Nazis in the mid-1930s, the partners sold the company to Ernst Volk and emigrated to Israel. Volk later bought the German based firm Trix, but operated Distler as a separate entity. Destroyed by bombing in 1945, the company began operations again after the Second World War. The toy division was sold in 1962 to a Belgian company who marketed Distler toys until 1968. Distler mastered the art of making lithographed tin penny toys which were sold through the 1930s. Comic and erratic action cars were part of a large automotive line along with airplanes and toy trains.

DOLL & CO.
Nuremberg, Germany
1868 – c. 1948

Tinsmith Peter Doll joined with J. Sondheim in 1868 for the manufacture of steam engines and accessories. Novelty toys and trains were later added to the line. The management changed hands several times before the company was sold to Fleischmann about 1938. The name was retained until about 1948.

HANS EBERL
Nuremberg, Germany
c. 1900–1928

Hans Eberl appears to have been most active from 1906 through 1914, when most of his automotive toys appeared with the trademark initials H.E.N. Many of his later automotive toys appear to be joint ventures or special orders from factory agents, such as Borgfeldt. The last Eberl toys to surface appear to be late 1920s.

GEBRUDER EINFALT
Nuremberg, Germany
1922 to present

Founded by brothers Georg and Johann Einfalt, the firm turned out many colorful lithographed tin, mechanical, comic and erratic action toys for export. Up to 1930, some toys can be found marked with the initials G.E. or G.E.N. Einfalt made a series of cheap, oversize penny toys for the American market. The autos and trucks without windups sold for 10¢ each through chain stores and mail order houses. After 1935, Einfalt used the trademark 'Technofix'. The company still remains in family control.

H. FISCHER & CO.
Nuremberg, Germany
c. 1908–31

An innovative company which devoted a large part of its business to 'no name' identity production. Geo. Borgfeldt of New York was a main customer, using the trademark 'Nifty' for identification. Lithographed tin toys with an unusual and erratic action were a specialty of the company. Fischer marketed some toys with its own trademark, a fish swimming through the letter A.

GEORG LEVY
Gely
Nuremberg, Germany
c. 1920–71

A partner with Hubert Kienberger until 1916, George Levy began toy production on his own about 1920. He was forced to flee the Nazis in 1934, and settled in England. The factory continued under German management, trading by the less-Semitic name of 'Nurnberger Blechspielwarenfabrikan,' meaning Nuremberg Tin Toys Factory. The new owner, Karl Ochs, kept the business running until 1971.

GREPPERT & KELCH
GUNDKA, G & K
Brandenburg, Germany

The partners called the factory Gundka-Werke and marked toys 'Gundka' or with the initials G & K. Small lithographed tin mechanical toys were a specialty of the firm. Products found in the United States date from about 1912 to 1930. The company closed during the Depression. It appears to have been most active around the early to mid-1920s.

S. G. GUNTHERMANN,
Nuremberg, Germany
1877 to present

Founder S. G. Gunthermann died in 1890. His widow married the company manager Adolf

Weigel, whose initials were added to the founder's in the company trademark. They were removed after Weigel's death in 1919. The company was sold to Siemens in 1965, and continues to operate.

HAUSSER
Ludwigsburg, Germany
1904–1955
Brothers Otto and Max Hausser initially produced wooden toys. Their composition (sawdust and glue) figures called 'Elastolin' covered a wide range from military to farm yard and wild animals and birds. Hausser made a fine line of military vehicles during the early to mid-1930s (some manufactured by Tipp), keeping pace with the military readiness taking place in Germany at the time. War products occupied the factories from 1942 through 1946. The factories returned to toys in 1946. Hausser switched from tin to plastic and synthetic materials after 1955. A later trademark is a house which incorporates the initial H.

J. L. HESS
Nuremberg, Germany
1886–1934
M. HESS
c. 1825–1886
One of Europe's oldest toy manufacturers, the company was founded by M. Hess and taken over by his son, John Leonard Hess, after the death of his father in 1886. It made lithographed tin mechanical toys, some with friction mechanisms called 'Hessmobiles' and bearing initials 'J.L.H.'

GEORG G. KELLERMANN
Nuremberg, Germany
1910 to the present
Using the trademark CKO, this manufacturer is probably best known in the United States for its penny toys and small lithographed, windup tin toys. The company was continued by Willy Kellermann after the death of his father Georg in 1931.

LEHMANN
Brandenburg, Prussia 1881 to present
Nuremberg, Germany 1851 to present
Founded in 1881 by Ernst Paul Lehmann. After his death in 1934, the firm was taken over by his cousin, Johannes Richter. Moving to West Germany after the Second World War, Richter still used the Lehmann name, started a new factory in Nuremberg in 1951. The original factory remains in operation.

LE RAPIDE
Paris, France
Early 1920s to 1954
Louis Rouissy, one of the heirs to the Nestlé Company (Swiss chocolate) marketed without success a rapid 0 gauge model train both in electric and clockwork. These toys are trademarked with initials L.R. Also automobiles that raced on tracks were a specialty of this firm.

GEBRUDER MARKLIN
Nuremberg, Germany
1859 to present
Founded in 1859 by Theodor Friedrich Wilhelm Marklin, a master sheet metal worker. When he was 42 years old, he and his wife, Caroline, began the manufacture of toys for doll house kitchens, using the name W. Marklin. Marklin died in 1886, and his wife took control of the company.

In 1888, their sons, Eugen and Karl Marklin, managed the company, changing the name to Gebruder Marklin. From 1892 to 1907, the company continued with E. Marklin and E. Fritz in charge. From 1907 to the present, the company has operated as Gebruder Marklin & Co.

Marklin, a name that is synonymous with originality and quality, is one of the world's oldest toy manufacturers.

F. MARTIN
Paris, France
1887–1919
Founded by Fernand Martin in 1887, the company produced a line of inexpensive, small, pressed tin toys. The figures were painted and wore clothing made of material. They were actuated by means of spring wound motors, rubber bands, or friction type mechanisms. A prestigious and well known toymaker with diverse interests outside his business, Martin won many medals of honor for his mechanical toys. The toys were so well-copied by his competition that experts claim it is virtually impossible to distinguish genuine Martin-produced toys from the fakes. Martin toys which are marked use the initials F.M. Some Martin trucks produced before the First World War were fitted with wind-up motors that performed double actions. They started and stopped while loads automatically tipped for dumping, then started up again. Following Martin's death in 1919, the company was acquired by Victor Bonnet et Cie.

JOHANN PHILIPP MEIER
Nuremberg, Germany
1879
A manufacturer of tin toys, the firm specialized in lithographed tin penny toys. A cart pulled by a dog was its trademark. These toys date from the early 1900s to 1917. Meier penny toys were imported into the U.S. in large numbers. Most were sold to Pennsylvania Germans for use in traditional Christmas gardens.

MOSES KOHNSTAM
MOKO
Furth, Germany
1875–1959
Moses Kohnstam was an important wholesale toy jobber with an extensive catalog. Distler, Einfalt, Gunthermann, Hoch & Bechmann and Meier were some of the companies included. Toys made to Kohnstam's order were marked with the name 'MOKO'. One of his sons, Julius, opened an English branch in 1890. When Moses died in 1912, his other two sons, Willi and Emil, took over the firm

but the the company was forced to close in 1933 like most Jewish businesses. Emil fled to England where he joined his brother. Willi remained in Germany and died there in 1934. Julius died in 1935, leaving Emil to run the English company with his son, Richard. Emil died in 1948, leaving J. Kohnstam, Ltd. to Richard. The Beatties hobby store chain is now part of Richard Kohnstam Ltd.

MULLER & KADEDER
M & K
Nuremberg, Germany
c. 1900 to present
Muller & Kadeder worked from the turn of the century, producing mostly unmarked mechanical tin toys, which were painted and lithographed. Most notable are the aeronautical carousels and comic characters, such as Buster Brown toys intended for the American market. Starting in the late teens, the company produced some lithographed automotive toys which were marked.

GEBRUDER RAUH
Nuremberg, Germany
The brothers Rauh worked at the turn of the century and manufactured lithographed tin mechanical toys, some driven by flywheels.

WILLIAM RISSMANN COMPANY
RI-CO
Nuremberg, Germany
1907–?
William Rissmann purchased a toy factory in 1907 and was registered as a toy train manufacturer and maker of tin mechanical toys. His products appeared in the late 1920s. RI-CO should not be confused with a Spanish toy firm of the same name. Rissmann's toys are usually marked with 'Germany', in addition to a trademark.

STOCK
Solingen, Germany
c. 1905 – 1930s
Founded by Walter Stock, the company produced a line of lithographed tin mechanical automotive and animal-drawn toys, as well as penny toys intended for promotional use in America. Stock toys are similar in concept to Lehmann designs. The trademark was a pair of crossed canes.

TIPP & COMPANY
Nuremberg, Germany
1912–71
Tipp was founded in 1912 by Miss Tipp and Mr. Carstens. Tipp left during the first year and was succeeded by Philip Ullman. In 1933, like many Jewish business owners, Ullmann was forced to flee to England, where he started the Mettoy Company. During this time, Tipp was placed under the management of a former Bing director. Military toys dominated the line until the plant closed in 1942. In 1948, the factory was returned to Ullmann under the Repatriation Act. The company closed in 1971. Philip's son, Henry, joined his father in business. Henry now lives in Switzerland in retirement.

Bibliography

The American Car since 1775. New York: *Automobile Quarterly*, 1971.

AUTObiography by Red Book–Blue Book. Chicago; National Market Reports, 1964.

Baecker, Carlernst and Dieter Haas. *Die Anderen Nürnberger*. Frankfurt, Germany: Hobby Haas,
Band 1, 1973.
Band 2, 1973.
Band 3, 1974.
Band 4, 1975.
Band 5, 1976.

Bentley, John, *Great American Automobiles*. New York: Bonanza, 1957.

Bolles, Leonard. *The History of New Bedford*. N.p.: n.p., 1892.

Borgeson, Griffith. *The Golden Age of the American Racing Car*. New York: Norton, 1966.

Bowers, Q. David. *Early American Car Advertisements*. New York: Vestal, 1966.

Burness, Tad. *Cars of the Early Twenties*. Philadelphia: Chilton, 1968.

———. *Cars of the Early Thirties*. Philadelphia: Chilton, 1968.

———. *American Car Spotter's Guide 1920–1939*. Osceola, WI: Motorbooks International, 1975.

———. *American Truck Spotter's Guide 1920–1970*. Osceola, WI: Motorbooks International, 1978.

Cars of the 30s. New York: Beekman, 1980.

Clymer, Floyd. *Historical Motor Scrapbook*. Los Angeles: n.p., No. 5, 1948: No. 6, 1950.

———. *Henry's Wonderful Model T 1908–1927*. New York: McGraw, 1955.

Dammann, George H. *Illustrated History of Ford*. Sarasota, FL: Crestline, 1971.

———. *70 Years of Chrysler*. Sarsota, FL: Crestline, 1974.

Davis, S. C. H. *Cars Cars Cars*. London: Hamlyn, 1967.

Eikelberner, George and Serge Agadjanian. *American Glass Candy Containers*. Belle Meade, NJ: 1967.

Feeny, Bill. *Later Toys*. Ligonier, PA: Bethlen, 1971.

Freeman, Ruth and Larry. *Cavalcade of Toys*. New York: Century, 1942.

Georgano, G. N., ed. *The Complete Encyclopedia of Motorcars*. New York: Dutton, 1968.

Gilbert, A. C. and Marshall McClintock. *The Man Who Lives in Paradise*. New York: Rhinehart, 1954.

The Great Toys of George Carette. London: New Cavendish, 1975.

Handbook of Gasoline Automobiles 1904–1905–1906. Introduction by Clarence P. Hornung. New York: Dover, 1969.

Handbook of Automobiles 1915–1916. New York: Dover, 1970.

Handbook of Automobiles 1925–1926. New York: Dover, 1970.

Hendry, Maurice D. *PIERCE-ARROW 'First among America's finest.'* New York: Ballantine, 1971.

Hertz, Louis H. *Messers Ives of Bridgeport*. Wethersfield, CT: Mark Haber, 1950.

———. *The Handbook of Old American Toys*. Wethersfield, CT: Mark Haber, 1947.

———. *The Toy Collector*. New York: Funk, 1969.

———. *Building and Collecting Model Automobiles*. New York: Crown, 1970.

Hibbs, David and Charles. *The History of British Bus Services*. Gt. Brit.: Newton Abbot, 1968.

Hillier, Mary, *Automata and Mechanical Toys*. London: Jupiter, 1976.

Karolevitz, Robert F. *This was TRUCKING*. Seattle, Superior, 1966.

Lewis, David L., ed. *The Automobile and American Culture*. Ann Arbor, MI: U of Michigan, 1980.

Maloney, James H. *Encyclopedia of American Cars 1930–1942*. Sarasota, FL: Crestline, 1977.

Matzke, Eric. *Greenberg's Guide to Marx Trains*. Sykesville, MD: Greenberg, 1978.

Meier, ——— and ——— Hoschek. *Over the Road*. Upper Montclair, NJ: Motor Buss Historical Society, [1975?]

McCall, Walter. *American Fire Engines since 1900*. Sarasota, FL: Crestline, 1976.

McClintock, Marshall and Inez, *Toys in America*. Washington, DC: Public Affairs, 1961.

McLaughlin, Terence. *Papier Mache*. New York: Larousse, 1975.

1904 Handbook of Gasoline Automobiles. Introduction by Ken Purdy. New York: Chelsea House, 1969.

Novelties in Metal. N.p.: New Bedford Board of Trade, 1889.

Olyslager Organisation. *American Cars of the 1930s*. London: Warne, 1973.

———. *Passenger Vehicles 1893–1940*. London: Warne, 1973.

Pressland, David. *The Art of the Tin Toy*. New York: Crown, 1976.

The Roaring 20's. Dallas, TX: Highland Enterprises, 1972.

Schroeder Jr., Joseph J. *The Wonderful World of Toys, Games and Dolls 1860–1930*. Chicago: Follett, 1971.

Stern, Philip Van Doren, *A Pictorial History of the Automobile*. New York: Viking, 1953.

Wagner, James K. *Ford Trucks since 1905*. Sarasota, FL: Crestline, 1978.

Weider, Robert and George Hall. *The Great American Convertible*. New York: Doubleday, 1977.

Weltens, Arno. *Mechanical Tin Toys in Colour*. Dorset, Eng.: Blandford, 1977.

Wendel, C. H. *Encyclopedia of American Farm Tractors*. Sarasota, FL: Crestline, 1979.

White, Gwen. *Toys and Dolls Marks & Labels*. Newton, MA: Branford, 1975.

Whitehouse, Patrick B. and John Adams. *Model and Miniature Railways*. Secaucus, NJ: Chartwell, 1976.

Wise, David Burgess. *Steam on the Road*. London: Hamlyn, 1973.

Wren, James A. and Genevieve J. *Motor Trucks of America*. Ann Arbor, MI: U of Michigan, 1979.

CATALOGS

Early original toy and automotive catalogs, flyers, and advertisements. Some are reprints. They include American Flyer, American National, Arcade (1903, 1924, 1925, 1928, 1930, 1931, 1932, 1933, 1936, 1940), Buddy L, Carlisle & Finch, Dent, Gibbs, Harris, Hill, Hubley, International Harvester, Ives, Kelmet, Kenton, Keystone, Kilgore, Kingsbury, Kingston, Lehmann, Mason & Parker, Neff-Moon, Strauss, Structo, Turner, Vindex, Weeden, Williams, and Wilkins.

Wholesale and retail store catalogs used for references including Boston Store (1905), Butler Brothers, California Notion and Toy Co. (1929/30), The Fair (1927), FAO Schwarz (1914, 1916, 1932), Sears, Roebuck Co. (1904, 1923, 1927, 1928, 1929, 1930), Selchow & Richter Co., Supplee-Biddle Hardware, Charles Smith Hardware (1904), Edward K. Tryon (1927), Montgomery Ward, and H. Wehmhoefer.

MAGAZINES (early issues)

Popular Mechanics, Playthings, Toys and Novelties (1908–1940 and 1944/45), *Bicycles and Novelties, Hardware Age, Horseless Age* (reprint: Volume 1, No. 1, Nov. 1895), *Youth's Companion* (1910, 1911, 1912), *Child Life* (1923, 1924, 1926), *Ladies Home Journal* (1908), and *Illustrated London News* Christmas 1957.

PUBLICATIONS (contemporary)

Cars and Parts, Old Cars Weekly, Antique Toy World.

ARTICLES

Bland, Ann. 'Arcade Toys. They look real.' *Spinning Wheel* May 1978.

Spong, Neldred and Raymond. 'American Friction Toys.' *Spinning Wheel* March 1977.

Wallbank, Lucy M. 'Weeden Toy Factory Known to Every Boy.' *Standard Times* [New Bedford, MA] 22 Oct. 1972.

OTHER SOURCES

A personal collection of original automobile manufacturer and customer catalogs, accessory catalogs and promotional material covering the subject from 1895 through 1942. Also, early studio photographs, newspapers and comic strip papers.

More information was culled from old public records, city directories, town histories and sources too numerous to include here.

Free Library of Philadelphia, Logan Square, Philadelphia.

The antique reference collection was an invaluable source of information for American and foreign automobiles, trucks and accessories.

Library of Antique Automobile Club of America, Hershey, PA.

A notable collection of automotive literature, catalogs and books, some very rare.

Encyclopaedia Britannica.

Index

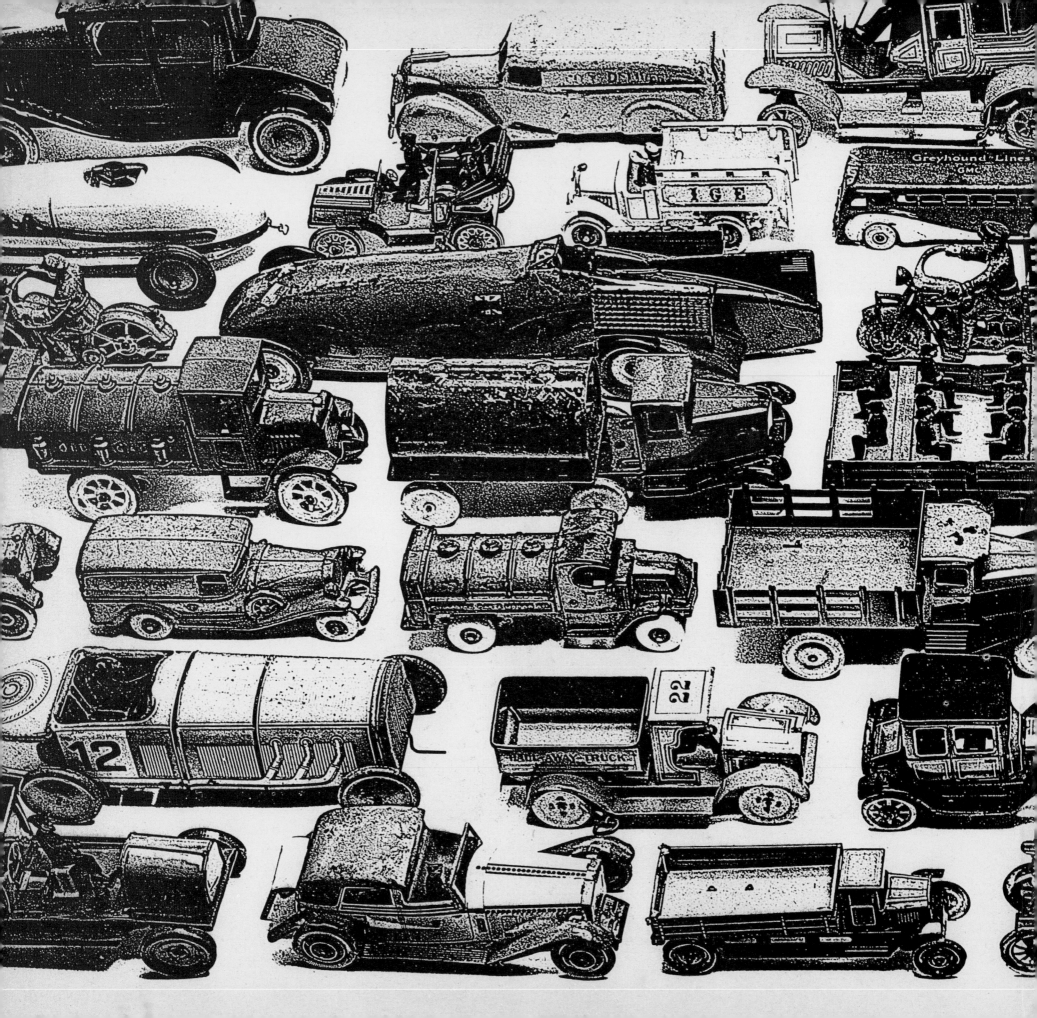